Romantics & Revolutionaries

REGENCY PORTRAITS FROM THE NATIONAL PORTRAIT GALLERY LONDON

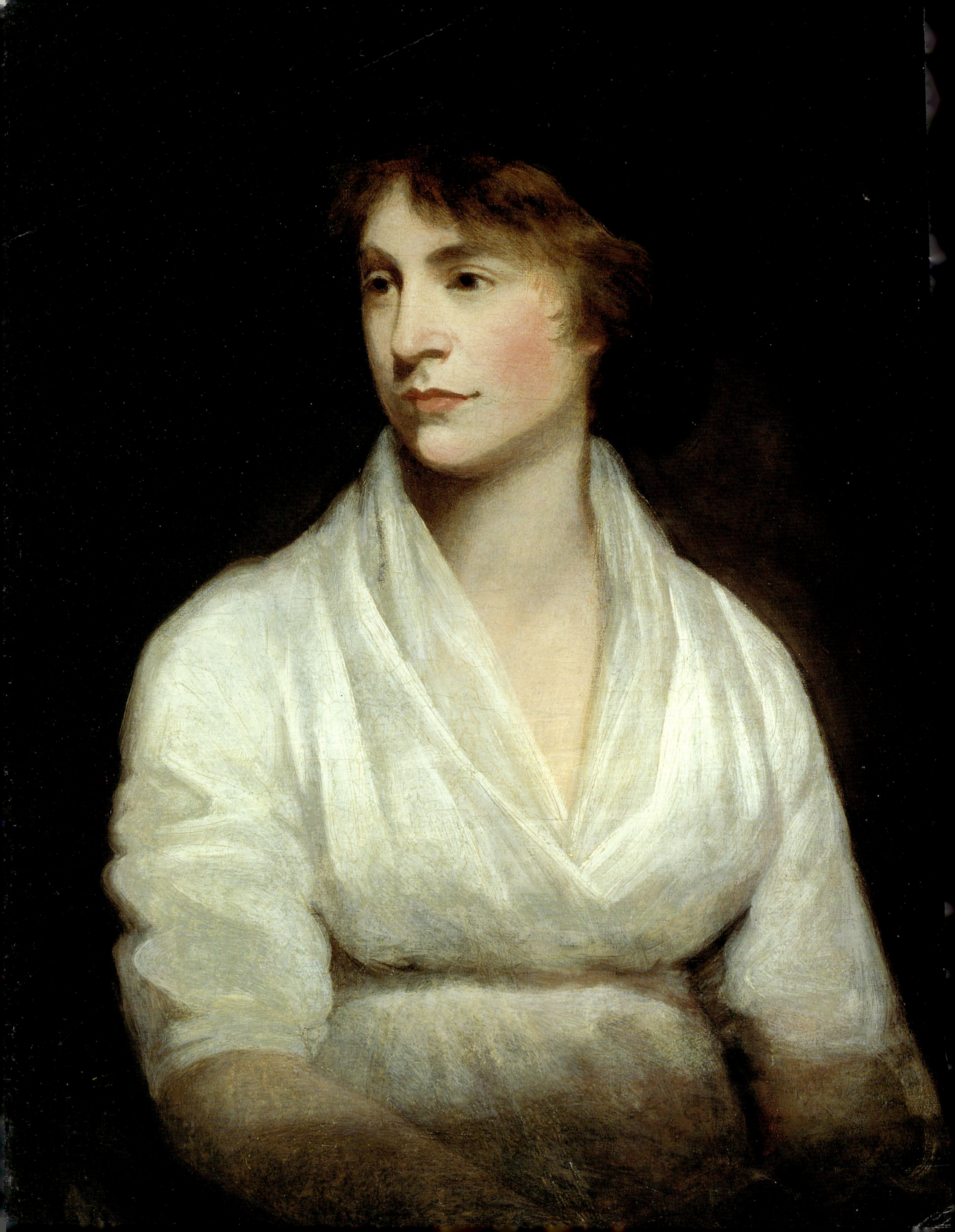

Romantics & Revolutionaries

REGENCY PORTRAITS FROM THE NATIONAL PORTRAIT GALLERY LONDON

INTRODUCTION BY

Richard Holmes

CATALOGUE ENTRIES BY

David Crane

Stephen Hebron & Robert Woof

NATIONAL PORTRAIT GALLERY

Published in Great Britain by National Portrait Gallery Publications,
National Portrait Gallery, St Martin's Place, London WC2H OHE

First published to accompany the American tour of the National Portrait Gallery's Regency paintings in 2002.

For a complete catalogue of current publications, please write to the address above, or visit our website on http://www.npg.org.uk/pubs

Some paintings may have been restored since this book went to press and colours of individual reproductions may therefore appear to differ from the originals.

ISBN 1 85514 337 2

A catalogue record for this book is available from the British Library.

PUBLISHING MANAGER: Celia Joicey
EDITOR: Louisa Hearnden
DESIGNER: Richard Foenander
PRODUCTION: Ruth Müller-Wirth

Printed in Hong Kong

FRONT COVER:
George Gordon Byron, 6th Baron Byron,
by Thomas Phillips (detail)

BACK COVER:

LEFT: Maria Anne Fitzherbert by Sir Joshua Reynolds
(detail reproduced by consent of the owners)

RIGHT: Napoleon Bonaparte by Benjamin Robert Haydon
(detail)

FRONTISPIECE:
Mary Wollstonecraft by John Opie (detail)

Contents

Foreword

In summer 2002, the National Portrait Gallery in London is showing a major retrospective of the work of the great, late eighteenth-century painter, George Romney. Since it is the first time that an exhibition has been organized of his work for a generation and since he was extremely prolific as an artist, it is a larger exhibition than we can easily accommodate in our normal exhibition gallery. We decided, therefore, to show Romney in the set of galleries which we normally devote to the display of our early nineteenth-century collection. This will give us an opportunity to refurbish those galleries to the highest standard and specification and to redisplay them making use of the latest techniques of interpretation.

Having decided to do this, the question arose: what should we do with the collection of early nineteenth-century portraits during the period of the exhibition? On a previous occasion when we used the top floor of the Gallery for an exhibition, a selection of our Romantic portraits was shown at The Wordsworth Museum, Dove Cottage, Grasmere. On this occasion, we felt that the best possible solution would be for the portraits to be shown in the United States at museums and galleries with a commitment to the display and interpretation of British painting, as a way of enabling those people who cannot easily see the portraits in London to see them on the other side of the Atlantic.

These are some of our greatest portraits. They are redolent of a period of exceptional significance in British literature and public life, the era of the Napoleonic Wars and of the early Romantic Movement, of Byron, Keats, Shelley and Wordsworth. They conjure up this period of history: its idealism, its interest in the imagination, its sense of confidence and wealth. This was the period when the architect John Nash was building his terraces alongside Regent's Park, when the Bank of England was being built in the City, and when the public face of Britain, as of America, was dominated by the imagery of Greece and republican Rome. But it was also a period when writers, as well as political thinkers, were influenced by a new belief in the metaphysical significance of nature, freedom and emotion. These portraits contribute importantly to our knowledge and understanding of the period.

The tour has necessarily been organised at relatively short notice and would certainly not have been possible without the help and assistance at every stage of David Setford of Art Reach International. In preparing the accompanying catalogue, we are greatly indebted to the contributions of Richard Holmes, the great biographer of Coleridge, to David Crane, author of recent books on Byron and Trelawny, and to Robert Woof and Stephen Hebron of The Wordsworth Trust, as well as to Louisa Hearnden for overseeing all aspects of its publication. I would like also to acknowledge the help and support of many people at the National Portrait Gallery. I hope that the exhibition will be seen by large numbers of people in the United States and that it will enrich their understanding of this period of British culture and public life.

CHARLES SAUMAREZ SMITH
Director, National Portrait Gallery, London

Directors' Foreword

Together the Georgia Museum of Art and the Yale Center for Studies in British Art, we welcome *Romantics and Revolutionaries: Regency Paintings from the National Portrait Gallery, London* to the United States. It represents the very heart of the collections of one of the United Kingdom's most venerable and adored institutions.

Replete with masterpieces, great artists and unforgettable historical characters, it goes without saying that it is a privilege to be able to work with, and bring to our visitors, such an exhibition. For us as Directors, and for our museums, such opportunities are rare. They help us not only with our critically important educational mission (and the cross-curricular opportunities afforded by this exhibition are legion), but also with our continual drive to find new audiences.

We would like to join together to thank the Trustees and staff of the National Portrait Gallery for their generosity in making this wonderful exhibition available to us. In particular, we are especially grateful to Charles Saumarez Smith, Director, Jacob Simon, Chief Curator, Lucy Peltz, Curator of Eighteenth Century Painting, Kathleen Soriano, Head of Exhibitions and Collections Management and Olivia Horsfall-Turner, Curatorial Assistant. Thanks to their wisdom, foresight and energy this opportunity has become a reality.

We should also mention the role of David Setford, and *ArtReach International*. *Romantics and Revolutionaries* represents *ArtReach*'s fourth exhibition to come to the United States, and we would like to wish this new and exciting venture continued success in the future.

Finally, we should thank our major underwriters and sponsors for their support. In Athens, we would like to thank the W. Newton Morris Charitable Foundation; the Friends of the Georgia Museum of Art; The Phillip and Irene Toll Gage Foundation; R.E.M./Athens, LLC; and Director's Circle members Mr. C. L. Morehead, Jr., Mr and Mrs Robert Burton, Mr Edward S. Hallman, and Mr and Mrs Richard Berkowitz. Without the generous support and farsighted commitment to our communities of these individuals and foundations, our visitors would not have the opportunity to appreciate this outstanding collection, and spend time with some of the most important figures of the early modern age.

WILLIAM UNDERWOOD EILAND
Director, Georgia Museum of Art

CONSTANCE CLEMENT
Acting Director, Yale Center for British Art

Introduction

The first thing you may notice is that almost no one – except those two fine elderly and argumentative gentlemen from the previous generation, George Washington and George III – *almost no one is wearing a wig.* On the contrary, we meet an explosion of highly personal and wildly expressive hairstyles. You may observe the curl, the crimped, the cropped; the long, the lank, the wind-lashed; the punk, the shaved, the shorn; the bubbly, the *bien-en-brosse*, and the frankly-couldn't-give-a-damn-my-dear (one of the most difficult effects to achieve, and first mastered by Lord Byron).

The disappearance of the powdered wig in England, some time after 1790, truly marked a revolution. The poet Robert Southey's hair seems to have been monstrously permed and then dangerously charged with electricity or revolution (vatic static). The painter Haydon's hair looks brutally razored from the stress of producing his great historical canvases (a razor he finally turned on his own neck). The philosopher Bentham's hair is fine and white and pragmatical, as befits a Utilitarian sage. The Prince Regent's is a masterpiece of casual dash and forward brushing (the Prinny style, manufactured daily for two hours by an entire team of court hairdressers at Carlton House).

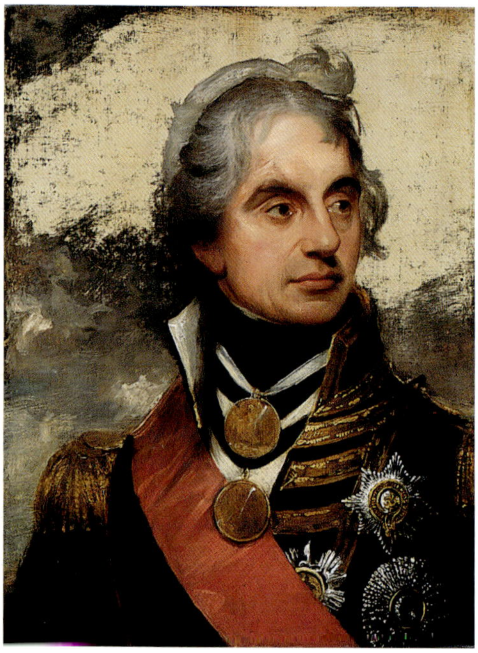

SIR WILLIAM BEECHEY, 1800
Horatio Nelson, Viscount Nelson (1758-1805)
Oil on canvas, 623 × 483mm (24½ × 19 ins)
NPG 5798

Overall, the effect is to make this gallery of Regency faces, of men and women who lived two hundred years ago, extraordinarily individualistic and modern. 'This is, emphatically, *the Age of Personality!*' exclaimed Coleridge. These personalities speak to us almost like contemporaries. Each face offers its story, and has that singular inner life we associate with Romanticism.

In no way is this limited to the poets or the painters. Look at the pale drawn cheeks, and intensely introspective face of John McAdam, sitting on a rock above a valley near Bristol. This was not a man who wrote revolutionary verse epics. This was a man who laid out hundreds of miles of smooth, 'macadamized' coaching road. As a result the Bristol to London mail of 1820, which a generation before had taken three days, now took ten hours and delivered the evening post the next morning at the breakfast table. This was its own kind of revolution, and indeed, a distinctly modern epic.

Constitutionally, the English Regency actually lasted less than a decade. It began in 1811, when King George III went definitively mad, and the Prince of Wales was appointed Prince Regent. It ended in 1820 when George III finally died and the Regent was crowned King George IV, to universal glee and mockery. But as a recognizable social period and a distinctive style in the arts and architecture, the English Regency flourished for more than thirty years. Its high phase was from 1803 (the resumption of the war against Napoleon) to 1834 and the passing of the Act against Slavery. The intervening years may be seen as marked by a series of symbolic conflicts: the Battle of Trafalgar (1805), the Battle of Waterloo (1815), the Massacre of Peterloo (1819), and the passing of the Great Reform Bill (1832). *(See Outline Chronology)*

Historically, the English Regency has been described in many ways. For political historians it is the 'Age of Reform', dominated by the campaign to overhaul the English Parliament (implacably opposed by most Tory politicians, despite the more liberal visions of George Canning) and to abolish black slavery throughout the new Empire (championed by the dying Wilberforce). For social historians it is the 'Age of Scandal', as exemplified by the Prince Regent and his four fat brothers, with their astonishing record of gambling, gluttony, and cast-off mistresses. The mistresses in fact show up rather well. Mrs Fitzherbert encouraged the Prince Regent in his architectural schemes. Dorothy Jordan bore his brother the Duke of Clarence ten children, while maintaining a brilliant career as a comic actress – often piquantly in drag – and sometimes paying the Duke's debts from her thespian earnings.

Again, for historians of style, the Regency is the 'Age of Extravagance', or the 'Age of Paradox' (Coleridge again turned a neat phrase here: 'the Motto is, Extremes Meet!'). The oriental excesses of the Brighton Pavilion, with its glittering domes and minarets, have to be set against the beautifully proportioned, blanched neo-classical stucco of Regent Street and Regent's Park. All were built by John Nash, under the Prince Regent's patronage. The London of the Regency dandies (who hero-worshipped Beau Brummell), or of the Regency Bucks and Fancy (who idolized the bare-knuckle prize-fighters like Jem Belcher and Tom Cribb) was also the London of learned societies (like the Zoological and Astronomical Societies) and earnest lecture institutes, like the Royal Institution where Humphry Davy held huge audiences spellbound with exploding gases and sparkling electricity. Many of these were also patronized by the Prince Regent.

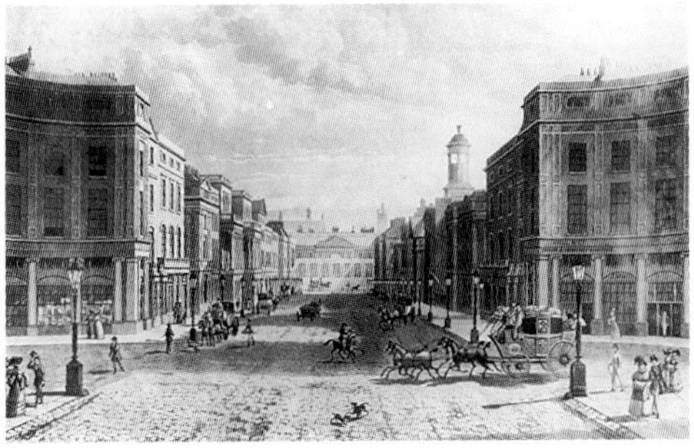

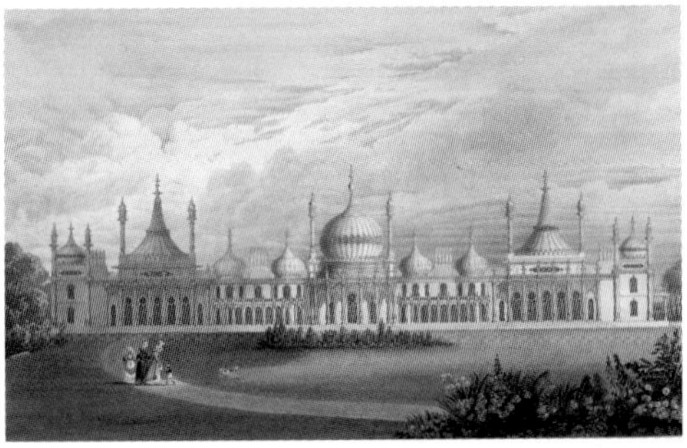

Lower Regent Street from Piccadilly, 1822
Published by R. Ackermann's Repository of Arts, 101 Strand, 1 May, 1822
Aquatint, 430 × 530mm
© Museum of London

View of the East front of the Royal Pavilion at Brighton
John Nash, 1826
Aquatint
© Brighton Museums

The present exhibition reflects something of all these contradictory elements. But it is first and foremost a brilliant showcase of what Coleridge called those 'emphatic personalities'. Many of them will be gloriously familiar names, whom one greets as old friends, though it is sometimes a shock to put a face to a name. Who would have thought the great socialist and kindly factory reformer Robert Owen, founder of New Harmony in Indiana, looked so like a mischievous pixie?

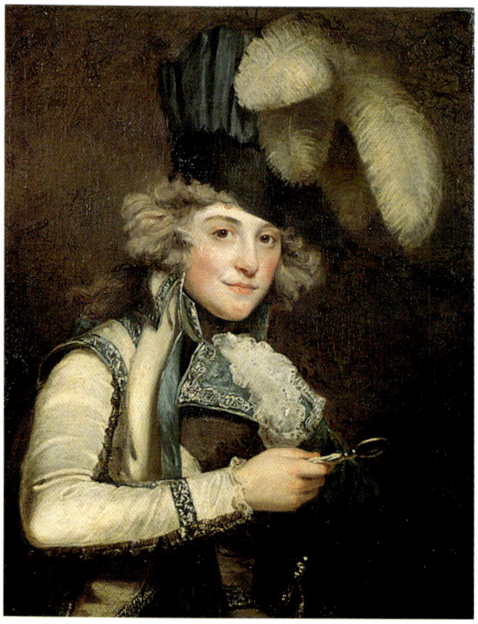

JOHN HOPPNER, exh. 1791
Dorothy Jordan (1762-1816)
Oil on canvas, 749 × 622mm (29½ × 24½ ins)
NPG L174
By courtesy of the Tate Gallery

This is the age of Lord Byron and Percy Bysshe Shelley, of Nelson and the Duke of Wellington, of Jane Austen and Mary Wollstonecraft, of Turner and Constable, of Edward Jenner and Sir Humphry Davy, and – naturally enough – of the Prince Regent and (among many other women) his separated wife Queen Caroline, gamely sporting her come-hither feathers. They are all here – over sixty lords and ladies, soldiers and statesmen, writers (many women) and painters, scientists and sportsmen, moral reformers and mistresses. And they are all very good company indeed.

In pictorial terms, they are also something of a surprise. Although this is the Romantic period, what is striking about so many of these portraits is precisely their lack of Romantic extravagance, sentiment or melodrama. The best workaday portrait painters of the Regency period – James Northcote, John Opie, Thomas Phillips, Henry William Pickersgill – favoured a direct, relatively plain, head-and-shoulders portraiture. Their palettes reflect the clothes chosen by their subjects, and tend to be cool, sober, and understated. The revolutionary philosopher, William Godwin, whose *Political Justice* (1793) set fire to the young minds of half his generation, is painted by Northcote with an almost Roman severity, a classical sage with the light of Reason glowing on (or from) his brow. The visionary poet, William Blake, who conversed with angels in his studio, is presented by Phillips as a successful small-businessman, with a fine clean neckcloth and a gold seal on a red ribbon at his waistcoat, with the engraver's burin poised ready in his hand.

There are a few intriguing stage props. Most of these are justified as professional trademarks: the fencing-master Henry Angelo's sword, Edward Jenner's vaccine cow, Sir Marc Brunel's faintly Dantesque tunnel under the Thames. But there are some subtle shocks, like the naturalist Charles Waterton's South American wild cat, its head mounted grotesquely on a plinth. (Why is the latter so oddly disturbing? Perhaps because, although it was painted in Philadelphia, it suggests a subliminal memory of the French guillotine.)

Every so often there is some outrageous coup de théâtre: Lord Byron sporting his Errol Flynn moustaches

HILAIRE LEDRU, 1835
Charles Green (1785-1870)
Oil on canvas, 359 × 289mm (14⅛ × 11⅜ ins)
NPG 2557

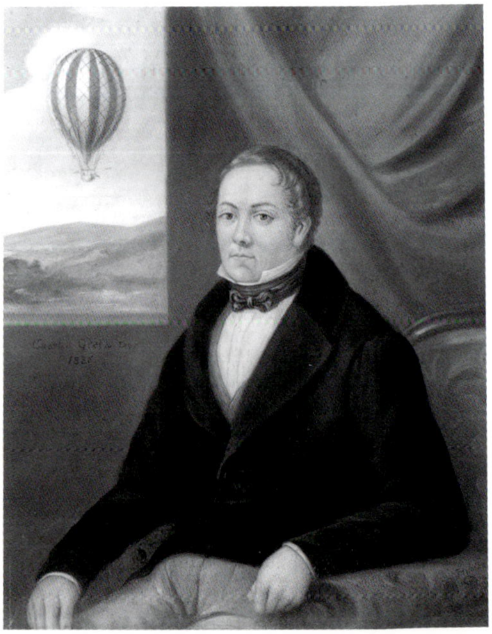

and Albanian turban; or Fanny Burney in her gravity-defying hat; or George IV bursting from his skintight silk breeches. Indeed most of Sir Thomas Lawrence's portraits, especially the unfinished ones of the Prince Regent and William Wilberforce, flaunt a fine aristocratic bravura. So, to a lesser extent, do those of his arch rival for the presidency of the Royal Academy, John Hoppner.

There is some natural drama in the sheer monumental dimensions of a few of these pictures: the portraits of Bentham, Pitt, Canning, or Nelson on his quarterdeck. Size matters, as the historical painter Haydon kept insisting in his wonderfully outspoken *Journals*. But the prevailing coolness and lack of rhetoric perhaps reflects a Regency style or mood. At its most extreme this was also expressed in the dandyism of Beau Brummel, who made a cult of immaculate understatement. His hallmarks were dark clothes, dry wit, studied nonchalance, and absolutely clean linen (with perhaps a hint of eau de Cologne).

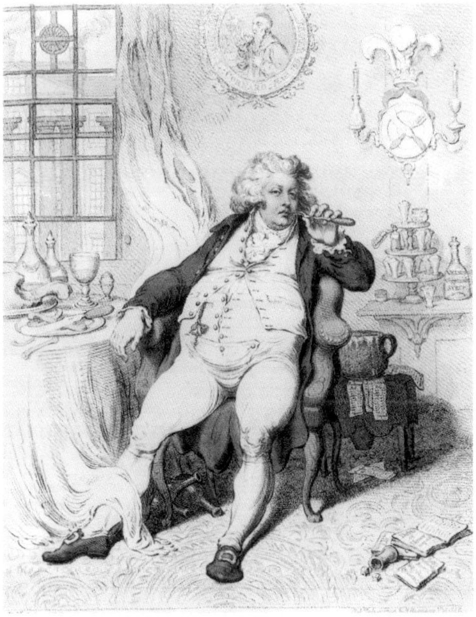

JAMES GILLRAY, 1792
'A Voluptuary Under the Horrors of Digestion' (George, Prince of Wales, later Prince Regent)
Coloured etching
NPG D9024

Nonetheless, it was still an age of personal display, and portraiture flourished during the Regency, the last generation before the daguerreotype photograph. There was a growing hunger for glamorous, humorous or erotic images. Boxers, balloonists, opera singers, dragoons or actresses reappeared as tinted pin-ups for the gentleman's folding wash-screen. Successful writers had their profiles engraved as frontispieces to their works. National figures achieved the apotheosis of being elevated to huge wooden pub signs, or received the fatal accolade of a cartoon by Gillray, Cruikshank or Rowlandson. These were reproduced by the thousand. Ironically, such celebrity, then as now, was prized, even by its victims. The Prince Regent paid vast sums to collect the originals of Gillray's cartoons of himself.

The leading painters of the day exhibited at the annual Royal Academy shows at Somerset House. But they also showed with commercial dealers, in their own studios, or even in specially hired halls and galleries around Piccadilly and Pall Mall. Most portraits began as private commissions, by friends, patrons, or business interests. But popular subjects quickly spread by means of commercial copies, or as engraved prints, etchings or mezzotints. These were sold in the flourishing print shops, the most popular being around Seven Dials and The Strand.

This period saw the rise of the first professional art critics. They were either wealthy connoisseurs and collectors, like Richard Payne Knight, (who also had a fine eye for erotica); or else they were working journalists like William Hazlitt, who wrote art criticism in monthly periodicals like the *London Magazine*. Hazlitt had been trained as a painter, and understood both the technicalities and the aesthetic problems posed

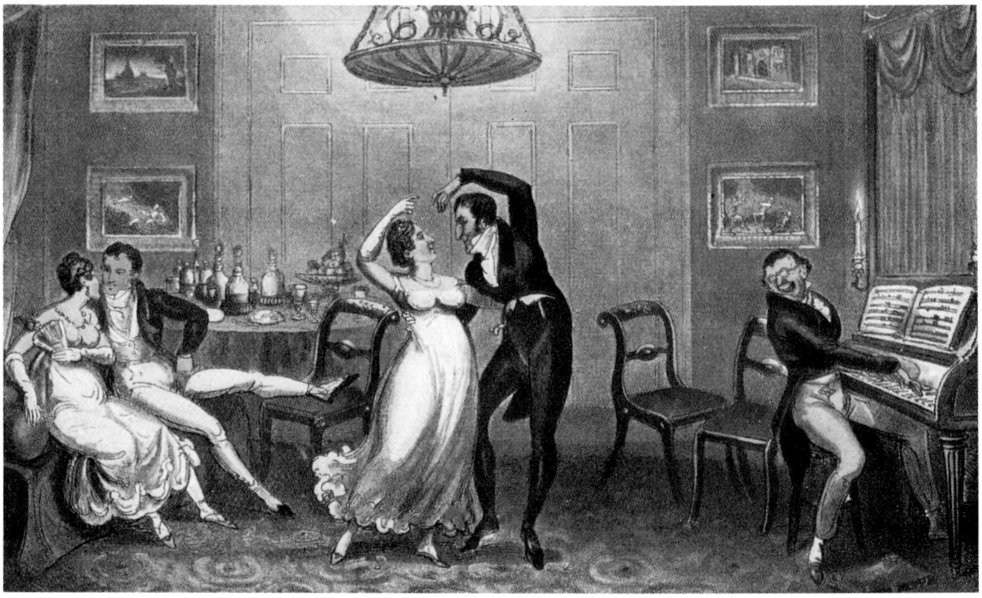

Illustration from Pierce Egan's 'Life in London'
George Cruikshank, 1821

by portraiture. He spent hours in the London studio of James Northcote, discussing the celebrities of the day. The result was his fascinating memoir, *Conversations of James Northcote, Esq., R.A.* (1827), a mixture of flippant Regency gossip, fine reminiscence, and serious technical discussion.

Another painter who wrote and spoke exceptionally well about Regency portraiture was John Opie. An imaginative and independent-minded man from the West Country (like the scientist Davy and the poet Coleridge), he travelled in France and was well known in radical circles. At the same time he rose rapidly to become Professor of Perspective at the Royal Academy, at the age of forty-four. Opie executed plain but wonderfully penetrating portraits of his friend Mary Wollstonecraft, his wife the beautiful novelist Amelia Opie, and his fellow artist Thomas Girtin. He died too soon, and his posthumous *Lectures on Painting* (1809), were edited with a haunting memoir by his widow.

Opie's paintings have a quiet strength that lies at the heart of Regency portraiture. They combine directness and dignity, with a particular kind of human warmth. He used rich but muted colours for his subjects' clothes (deep browns, dark Titian reds, shadowy blues

JOHN OPIE, 1785
Self-portrait (1761-1807)
Oil on canvas, 743 × 622mm (29¼ × 24½ ins)
NPG 47

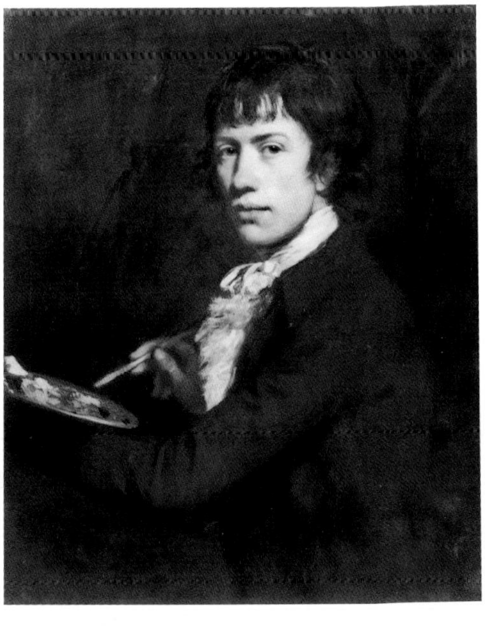

and greens), but rendered up their faces with a vivid, tender, living bloom. His best portraits achieve a characteristic Romantic intimacy. They show subjects whom he knew well, with familiarity and affection, but bestowing upon them an intense and arresting inner life of their own.

Yet this prevailing sense of human intimacy, hides a larger social mystery. Regency England presents an enigma. Here was an immensely elegant society, which was also singularly drunken and dissolute. Here was a cool and self-confident society, which was also turbulent, violent and highly unstable just beneath the surface. Here was the most civilized society in Europe (the proponent of the waltz, the flushing water closet, and the seaside watercolour), which also widely condoned the pistol-duel, the bare-knuckle prizefight, and the teenage prostitute in the park (probably Regent's Park). The confident, civilized Regency world is well represented in these pictures. But the other England, defined by a powerful sense of social trauma, of economic crisis and gathering political anger, is scarcely visible. We have to imagine this other world existing just outside the picture frames.

From 1811, Luddite weavers, who broke up the newly mechanized looms, terrorized the north of England and were subdued by a standing militia larger in numbers than the army that Wellington commanded in the Spanish Peninsular War. From 1815 three-quarters of a million wartime veterans (many with appalling loss of limbs) were jobless and frequently homeless. From 1817 high post-war taxes and bad-weather harvests, produced an enormous number of bank and business bankruptcies across England. Among these (for example) was Coleridge's publisher Rest Fenner, who defaulted on every book royalty that Coleridge had earned since 1815, and Walter Scott's publisher Ballantyne who left the novelist with £114,000 of personal debts in 1826.

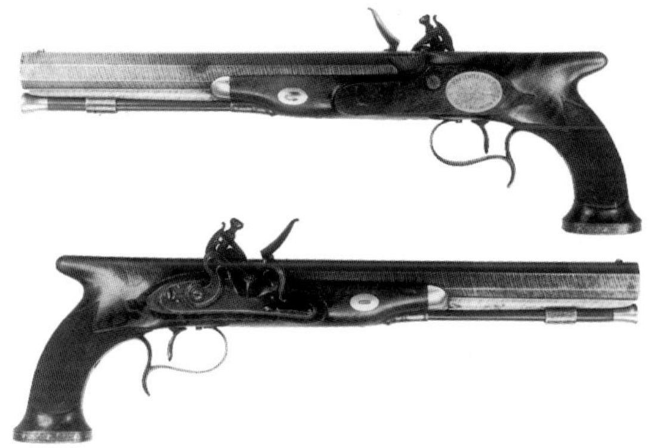

W. A. JONES, LONDON
Duelling pistols, *c.* 1815
Engraved: 'Presented to H. G. The Duke of Wellington K. G.' and 'By the Honorable East India Company'
© The Museum of London

The persistent violence of the period is striking. It is often forgotten that the English Regency saw the only successful assassination of a serving British Prime Minister, the Right Honourable Spencer Perceval, who was shot dead in the lobby of the House of Commons in May 1812. In 1819 it saw the massacre of the families attending a rally for parliamentary reform, at St Peter's Field near Manchester (which became known as Peterloo). The London *Times* reported 400 people seriously wounded with sabre cuts, and twelve people actually killed, among whom were a mother and her baby. It also saw one of the few serious attempts to kill the entire British Cabinet, in the Cato Street Conspiracy of February 1820.

The depth of feeling against the royal and the political establishment is astonishing. It produced some of the most biting social satire that Britain has ever known. The cartoons of Gillray and Rowlandson are famous for their savagery and sexual innuendo. But the protest and mockery are also stinging in the satiric poems of Byron

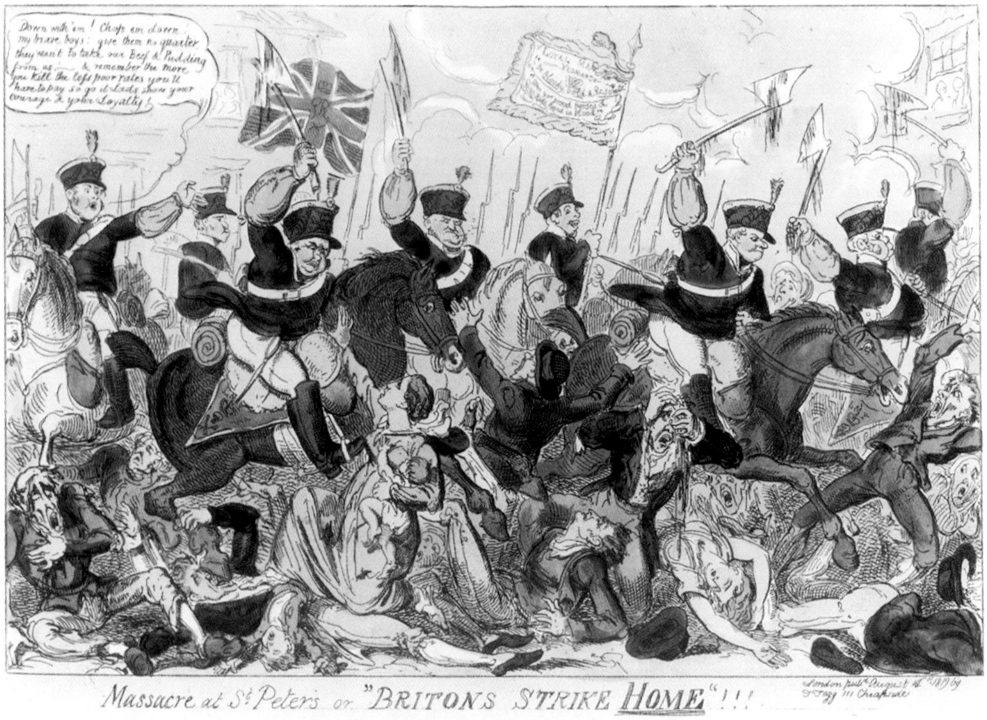

The Massacre at St Peter's or 'Britons Strike Home!!!'
I.R. or G. Cruikshank, 1819

and Shelley, in the comic novels of Peacock, and in the punchy newspaper writing of Hazlitt and Cobbett. Many radical writers and editors – including Leigh Hunt, Richard Carlile, and Cobbett were imprisoned for 'libelling' the Prince of Wales. Shelley had to be safely in Italy when he wrote his furious sonnet defining "England 1819":

> An old, mad, blind, despised, and dying king, -
> Princes, the dregs of their dull race, who flow
> Through public scorn, - mud from a muddy spring, -
> Rulers who neither see, nor feel, nor know,
> But leech-like to their fainting country cling,
> Till they drop, blind in blood, without a blow, -
> A people starved and stabbed in the untilled field, -
> An army, which liberticide and prey
> Makes as a two-edged sword to all who wield, -
> Golden and sanguine laws which tempt and slay;
> Religion, Christless, Godless - a book sealed, -
> A Senate, - Time's worst statute unrepealed, -
> Are graves, from which a glorious Phantom may
> Burst, to illumine our tempestuous day.

For Shelley, "Time's worst statute" was the unreformed and unrepresentative House of Commons (like Cobbett and Bentham, he wanted universal suffrage). His 'glorious Phantom' was Liberty herself. Significantly he imagined her in his other poems, not like the flouncy young "Marianne" (the Republican symbol of France), but as a beautiful mother with a child in her arms. But even for a radical and expatriate like Shelley, she was a specifically English Liberty. This was, despite everything, a profoundly patriotic ideal. For a new and vocal sense of patriotism, and intense national pride, was also an absolutely defining force in the Regency across all classes.

This is already clear from the career of Horatio Nelson, each of whose victories from the Battle of the Nile (1799) onwards, was celebrated by huge popular demonstrations throughout the country (even Gillray made him glamorous, swiping French crocodiles with his one arm swinging a heart-of-oak cudgel). When Nelson died, Englishmen wept openly in the streets – not only in London, and Bristol, and Norwich; but also where he had been romantically stationed with Lady Hamilton in Naples. It is intriguing that Nelson gave the huge portrait by Guy Head, painted in Naples and showing a phallic sword thrust suggestively into the furled French colours, as his personal gift to 'beloved Emma'. Robert Southey's brilliant, all-action biography of Nelson (1813), with its patriotic rhetoric ('England expects that every man will do his Duty!') became one of the bestsellers of the age.

The cult and rhetoric of patriotic heroism spread right through Regency society. In 1822 a national subscription (ladies-only) paid for the erection of a naked statue of Achilles, in honour of the Duke of Wellington at Hyde Park Corner in London. It's still there, like Nelson's Column in Trafalgar Square (1842); and there are still more 'Wellington' and 'Nelson' pub signs than any others in England. The British came to regard their soldiers, their sailors, their poets, their painters and their inventors (rather than their pure scientists) as unquestionably the finest in the world.

The British traveller abroad was renowned for his legendary sangfroid, and also for his legendary arrogance. Washington Irving, observing him in America wrote: 'English travellers are the best and the worst in the world. When no motives of national pride or interest intervene, none can equal them for philosophical views of society...but when either the interest or reputation of their own country comes in collision with another, they go to the opposite extreme in the indulgence of splenetic remarks and an illiberal spirit of ridicule.' (*The Sketch Book of Geoffrey Crayon, Gent.* 1822)

This was putting it only too politely. When the prizefighter Jem Belcher's brother, Tom Belcher, wrote a popular handbook on *The Art of Boxing, or Science of*

GEORGE ROMNEY, *c.* 1786
Emma, Lady Hamilton (1765-1815)
Oil on canvas, 737 × 597mm (29 × 23½ ins)
NPG 294

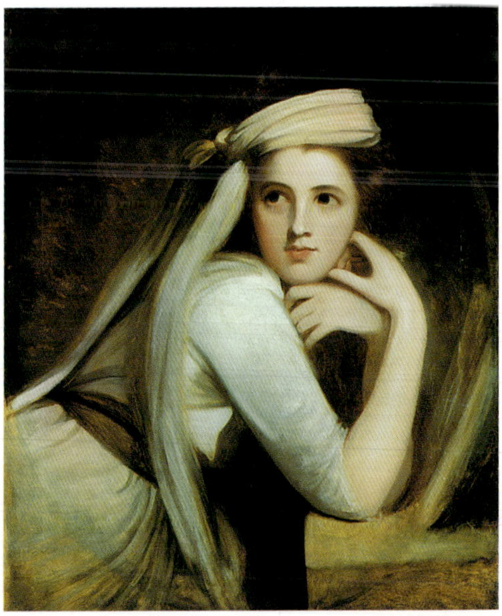

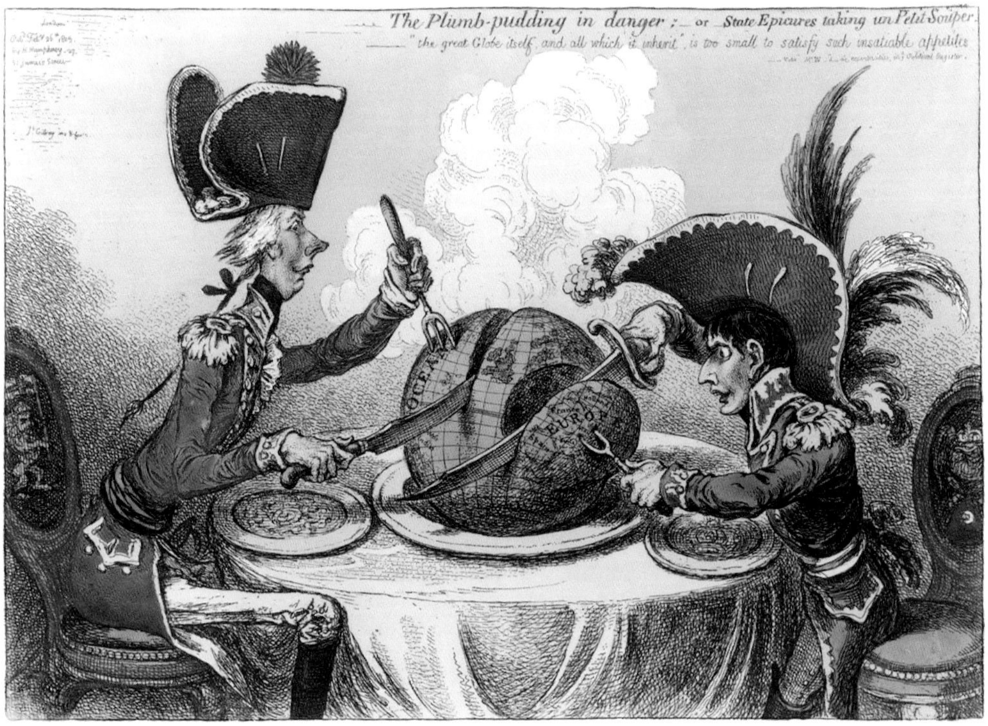

JAMES GILLRAY, 1805
'The Plumb-pudding in danger; – or – State Epicures taking un Petit Souper'
Coloured etching
NPG D11190

Manual Defense (*c*.1820), he concluded cheerfully: 'The advantages Englishmen possess over foreigners, from their knowledge of Boxing, are no inconsiderable motives to recommend it.'

This proud, national spirit of the English Regency can be seen as the underlying force that unified so many of its apparent paradoxes. It was essentially a wartime, and then a post-war phenomenon. The first half of the Regency period (1803-1815) had passed in a long, bitter conflict with England's traditional enemy France, culminating in the stunning victory of Waterloo against Napoleon. England was now, for the first time, the master of Europe. The second half of the Regency (1816-1834) began in a mood of heady victory, and a sense of the vast seaborne Empire – the pink on the Pudding – stretching out to Canada, India, Australia and beyond. But this jubilation quickly generated another mood of angry self-questioning and self-mockery. What exactly was victory for, and who had gained by it?

What followed was a growing, vociferous demand for a juster, more generous and more inclusive post-war society. As England had achieved greatness, she must now act in a great-hearted way. She must reform her Parliament, emancipate her Catholic citizens from civil restrictions, and set the whole world an example by destroying her own share in the global slave trade. It had, after all, been very considerable. At the end of the eighteenth century, about 60% of the trade between Africa, America and the West Indies was aboard British ships, exporting more than 40,000 blacks annually.

In the historic slave trade debates of 1807, the rhetoric of Regency patriotism is already clear. The Bishop of Durham admonished the House of Lords: 'We are a people more favoured by Heaven than any other nation has been since the commencement of Time...But we should beware how we forfeit the protection of Providence by [this] continual injustice: for if we do we shall look in vain hereafter for the glories of the Nile and Trafalgar.'

The influential British historian Linda Colley, now a Professor at Yale University, has seen in this spirit the historic emergence of a quite new and unifying sense of national identity. For her it was defined against the traditional enemy France, 'the Catholic Other', and it was essentially Protestant and masculine. 'There was a sense at this time, as perhaps there still is, in which the British conceived of themselves as essentially a "masculine" culture – bluff, forthright, rational, down-to-earth to the extent of being philistine – caught up in an eternal rivalry with an essentially "effeminate" France – subtle, intellectually devious, preoccupied with high fashion, fine cuisine and etiquette, and so obsessed with sex that boudoir politics were bound to direct it.' (*Britons: Forging the Nation*).

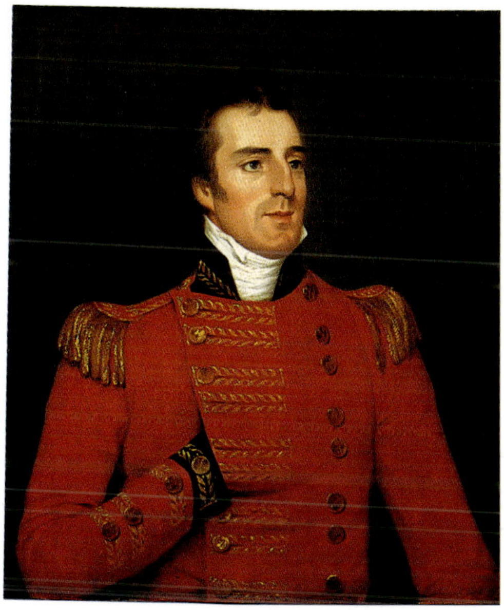

ROBERT HOME, 1804
Arthur Wellesley, 1st Duke of Wellington (1769-1852)
Oil on canvas, 749 × 622mm (29½ × 24½ ins)
NPG 1471

There is much truth in this; and yet perhaps it oversimplifies. The upper-class English admiration for certain things French paradoxically grew during the Regency. Well-off English visitors flocked to Paris during the peace of 1802, and again immediately after Waterloo. English admiration for French clothes, furniture, wine, painting, pure sciences, philosophy, and indeed sexual good manners, always resurfaced after temporary setbacks.

Coleridge wrote wartime essays describing Voltaire as a French hairdresser, Rousseau as a political fanatic, and suggesting that Napoleon might usefully be assassinated. But less than a decade later, Humphry Davy had been proudly elected to the French *Institut Impérial* for his achievements in chemistry; Shelley had made a dreamy pilgrimage to 'Rousseau country' with Byron; and Hazlitt had embarked on Napoleon's biography.

Towards the end of the Regency, the young Edward Bulwer Lytton started a flourishing new genre, by writing a book precisely about the nature of the emerging national identity: *England and the English* (1833). The subtle counterpoint between French and English characteristics became a central theme. One might note that this has continued right down to the most tortuous modern negotiations within the

European Union. 'We may observe the different form of the national vanity in the inhabitant of either country by comparing the eulogia which the Frenchman lavishes on France, with the sarcastic despondency with which the Englishman touches upon England.' (Lytton, p.6). That the book was published in Paris, by Galignani, and dedicated to The Prince Talleyrand, was a nice example of English humour.

The apparent 'masculinity' of the Regency culture is also belied by the increasingly pervasive influence and brilliance of its women writers. Clearly Jane Austen's novels defined a new kind of civilized, middle-class Englishness. Their wit and playfulness put a whole generation of readers on its mettle. 'It is a truth universally acknowledged, that a single man in possession of a good fortune, must be in want of a wife.' This famous ironic opening to *Pride and Prejudice* (1813) gently raises so many profound questions about love, marriage, property, security and sexual desire.

Austen modestly claimed to be painting literary miniatures on a 'little bit (two inches wide) of Ivory'. But like all great art they have become universal, and in our own time have transferred successfully to television and film (possibly helped by the Regency cleavage). Her own quaint portrait miniature, by her sister Cassandra, has rightly become one of the most celebrated and treasured images of the Regency.

But women writers were not necessarily modest, or content to work within drawing-room conventions. Mistresses now began to take revenge through publishing confessional novels (such as Lady Caroline Lamb's *Glenarvon* (1816) against Byron); or through circulating scandalous diaries, such as Harriette Wilson's notorious *Memoirs* of 1825, which elicited the immortal reply from the Duke of Wellington: 'Publish and be damned!'.

Perhaps these were mere Regency tittle-tattle. But Mary Wollstonecraft's *The Rights of Woman* (1792) is now recognized as one of the founding texts of modern Feminism. Her husband, the anarchist philosopher William Godwin, intended to extend her influence by writing an astonishingly frank biography immediately after her untimely death (aged 38) in 1797. He worked with the tender portrait by John Opie above his desk. She hardly looks like the woman Horace Walpole called 'a Hyena in petticoats'.

But Godwin's book so deeply shocked readers with its personal revelations (a Paris love affair, an illegitimate child, two suicide attempts, and death in childbirth) that Mary's reputation was apparently ruined for a generation. Nonetheless her views continued strongly to infiltrate contemporary thinking, not least through humorous novels by her beautiful friend Amelia Opie, and by her sprightly critic the diarist Fanny Burney who wrote *The Wanderer, or Female Difficulties* (1814). Burney also wrote an extraordinary harrowing and courageous account of her own surgical treatment for breast cancer without anaesthetic.

Wollstonecraft's daring and originality bore other fruit. Her daughter Mary ran away to France at 16 with the poet Shelley, and four years later wrote *Frankenstein, or the Modern Prometheus* (1818). First popularized through Regency stage productions in the 1820s, this novel eventually became one of the prophetic books of the century. It not only launched the modern genre of science fiction, but for the first time seriously questioned the human impact of scientific research. Many of the passages describing young Frankenstein's education at Ingolstadt were based on Humphry Davy's actual lectures and scientific speculations in London.

Mary Shelley's intellectual achievement in writing *Frankenstein* at such a young age (for unlike the horror films it later inspired, it is essentially a book of ideas) might seem inexplicable. But her genius flowered within one of the great dynamic periods of English literary creativity, surrounded by an extraordinary inner circle of writers (Godwin and Mary Wollstonecraft, Shelley and Byron, Davy and Coleridge), all of whom she knew personally – except, tragically, her own mother.

Starting with *The Lyrical Ballads* (1798) by Wordsworth and Coleridge, the thirty or so years of the English Regency witnessed one of the great productive epochs of English imaginative literature. Poetry, novels, essays, diaries, confessions and memoirs poured from the press. It is no coincidence that nearly a third of the portraits in this exhibition are those of writers. It is really they, if anyone, who have finally come to represent the 'Spirit of the Age'. It is they who have become the familiar icons of British genius, now recognizable across half the globe.

Moving from picture to picture, looking deep into their individual faces, and recalling the strange fragments of their extraordinary lives, one asks why this should be so? One answer was provided by Mary's husband, Percy Bysshe Shelley. It appears not in a poem, but in an essay written privately in Italy in 1820. It was entitled *A Philosophical View of Reform*, but it is really a sublime poetical view of the whole English Regency and what it promised.

> It is impossible to read the productions of our most celebrated writers, whatever may be their system relating to thought or expression, without being startled by the electric life which there is in their words. They measure the circumference or sound the depths of human nature with a comprehensive and all-penetrating spirit at which they are themselves perhaps most sincerely astonished, for it is less their own spirit than the spirit of their age.
>
> They are the priests of an unapprehended inspiration, the mirrors of gigantic shadows which futurity casts upon the present; the words which express what they conceive not; the trumpet which sings to battle and feels not what it inspires; the influence that is moved not, but moves. Poets and philosophers are the unacknowledged legislators of the world.

RICHARD HOLMES

An Outline Chronology of the English Regency

RICHARD HOLMES

1785 Prince of Wales secretly marries Mrs Fitzherbert

1788 First Regency crisis: George III temporarily insane

1795 Prince of Wales officially marries Caroline of Brunswick

1800 Prince of Wales becomes first President of the Royal Institution

1801 Edward Jenner: *On the Origin of the Vaccine Innoculation*

1802 Peace of Amiens
Edinburgh Review (Whig liberal) launched

1803 Resumption of war with France

1804 Napoleon crowns himself Emperor

1805 Battle of Trafalgar, death of Nelson
Gillray: *The Plumb-pudding in danger* (cartoon)

1806 Death of Fox and Pitt
Napoleon wins the Battle of Austerlitz

1807 Peninsular War begins
Abolition of the British Slave Trade
William Wordsworth: *Poems in Two Volumes*

1808 Dalton: *New System of Chemical Philosophy* (atomic theory)
Bramah: improved model of the flush water closet

1809 *Quarterly Review* (Tory) launched
Disastrous Walcheren expedition against the French
Castlereagh and Canning fight duel

1810 Cribb boxes Molineux (black fighter from NewYork)

1811 Regency officially declared on George III's madness
Extravagant Carlton House celebrations
Luddite riots in North of England begin

1812 Assassination of Prime Minister, Spencer Perceval in the Commons
Castlereagh appointed Foreign Secretary (until 1822)
Byron's *Childe Harold's Pilgrimage*
British troops burn down the White House, Washington

1813 Robert Southey: *Life of Nelson*
Robert Southey becomes Poet Laureate
The waltz becomes à la mode

1814 Jane Austen: *Mansfield Park*
Fanny Burney: *The Wanderer, or Female Difficulties*
The Times installs steam printing presses

1815 Battle of Waterloo, 'a damn close-run thing' (Wellington)
Davy invents the Miners' Safety Lamp (no patent)

1816 Beau Brummell exiled in Boulogne (d.1840)
Coleridge: *Christabel, Kubla Khan and The Pains of Sleep*
Jane Austen: *Emma* (dedicated to the Prince Regent)

1817 Death of Princess Charlotte
Widespread business bankruptcies
Walter Scott: *Rob Roy*
Exhibition of the Elgin Marbles at the British Museum

1818 Mary Shelley: *Frankenstein, or, The Modern Prometheus*
Thomas Love Peacock: *Nightmare Abbey*

1819 Peterloo Massacre
Shelley: "Ode to the West Wind"
John Keats: "Ode to a Nightingale"

1820 Prince Regent crowned George IV
Cato Street Conspiracy to assassinate the Cabinet
Astronomical Society founded
Pierce Egan: *Life in London* (illustrated by George Cruikshank)
Trial of Queen Caroline
Charles Lamb: *Essays of Elia*

1821 De Quincey: *Confessions of an English Opium Eater*
Greek War of Independence begins
John Constable paints *The Hay Wain*

1822 George IV opens the Brighton Pavilion (John Nash)
Suicide of Foreign Secretary, Lord Castlereagh
Hyde Park monument to the Duke of Wellington

1823 First stage production of *Presumption, or the Fate of Frankenstein*

1824 Death of Lord Byron at Missolonghi
Athenaeum Club, Pall Mall founded
Westminster Review (Benthamite) founded
George IV opens the National Gallery

1825 Hazlitt: *The Spirit of the Age*
Legal recognition of Trade Unions

1826 Zoological Society founded

1827 Death of Canning
London University founded

1828 Thomas Arnold appointed headmaster of Rugby school

1829 Catholic Emancipation
Duke of Wellington fights duel

1830 Accession of William IV, 'the Sailor King'
William Cobbett: *Rural Rides*
Stephenson 's 'Rocket' runs down Huskisson

1831 Parliamentary Reform Bill rejected
Bristol riots
Darwin departs on *HMS Beagle*

1832 Great Reform Act

1833 British Association for the Advancement of Science founded
Bulwer Lytton: *England and the English*

1834 Abolition of slavery in the British Empire
Houses of Parliament burnt down (accidentally)

1837 Accession of Queen Victoria

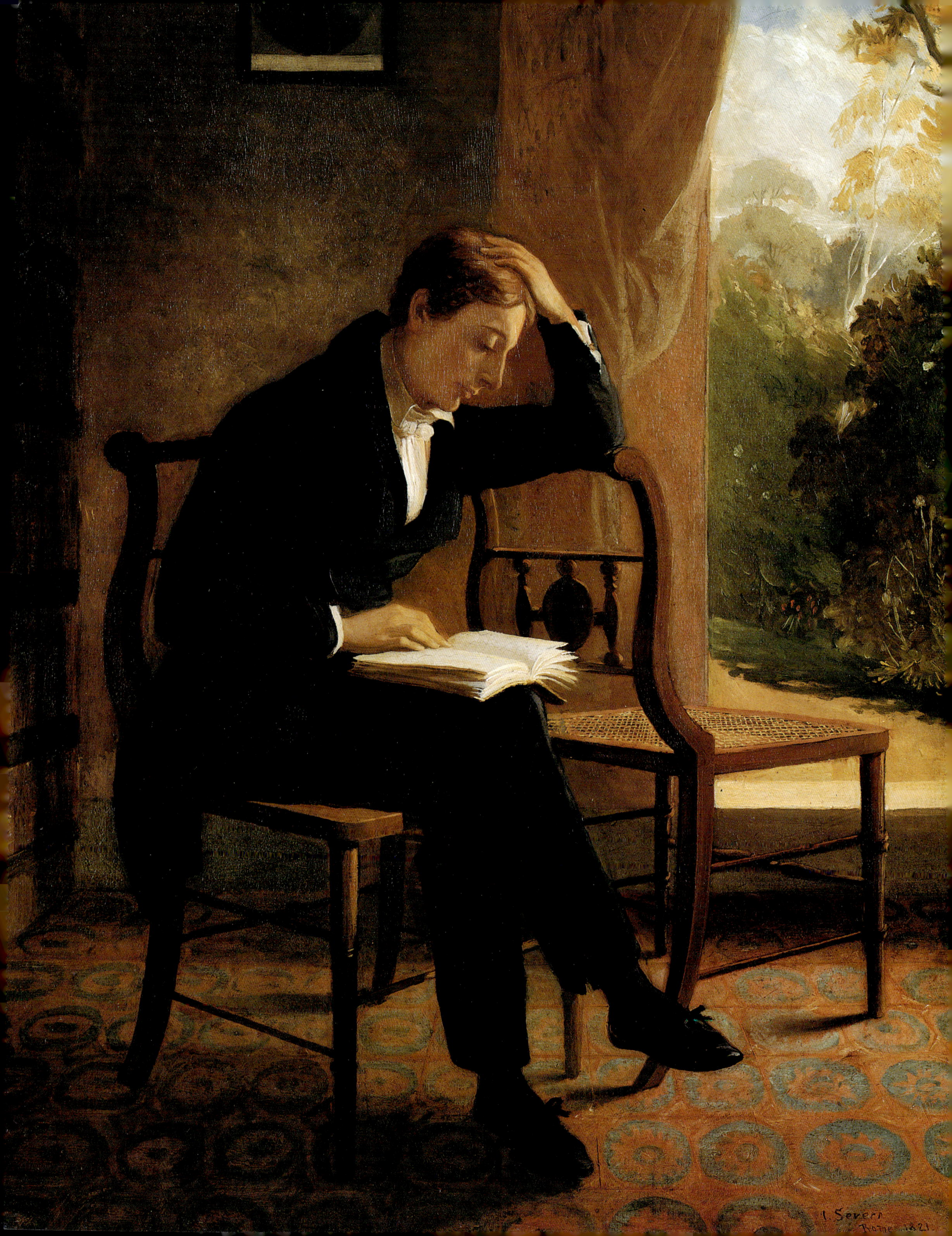
I. Severn
Rome 1821

Poets & Visionaries

JOSEPH SEVERN, 1821-23

John Keats (detail)
(1795-1821)

Oil on canvas, 565 × 419 mm (22¼ × 16½ ins)
(NPG 58)

BENJAMIN ROBERT HAYDON, 1842

William Wordsworth

(1770-1850)

Oil on canvas, 1245 × 991 mm (49 × 39 ins)
NPG 1857

This portrait of Wordsworth on Helvellyn was the culmination of a long association between the poet and the artist, Benjamin Robert Haydon. In 1815 Haydon had made a life mask of Wordsworth, and subsequently several sketches, including one in 1818 which Wordsworth called 'the brigand', and his brilliant 1819 study for the figure of Wordsworth in the large history painting, *Christ's Entry into Jerusalem* (1820). Hazlitt considered this last image to be 'most like the poet's drooping weight of thought and expression'.

In 1840 Haydon sent Wordsworth an etching of his painting of his other great hero, the Duke of Wellington. In return Wordsworth sent a sonnet, which he told Haydon, 'was actually composed while I was climbing Helvellyn'. Thus Wordsworth himself probably inspired Haydon to compose his portrait of the poet, deep in thought, on Helvellyn. He would also have had in mind a sonnet by Keats, 'Great spirits now on earth are sojourning', which described Wordsworth as

> . . . of the Cloud, the Cataract, the Lake
> Who on Helvellyn's summit wide awake
> Catches his freshness from archangel's wing. . .

More than simply a likeness, Haydon's picture here has the qualities of one of his history paintings: a recognisably heroic figure is depicted in the landscape of his deeds. On seeing it Elizabeth Barrett was inspired to write a sonnet that concludes:

> *He* with forehead bowed
> And humble-lidded eyes – as one inclined
> Before the Sovran thoughts of his own mind,
> And very meek with inspirations proud; –
> Takes him his rightful place, as Poet Priest
> By the high altar, singing Prayer & Prayer
> To the yet Higher heavens – a Vision free
> And noble, Haydon, hath thine Art releast
> No Portrait this with Academic air!
> And this is the Poet & his Poetry.

RW & SH

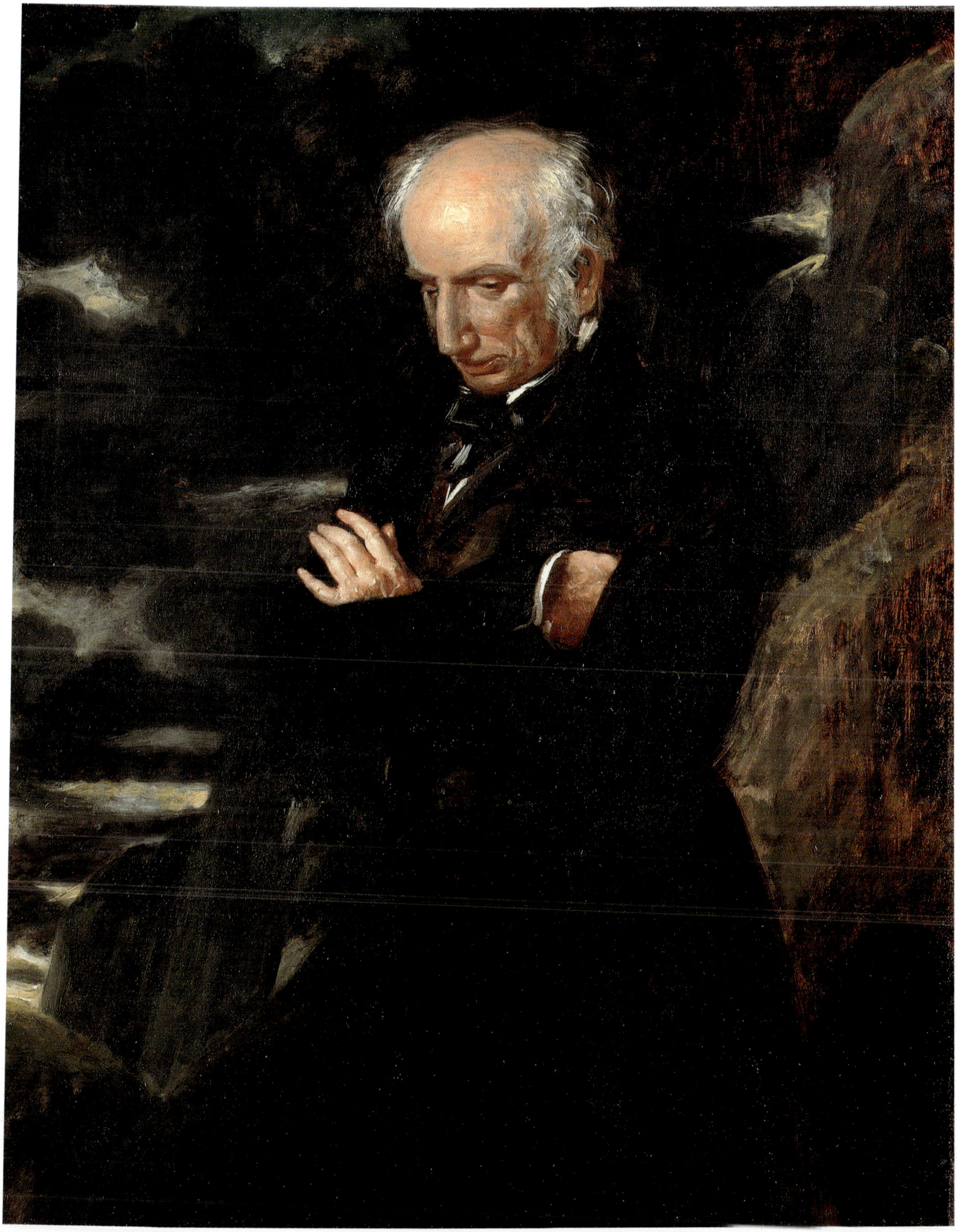

PETER VANDYKE, 1795

Robert Southey

(1774-1843)

Oil on canvas, 546 × 445 mm (21½ × 17½ ins)
(NPG 193)

Few people read Southey today, but in his lifetime he was one of England's best-known men of letters – a poet, historian, essayist and critic, and, for thirty-two years, Poet Laureate.

In his youth he was a Radical. With Coleridge, he planned the scheme of Pantisocracy, and in 1794 wrote two radical plays, *Wat Tyler* and (with Coleridge) *The Fall of Robespierre*. In 1803, after journeys to Portugal and then Spain, he moved to Greta Hall in the Lake District, where he spent the rest of his life. Surrounded by his enormous library, he worked with great industry. He wrote verse epics including *Thalaba the Destroyer* (1801) and *The Curst of Kehama* (1810). He also branched out into other kinds of writing, publishing, for instance, histories of Brazil and the Peninsula War, and biographies of Nelson, Wesley, Bunyan and Cowper.

As he grew older, Southey became an establishment figure and attacked younger writers like Shelley and Byron in the Tory periodical, the *Quarterly Review*. 'He wooed Liberty as a youthful lover', wrote Hazlitt, 'but it was perhaps more as a mistress than a bride; and he has since wedded with an elderly and not very reputable lady, called Legitimacy'. Byron mocked him in *The Vision of Judgement* (1822), a parody of Southey's own *A Vision of Judgement* (1821), written a year earlier to commemorate the death of George III:

> He said – (I only give the heads) – he said
> He meant no harm in scribbling: 'twas his way
> Upon all topics: 'twas, besides, his bread,
> Of which he butter'd both sides: 'twould delay
> Too long the assembly (he was pleased to dread),
> And take up rather more time than a day,
> To name his works – he but would cite a few –
> 'Wat Tyler' – 'Rhymes on Blenheim' – 'Waterloo'

Vandyke's portrait of the youthful Southey was, together with that of Coleridge above, commissioned by their friend the Bristol publisher Joseph Cottle.

RW & SH

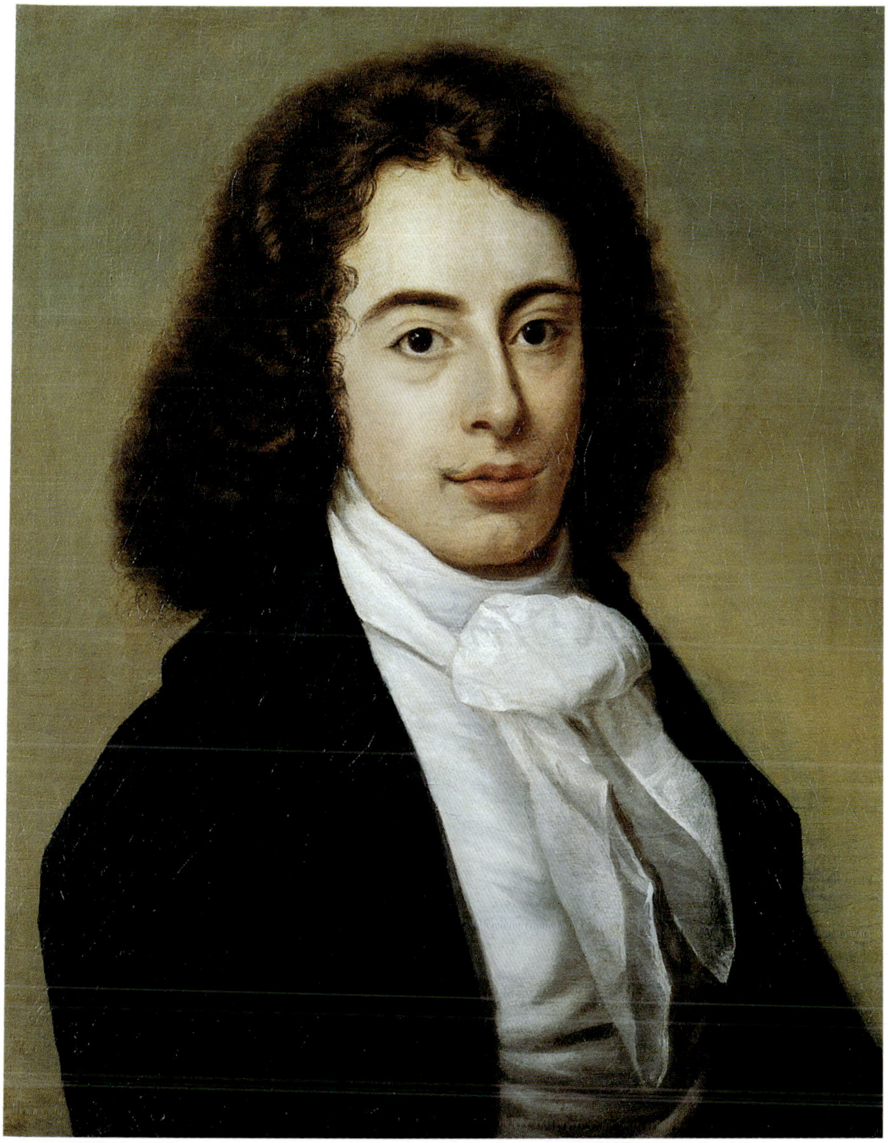

PETER VANDYKE, 1795

Samuel Taylor Coleridge

(1772-1834)

Oil on canvas, 559 × 457 mm (22 × 18 ins)
(NPG 192)

To Wordsworth he was 'The rapt One, of the godlike forehead, / The heaven-eyed creature', to Charles Lamb, 'an Archangel a little damaged'. This portrait of the poet, critic, philosopher and brilliant talker Samuel Taylor Coleridge dates from 1795, and shows him as the inspired youth of Romanticism. With his friend and future brother-in-law Robert Southey he had hatched a scheme, which they called 'Pantisocracy', to establish an ideal community in New England, and in 1795 he was delivering radical lectures in Bristol. He was just about to form the most important friendship in his life, with William Wordsworth, and write a series of extraordinary poems: 'The Rime of the Ancient Mariner', 'Kubla Khan', 'Frost at Midnight' and 'This Lime-Tree Bower my Prison'. His and Wordsworth's revolutionary publication, *Lyrical Ballads* would appear three years later in 1798.

'He is a wonderful man,' wrote Dorothy Wordsworth, 'pale and thin, has a wide mouth, thick lips and not very good teeth, longish, loose-growing half-curling rough black hair. But if you hear him speak for five minutes you think no more of them. His eye is large and full, not dark but grey; such an eye as would receive from a heavy soul the dullest expression; but it speaks every emotion of his animated mind; it has more of the "poet's eye in fine frenzy rolling" than I ever witnessed. He has fine dark eyebrows, and an overhanging forehead.'

A failed marriage, opium addiction, and the persistent feeling that the Muse had abandoned him marred Coleridge's later life. His later works include *Dejection: An Ode* (1802) and *Biographia Literaria* (1817). After learning of his death in 1834 Wordsworth remarked, 'he was the only *wonderful* man I ever knew'.

RW & SH

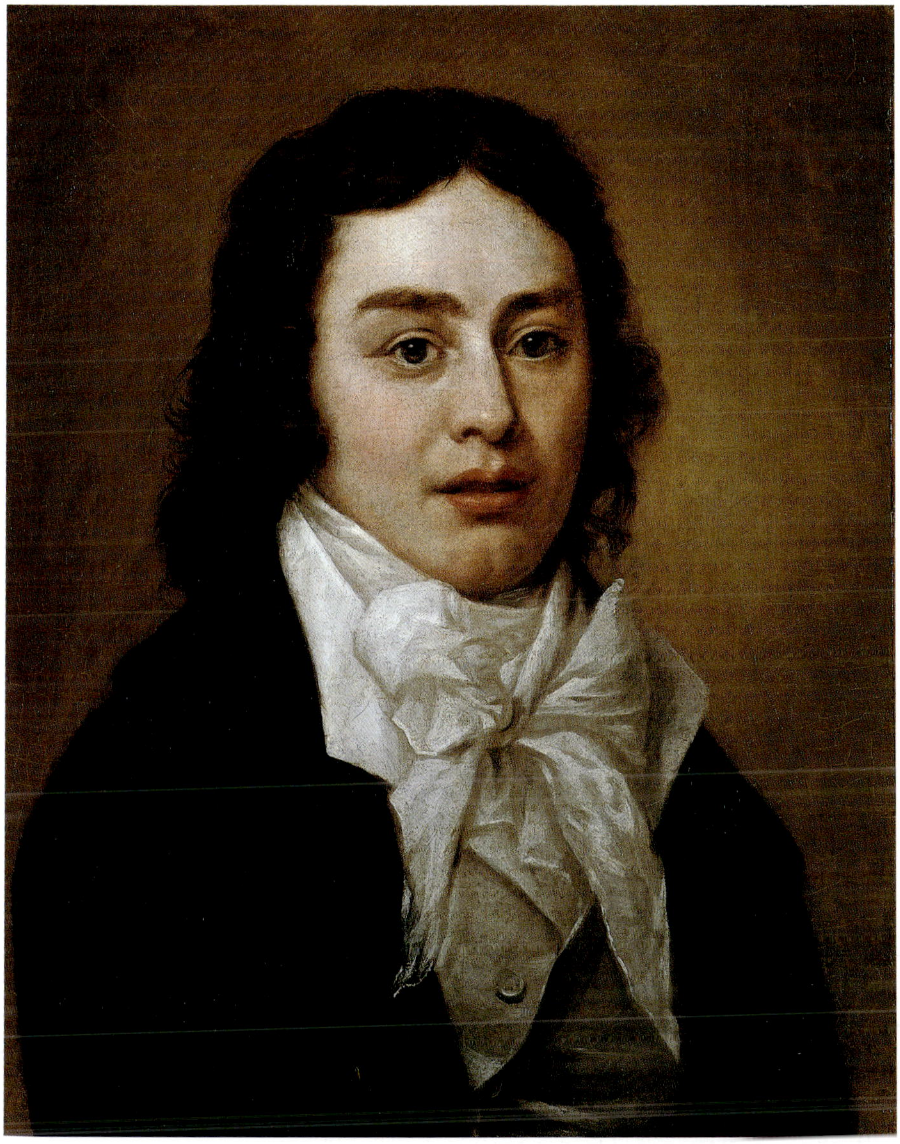

Samuel Taylor Coleridge

(1772-1834)

Oil on canvas, 1143 × 876 mm (45 × 34½ ins)
(NPG 184)

It is arguable that no man had a greater impact on the cultural life of the nineteenth century than Samuel Taylor Coleridge. In superficial ways the poetry and personality of Byron might have made a far more obvious impression, but as J.S. Mill noted, it is Coleridge and Bentham who were the seminal figures, their influence percolating down through their disciples until it was part of the air, breathed by men and women who would not have recognised the source of their beliefs.

If Coleridge's influence is a subtle and elusive thing, however, the impact of his person was startlingly immediate. 'His complexion was at that time clear, and even bright', Hazlitt later recalled of their first meeting, brilliantly anchoring his subsequent disenchantment to the details of Coleridge's physiognomy. 'His forehead was broad and high, light as if built of ivory, with large projecting eyebrows, and his eyes rolling beneath them like a sea with darkened lustre ... His mouth was gross, voluptuous, open, eloquent; his chin good-humoured and round; but his nose, the rudder of the face, the index of the will, was small, feeble, nothing – like what he has done.'

Even in middle age, when opium and metaphysics had taken their toll, the effect could be just as impressive. 'So far as I can judge the likeness is a true one', Coleridge's American friend Washington Allston confessed sadly of his stiff portrait, 'but it is Coleridge in repose ... it is not Coleridge in his highest mode – the poetic state. When in that state no face I ever saw was like his, it seemed spirit made visible, without a shadow of the physical upon it. But it was beyond the reach of my art.'

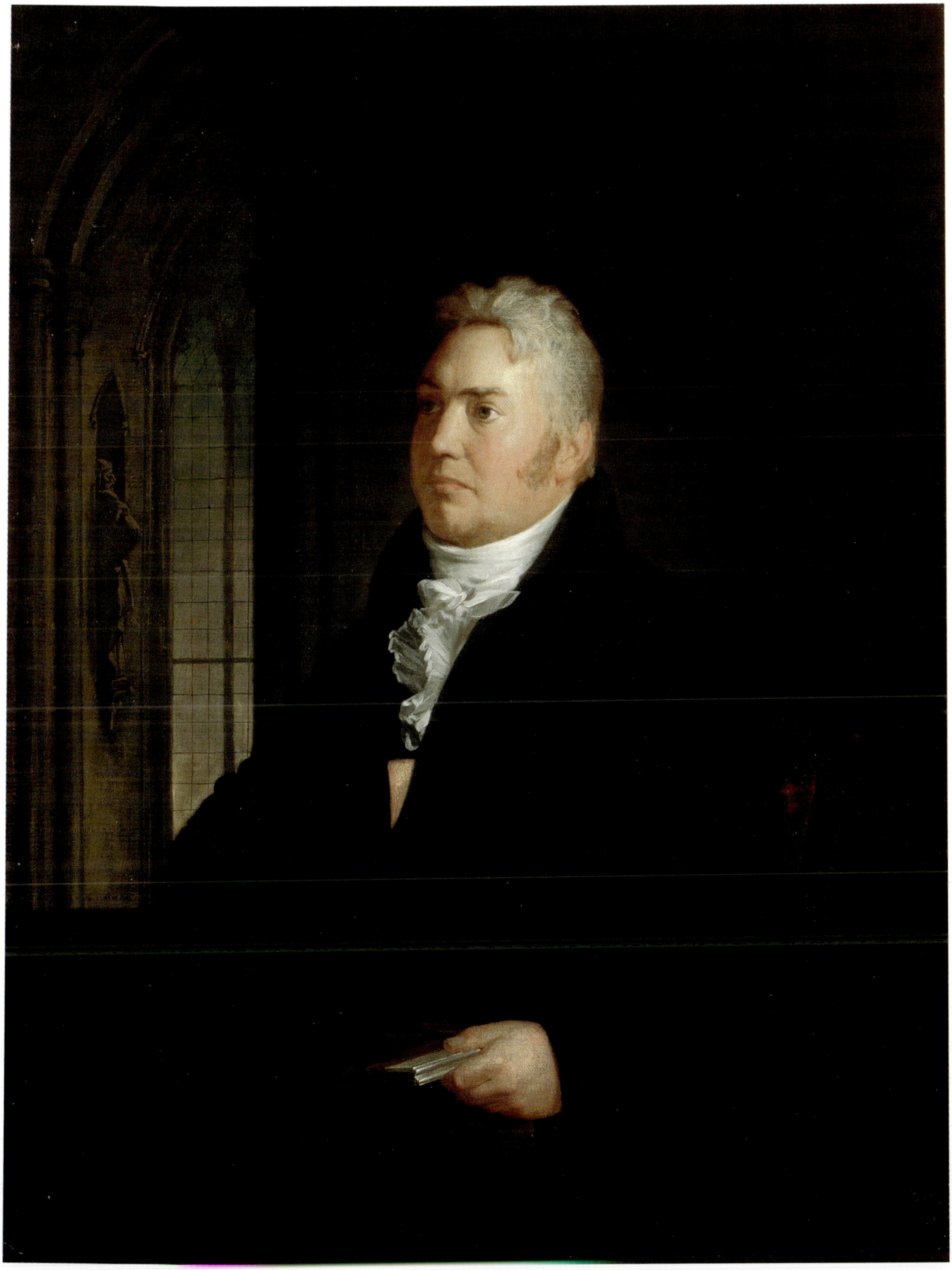

SIR JOHN WATSON-GORDON, *c.*1845

Thomas De Quincey

(1785-1859)

Oil on canvas, 1273 × 1013 mm (50⅛ × 39⅞ ins)
(NPG 189)

The son of a wealthy merchant who died when he was young, De Quincey ran away from Manchester Grammar School at the age of seventeen, and after a summer wandering in Wales spent a desolate winter on the streets of London. After a reconciliation with his guardians he went up to Oxford University, but as soon as he came into his inheritance he made his way to the Lake District, where he became an intimate of the Wordsworth household and finally settled in Dove Cottage.

A man of great conversational charm and compulsive generosity, De Quincey soon exhausted his inheritance, and, with a wife to support, gave up the life of a gentleman scholar for that of a writer. Since 1804 he had been taking opium in ever-increasing doses, and in 1821 he published his *Confessions of an English Opium Eater* (1821), a brilliant account of his early experiences and the effects of addiction. It has become one of the classic texts of English Romanticism.

A Tory in politics and conservative in temperament, De Quincey was in many ways, however, an improbable prophet of Romantic excess. From its first publication in the *London Magazine*, *Confessions* was a success, but it made little money and from 1828 he lived with his family in Edinburgh, where he sustained life in the face of ill health and addiction with that mix of hack writing and perceptive criticism that is probably truer to his nature and talents. His essay *On the knocking at the Gate in Macbeth* is as good as anything written on the play.

It is this De Quincey, the small, shy, courteous figure of Edinburgh legend, that Sir John Watson-Gordon (history turned portrait painter and Scotland's successor to Raeburn) has captured in this portrait.

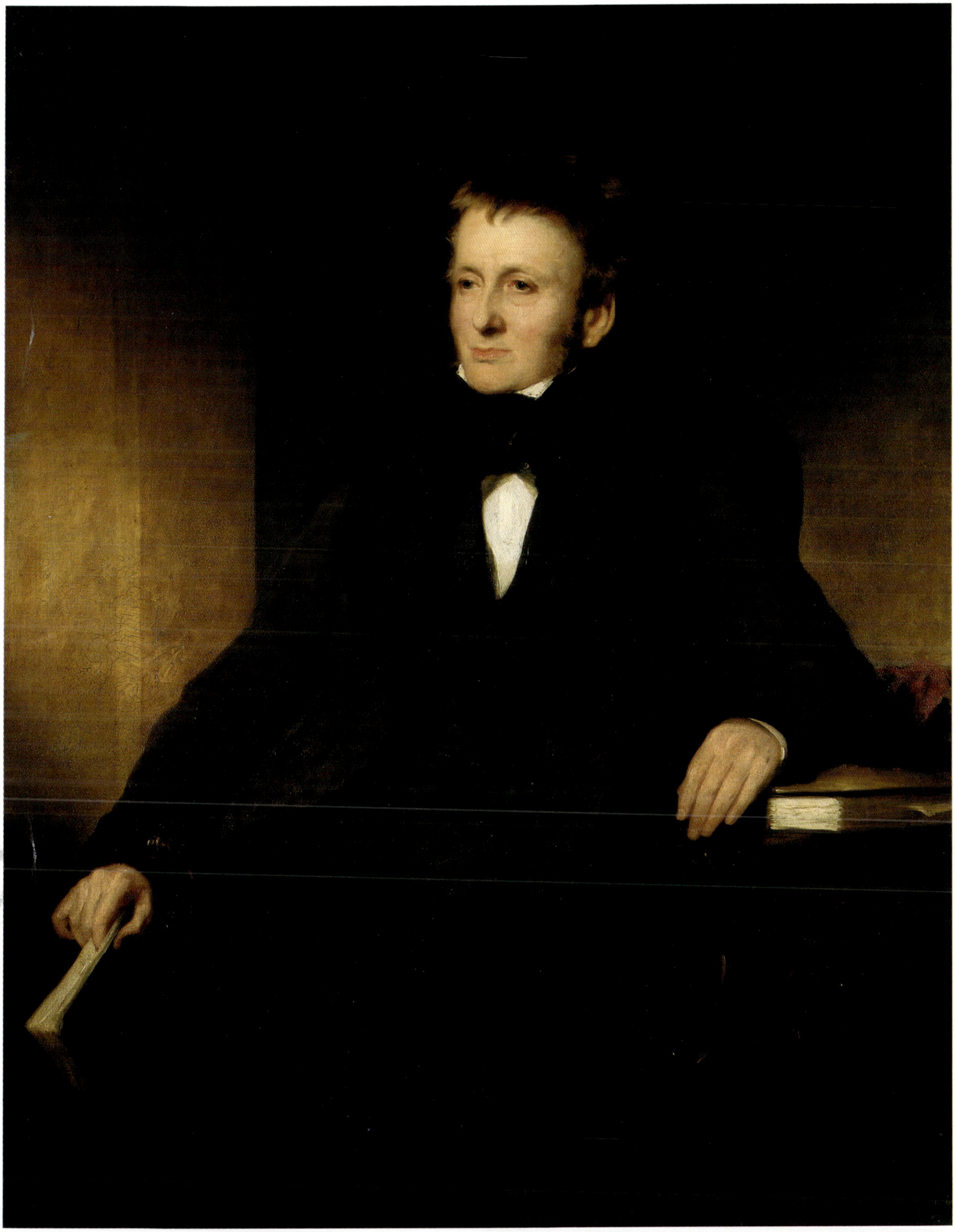

WILLIAM HAZLITT, 1804

Charles Lamb

(1775-1834)

Oil on canvas, 762 × 622 mm (30 × 24½ ins)
(NPG 507)

To Wordsworth, writing about Lamb after his death, he was 'the frolic and the gentle'. To Coleridge, a lifelong friend from their days together at Christ's Hospital school, he was 'my gentle-hearted Charles'. The public knew him as a fine essayist, a sympathetic critic, and an occasional poet.

Lamb spent almost his entire life in London, a city he loved: 'I have passed all my days in London until I have formed as many and intense local attachments, as any of you mountaineers can have done with dead nature', he wrote to Wordsworth in 1801. For thirty years he worked at East India House. He never married, but lived with and cared for his sister Mary, a manic depressive, who in 1796 had killed their mother in a fit of madness.

Early in his writing career Lamb published some poetry, a prose romance and a tragedy, *John Woodvil* (1801). His first real success was the collection of prose adaptations of Shakespeare for children, *Tales from Shakespeare* (1807); he wrote the tragedies, his sister the comedies and histories. Between 1820 and 1823 he was a regular contributor to the *London Magazine*, writing a series of popular essays under the name 'Elia'. The collected *Essays of Elia* was published in 1823 and 1833.

Witty, fun-loving and affectionate, Lamb was a good friend and companion. 'It was indeed an immortal evening', wrote Haydon in his diary after one memorable dinner in 1818, 'Wordsworth's fine intonation as he quoted Milton and Virgil, Keats's eager inspired look, Lamb's quaint sparkle of lambent humour, so speeded the stream of conversation, that in my life I never passed a more delightful time'.

This is one of Hazlitt's last pieces of portraiture, and shows Lamb dressed as Velázquez's 'Philip IV'. Crabbe Robinson described it in his diary as 'certainly the only painting by Hazlitt that I ever saw with pleasure'.

RW & SH

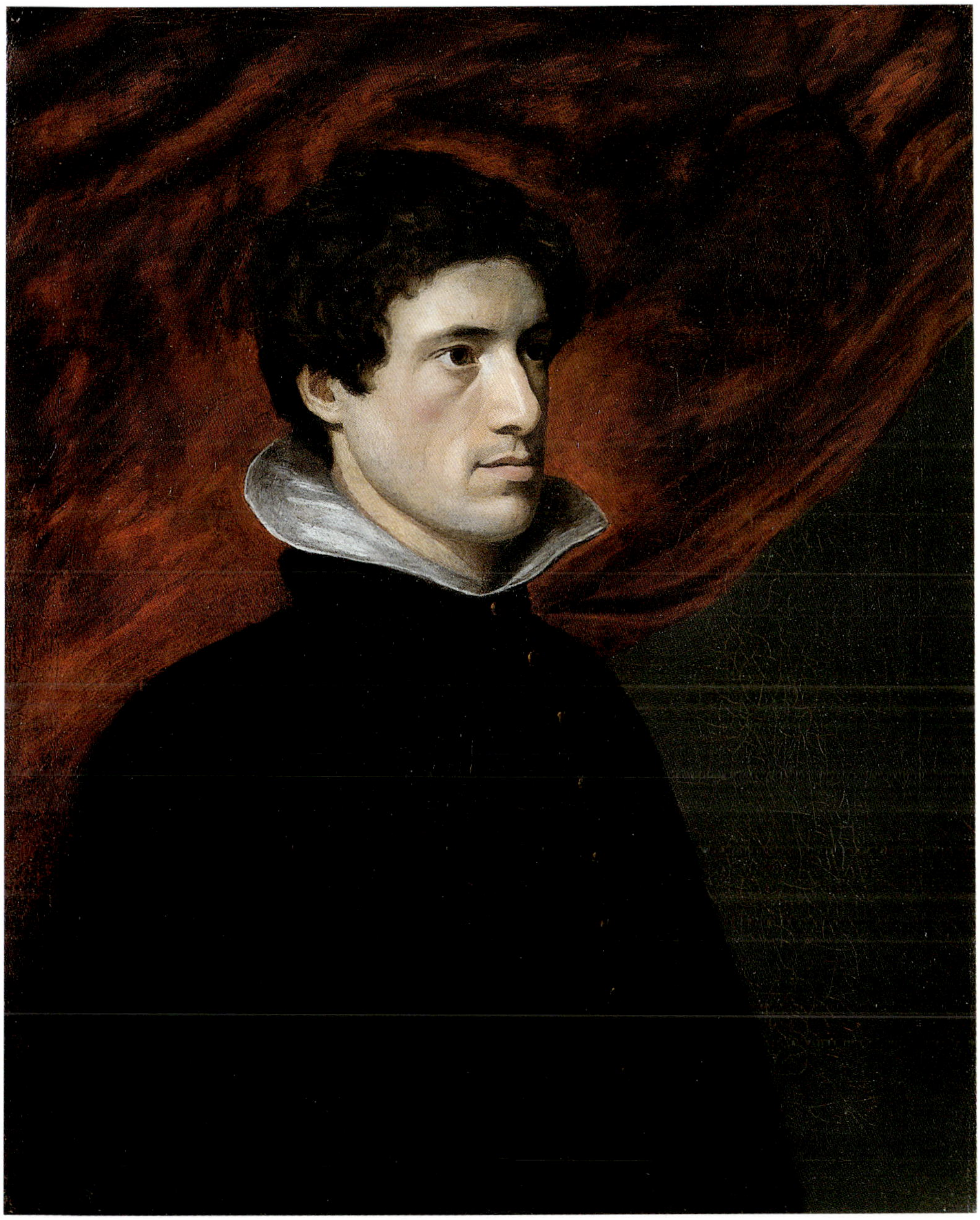

SAMUEL LAURENCE, *c.*1837

James Henry Leigh Hunt

(1784-1859)

Oil on canvas, 1118 × 905 mm (44 × 35⅝ ins)
(NPG 2508)

Poet, essayist, journalist and critic, Leigh Hunt is unfortunate to be remembered now for his mean-spirited biography of Byron and as the model for Dickens's Harold Skimpole. A lifetime's partiality to his friends' money always made him vulnerable to criticism, but in his youth at least, Hunt was one of the most courageous and gifted writers in the liberal cause. He was an independent and perceptive champion of literary talent – he introduced Keats to Shelley – and a constant thorn in the side of a repressive government .

The son of an 'unsteady preacher', Hunt was educated at Christ's Hospital, where Coleridge and Lamb had previously been at school. In his *Autobiography* (1850) he described himself as an 'ultra sympathising and timid boy', but underneath the famous Hunt manner and gentleness so brilliantly caricatured by Dickens was a resilience that Laurence's portrait captures intelligently.

Haydon called Hunt 'as fine a specimen of a London editor as could be imagined', and painted him to match, but Laurence's portrait is more subtle. Although painted when Hunt was in his mid fifties, it is possible to glimpse the young man who mercilessly pilloried the Prince of Wales, and who received Byron and Shelley in a gaol cell filled with flowers in the almost unnaturally young-looking face. Hunt's son thought it 'by far the best existing portrait' of his father. With the exception of a miniature by Joseph Severn and a lost chalk drawing, no artist, Thornton Hunt claimed, knew him well enough to do him justice. 'He was rather tall', he wrote in the preface to his father's *Autobiography*, 'as straight as an arrow, and looked slenderer than he really was. His hair was black and shining, and slightly inclined to wave; his forehead was straight and white, his eyes black and sparkling, his general complexion dark.'

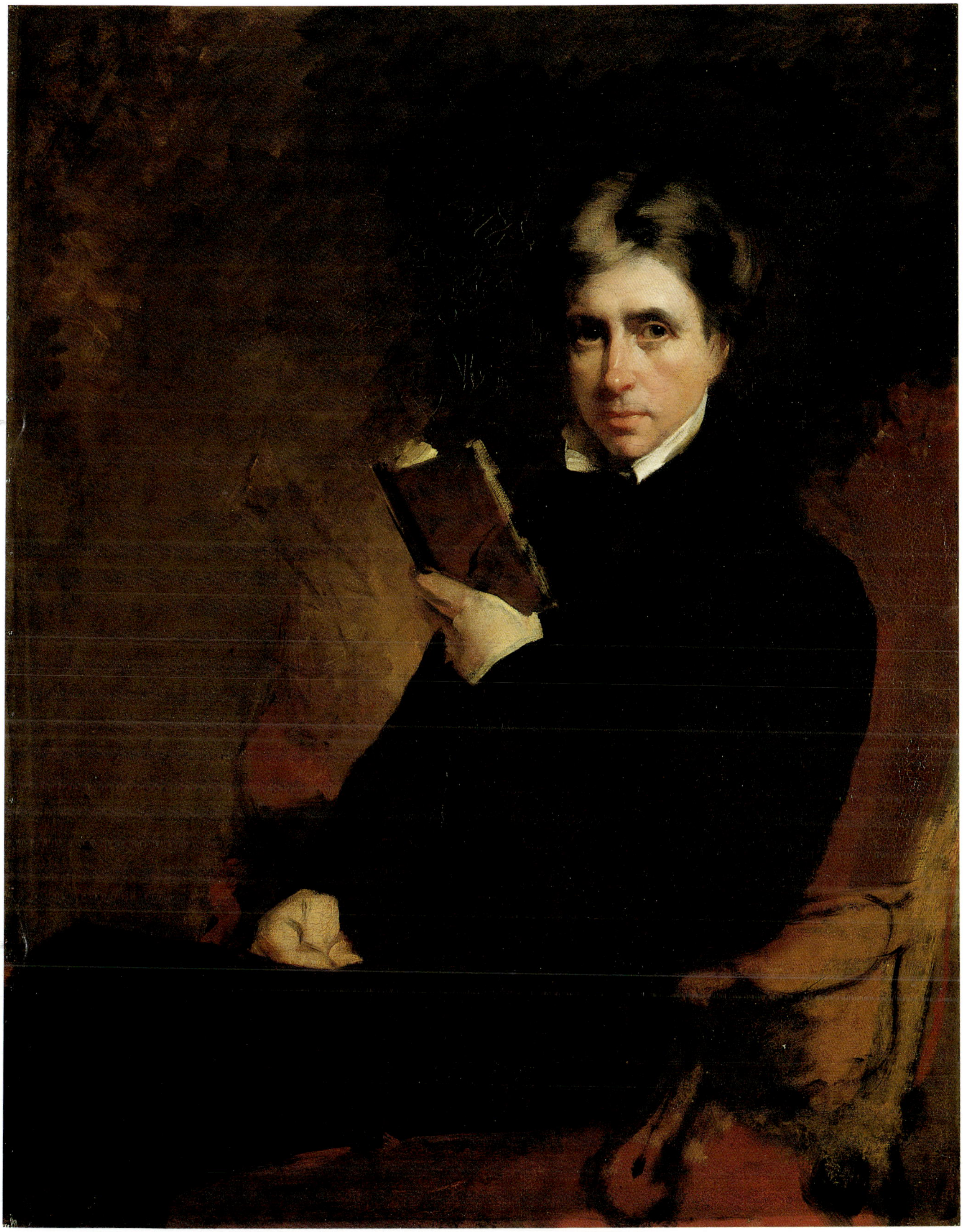

Benjamin Robert Haydon

(1786-1846)

Oil on canvas, 686 × 572 mm (27 × 22½ ins)
(NPG 510)

If Benjamin Haydon had been half as good a painter as he was a writer, his life would have taken a very different course. He has left behind him a wonderfully entertaining journal, but there was always such a fatal gap between ambition and artistic performance, between his towering sense of his own genius and the indifference of a philistine England to his paintings, that he has come down as one of the tragicomic figures of the age.

As the friend of Wordsworth, Keats, Lamb and Hunt, and the champion of the Elgin Marbles, Haydon has his place in the history of English Romanticism, but after one or two early successes, his career as a history painter was a failure. As a young man he had announced that he would paint like Titian and draw like Raphael, but as disappointment followed disappointment and he went in and out of prison for debt, his life spiralled downhill towards misery, ending with a savagely botched suicide that seemed typical of everything that had gone before. 'Poor Haydon', Elizabeth Barrett wrote, 'Think what an agony life was to him, so constituted! – his own genius a clinging curse! the fire and clay in him seething and quenching one another...Tell me if Laocoon's anguish is not an infant's sleep, compared to his.'

Haydon always identified with fallen genius, and particularly with Napoleon, but as Aldous Huxley pointed out, it is more suitably Mussolini that he resembles in the 1825 portrait by his pupil Georgiana Zornlin. 'The vast and noble brow, enlarged and ennobled by incipient baldness beyond the limits of verisimilitude', wrote Huxley, 'those flashing eyes; that square strong jaw; that wide mouth with its full, floridly sculptured lips; that powerful neck – are not those Il Duce's very features?'

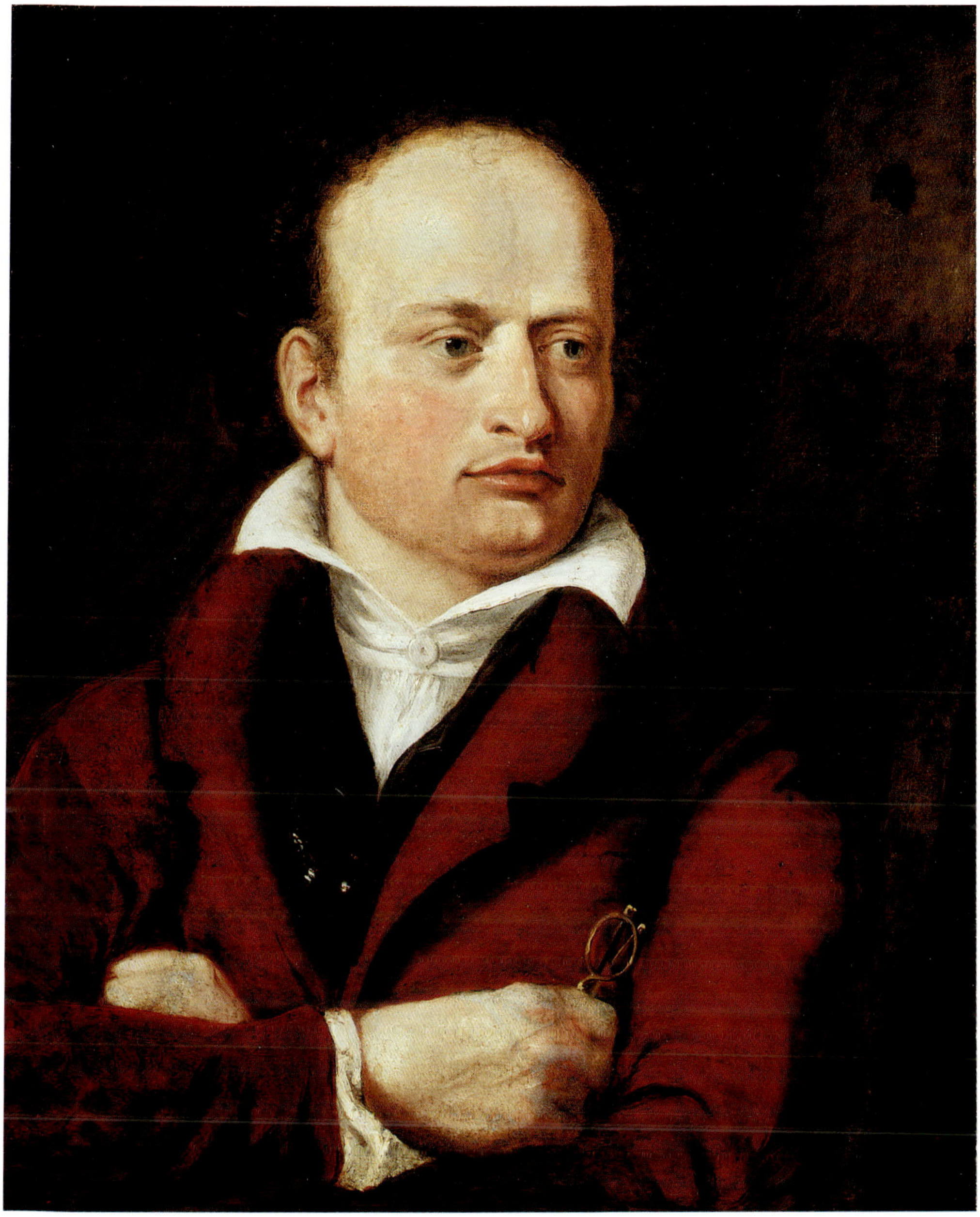

JAMES NORTHCOTE, 1778

Henry Fuseli

(1741-1825)

Oil on canvas, 778 × 645 mm (30⅝ × 25⅜ ins)
(NPG 5469)

Henry Fuseli was born in Switzerland and was a Zwinglian minister when a meeting with Rousseau confirmed his growing disenchantment with religion and put an end to his vocation. Fuseli's early cultural interests had been largely literary, but with the encouragement of Reynolds he turned in his late twenties to painting. From 1770-8 he lived and worked in Italy, falling under the influence of Michelangelo and becoming a prominent member of a group of artists that included Alexander Runciman.

Fuseli had first visited England in 1764, and in 1780 settled permanently in London, where for more than forty years he managed to combine an exotic reputation and taste for pornography with an effortless conquest of the artistic establishment. After his death there was a profound reaction against his art that only ended with the Aesthetic Movement, but the intensity of his imagination, the disturbing nature of his subject matter, and the clarity of his draughtsmanship give him an important place among the artists of his period.

'I fancied Fuseli himself to be a giant' Benjamin Haydon wrote of him, as so often achieving with a pen portrait a vividness that eluded him with a brush. 'I heard his footsteps and saw a little bony hand slide round the edge of the door, followed by a little white-headed lion-faced man in an old flannel dressing-gown tied round his waist with a piece of rope and upon his head the bottom of Mrs Fuseli's workbasket.' Northcote, not always the most generous of men, more prosaically thought Fuseli's manner less 'that of a gentleman, but more like that of a Swiss valet.'

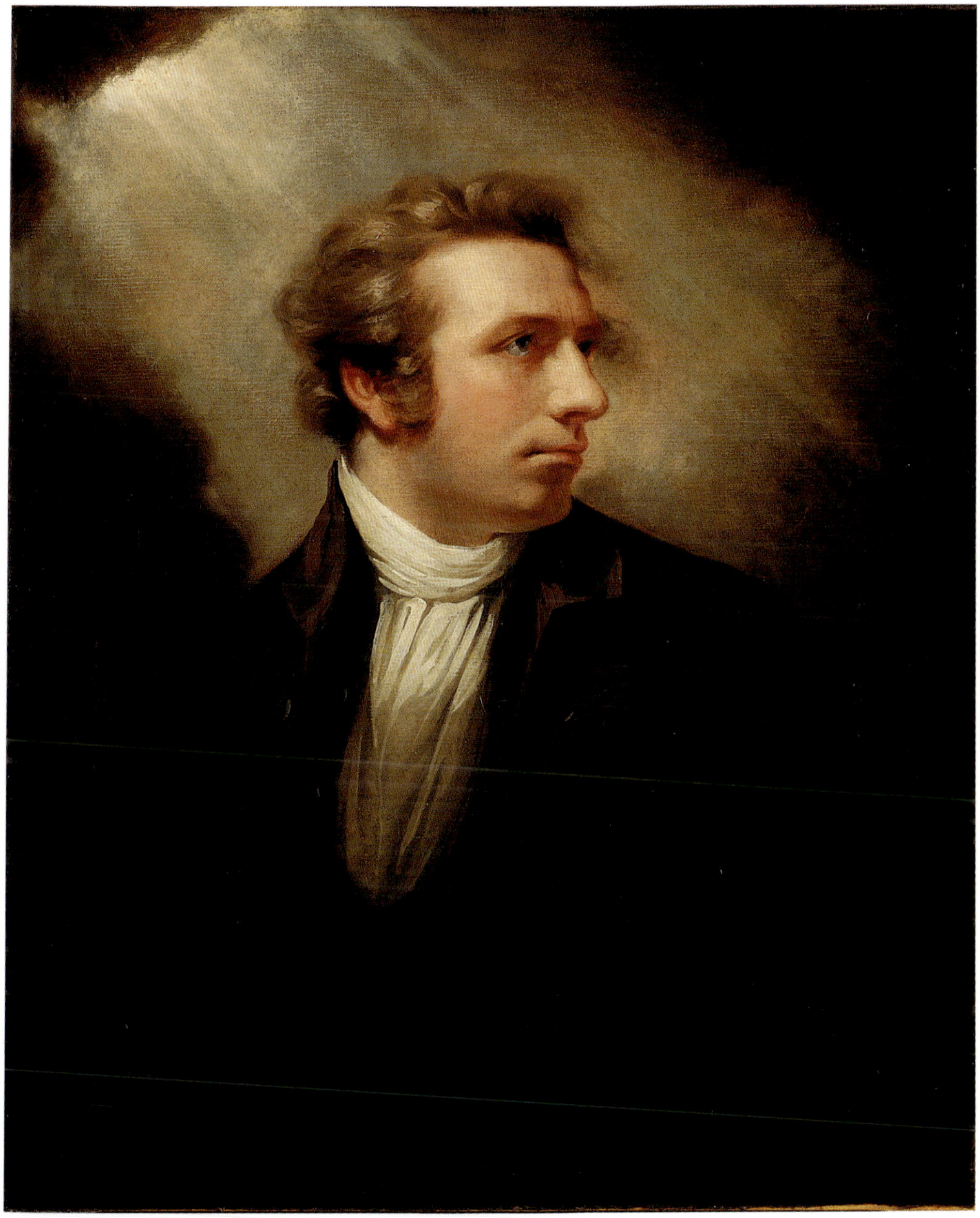

THOMAS PHILLIPS, 1807

William Blake

(1757-1827)

Oil on canvas, 921 × 720 mm (36¼ × 28⅜ ins)
(NPG 212)

Engraver, painter, poet, visionary and prophet of the modern age, Blake is perhaps the most distinctive of all the English Romantics, at once astonishingly original, and yet deeply rooted in the radical, dissenting tradition from which he came.

There are Romantic writers who could paint, like Hazlitt, and there are painters who could write, like Haydon, but Blake is unique in being equally important in both spheres. Apprenticed to James Basire and trained as an engraver, Blake wanted to find a method of uniting word and image in one integrated form, and in *Songs of Innocence and of Experience* (1794) he developed the technique of relief etching – the text etched in reverse, the illustration later coloured by hand – for which he is best known.

With his idiosyncratic, obscure and changing mythology, Blake is not an easy poet. 'That which can be made Explicit to the Idiot is not worth my care', he wrote, and during his lifetime he received little notice and was often poor. In his later years John Linnell and Samuel Palmer brought him some belated recognition as a painter, but it is only in recent times that the great prophetic poems of his maturity – as opposed to his more accessible lyrics – have attracted the sustained attention they deserve.

Phillips's portrait shows Blake at the age of fifty, the awkwardness of the pose suggesting a latent energy, the eyes fixed, as they always were, on some transcendent reality. Phillips recalled how Blake had described a vision of the Archangel Gabriel descending through the ceiling as he sat to him. 'His stature mean', Thomas Dibdin described Blake, 'his head big and round, his forehead broad and high, his eyes blue, large and lambent – such as my friend, Mr Phillips, has represented him upon his imperishable canvas.'

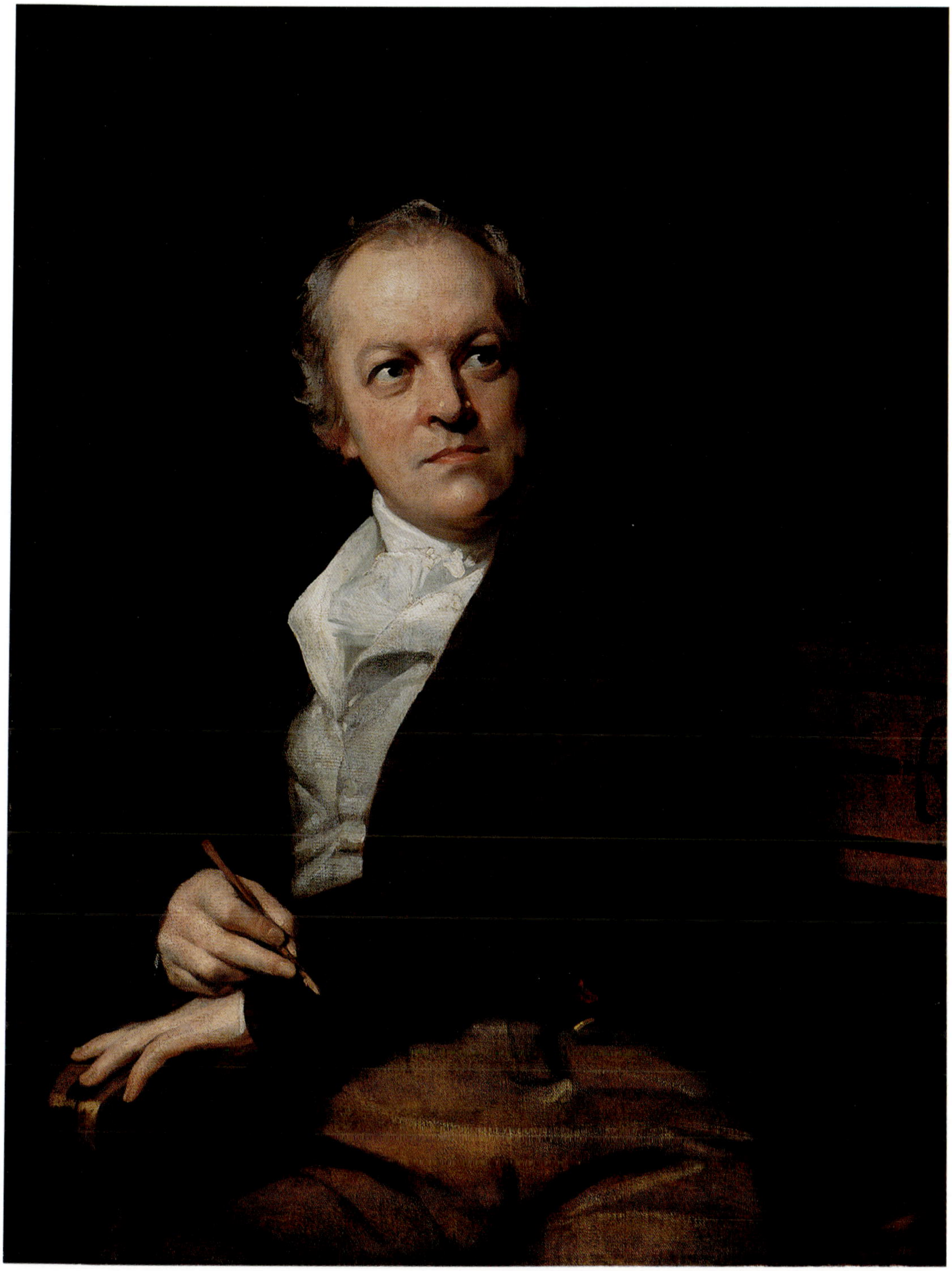

JOHN OPIE, 1798

Amelia Opie

(1769-1853)

Oil on canvas, 743 × 622 mm (29¼ × 24½ ins)
(NPG 765)

The devoted daughter of a Norwich doctor, the successful novelist and poet Amelia Opie – née Alderson – was brought up in that provincial, Unitarian tradition that had such profound influence on the intellectual and political climate of eighteenth-century Britain.

She gravitated to London in time to attend the 1794 treason trials, provoked by government fears of revolutionary France, allegedly clambering over the barrister's table at the Old Bailey to kiss Horne Tooke when he was acquitted. In the months ahead she became a vivid and attractive figure in London's radical circles. She was wooed by Thomas Holcroft and fell in love with Godwin – her complex feeling for him and Mary Wollstonecraft would surface a decade later in her best known novel, *Adeline Mowbray* (1804) – before she finally married the self-taught Cornish history and portrait painter, John Opie in 1798.

They were not to be married long, however. Opie died in 1807, the year after he had been elected Professor of Painting at the Royal Academy, and Amelia returned to Norwich. There she continued to write prolifically, carried on her literary correspondence (Madame de Staël, Scott, Lafayette and Sydney Smith were among her friends), looked after her father, became a Quaker and immersed herself in philanthropic works without ever losing her fondness for the world. She paid her own tribute to her husband with a biography of him published in 1809, and this portrait is Opie's tribute to her. It has been said that he was always a better painter of men than women, but in the peculiar intimacy of this portrait done to celebrate their marriage, in the unabashed and challenging frankness of her stare, he has wonderfully captured one of the great beauties of Romanticism and a woman of intelligence and spirit.

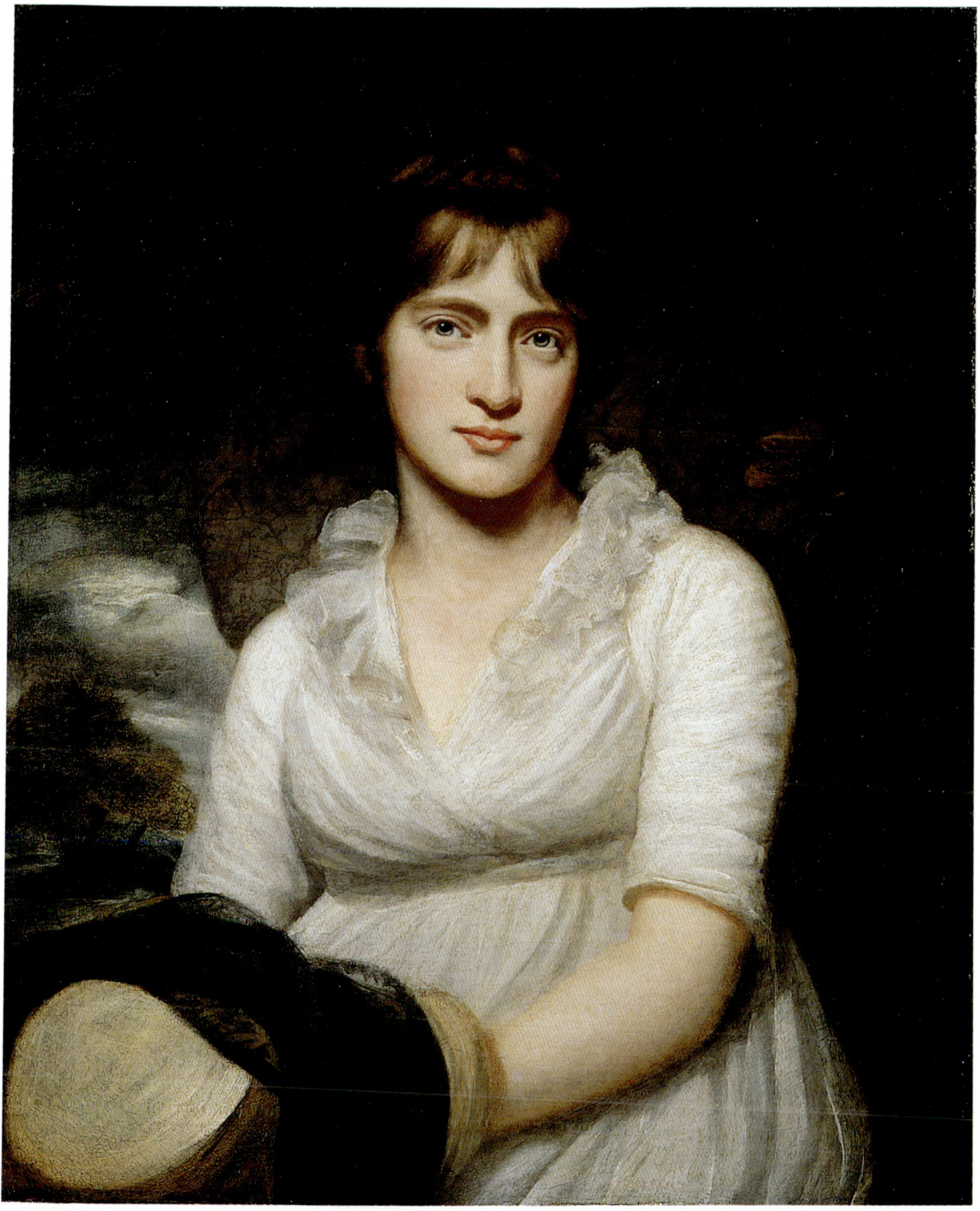

JAMES NORTHCOTE, 1802

William Godwin

(1756-1836)

Oil on canvas, 749 × 622 mm (29½ × 24½ ins)
(NPG 1236)

In the early manhood of Wordsworth and Coleridge, William Godwin was arguably the most famous of English writers. In his two volume *Political Justice* (1793), Godwin based his radicalism on an optimistic belief in human reason as a means to dispense with authoritarian controls and government machinery. Naturally reform could not be based on anything as unreasonable as violence: for him the French Revolution was not the model.

Godwin was also a novelist. His *Caleb Williams* (1794) suggests that the oppression of the hero Caleb derived from the organization of society. His subtitle, *Things As They Are*, indicates that Godwin's purpose was to analyse and demonstrate the faults of contemporary society.

In *Political Justice*, Godwin argued against the institution of marriage but he was to contradict his theories when in 1797 he married the pregnant Mary Wollstonecraft, whose *Vindication of the Rights of Woman* (1792), established her as the first British feminist. Mary died in childbirth in September 1797 and Godwin was left with two children, Mary's daughter from a previous relationship, Fanny Imlay, and the infant Mary. His marriage to Mary Jane Clairmont in 1803 emphatically domesticated him, for she, a widow, already had two children; a fifth child William, was born to them in 1805. Godwin needed money and enterprisingly published a series of children's books with his new wife. Among their authors were Charles and Mary Lamb.

James Northcote, the painter, both the pupil and biographer of Sir Joshua Reynolds, could appreciate Godwin as a fellow writer. Northcote throws the emphasis of this portrait upon the head, which befits Godwin, who believed in progress based on Reason. A Roman, perhaps republican, poise is discernible. Godwin like the portrait: 'The principal memorandum of my corporal existence that will remain after my death'. It was begun in 1801 and completed the following year.

RW & SH

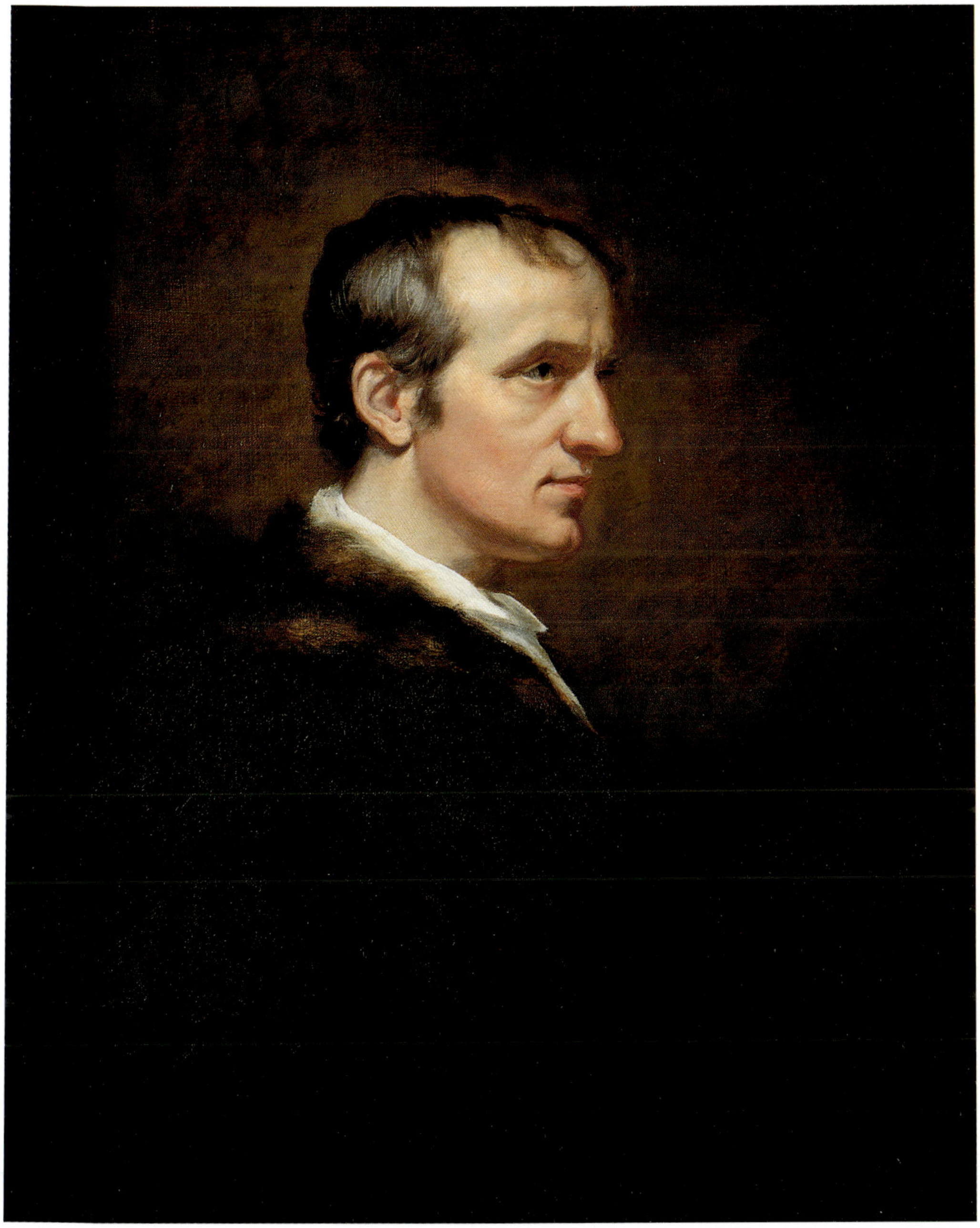

JOHN OPIE, *c.* 1797

Mary Wollstonecraft

(1759-1797)

Oil on canvas, 768 × 641 mm (30¼ × 25¼ ins)
(NPG 1237)

The wife of the philosopher William Godwin, and the mother of Mary Shelley, Mary Wollstonecraft stands in her own right as one of the major figures of the period. Half Irish by birth and wholly Irish by temperament, Mary Wollstonecraft ran a school and travelled on the Continent before settling in London in 1787, where she became a part of the radical circle that gathered around the publisher Joseph Johnson and included Blake, Fuseli, Paine and Godwin.

Mary Wollstonecraft was in Paris during the French Revolution, and had a child by the American Gilbert Imlay, but after being abandoned by him and attempting suicide, she fell in love with Godwin, and at the age of thirty-eight died giving birth to a second daughter. The influence of the mother she never knew on the future Mary Shelley was a profound and moving one, but her claims to a wider importance rest on her authorship of *The Rights of Woman* (1792), her stories, travel writing and journalism, and her seminal ideas on education. 'In the cause of half the human race', Mary Hays wrote of her, 'she stood forth, deprecating and exposing, in a tone of impassioned eloquence, the various means and arts by which women had been forcibly subjugated, flattered into imbecility, and invariably held in bondage.' She is now regarded as one of the founders of modern British Feminism.

'Everything I ever saw for the first time always disappointed me', said Amelia Alderson, later the artist's wife, 'except for Mary Wollstonecraft and the Cumberland Lakes'. Opie's portrait, painted in about 1797, when she was pregnant with her second child, captures something of the presence and force of personality memorably recorded by Godwin in his controversial biography of his wife.

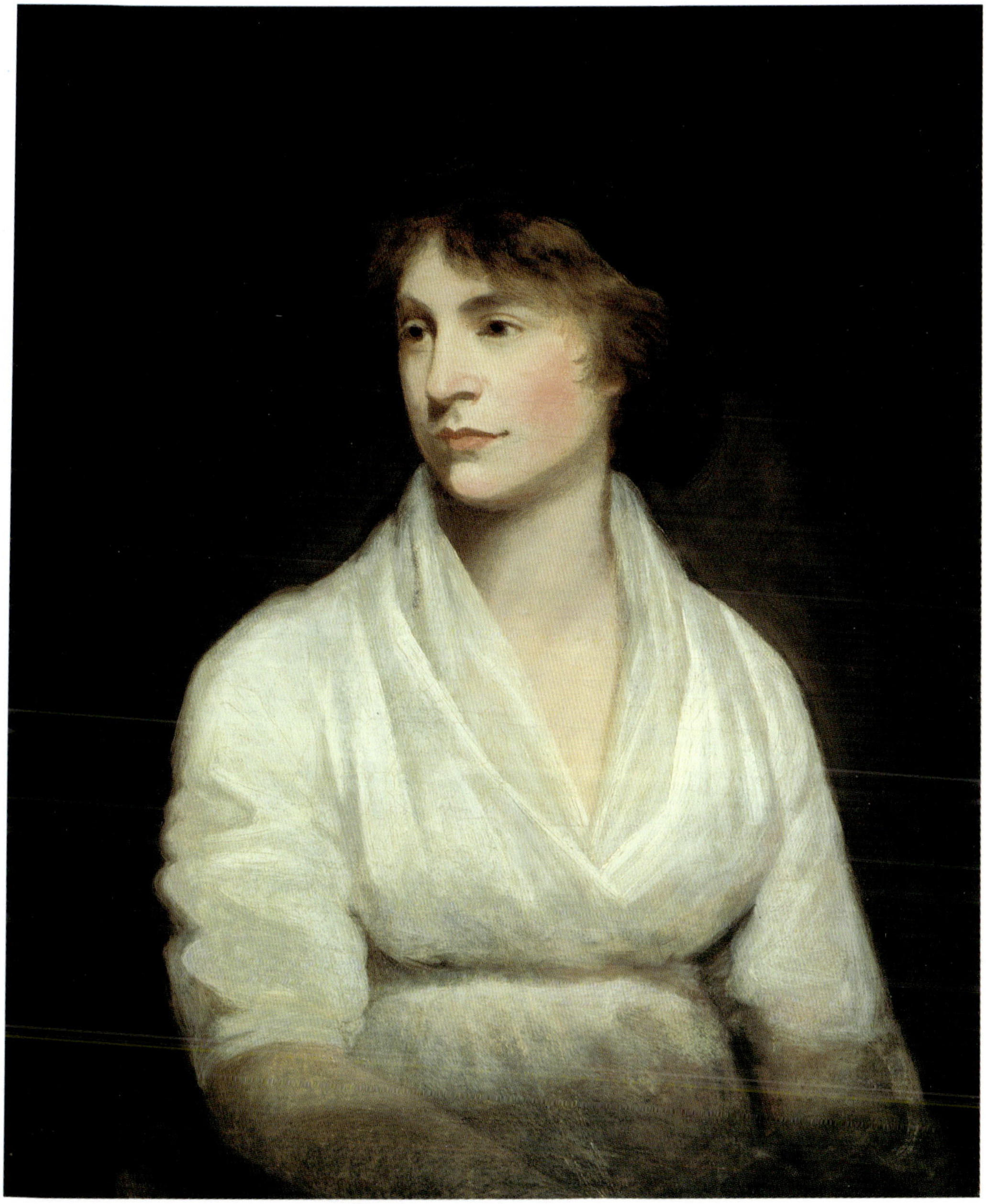

RICHARD ROTHWELL, *c.*1840

Mary Wollstonecraft Shelley

(1797-1851)

Oil on canvas, 737 × 610 mm (29 × 24 ins)
(NPG 1235)

Mary Shelley was the daughter of two of the best-known figures of the Enlightenment, and the wife of one of Romanticism's greatest poets. She was also a gifted author in her own right. Her mother, Mary Wollstonecraft, died only a few days after her birth, and her father, William Godwin, largely brought her up.

In 1814, aged only sixteen, Mary eloped to the continent with Percy Bysshe Shelley. In 1816, she and Shelley were neighbours of Byron on the shores of Lake Geneva, and visited him at the Villa Diodati; here she began her most famous work, the novel *Frankenstein* (1818). Later that year, following the suicide of Shelley's first wife, she and Shelley married. Between 1818 and 1822 they lived abroad, living successively at Milan, Venice, Rome, Florence, Pisa and Lerici, until Shelley's death in 1822. Of their three children together only one, Percy Florence, survived infancy. Mary returned with him to England in 1823.

The second half of her life, spent in England, was quiet and relatively uneventful. The portrait here shows her as a sedate widow in her forties, after she had published further novels, including *The Last Man* (1826), *Lodore* (1835) and *Falkner* (1837), and was living with her son in Boscombe Manor, the family home near Bournemouth. It hung over the fireplace in the Shelley 'sanctum' at Boscombe, together with the portraits of Godwin and Mary Wollstonecraft. When it was exhibited in the Royal Academy exhibition in 1840, the catalogue printed Shelley's description of Mary in the Dedication of *The Revolt of Islam:*

> How beautiful and calm and free thou wert
> In thy young wisdom, when the mortal chain
> Of Custom thou didst burst and rend in twain,
> And walked as free as light the clouds among . . .

RW & SH

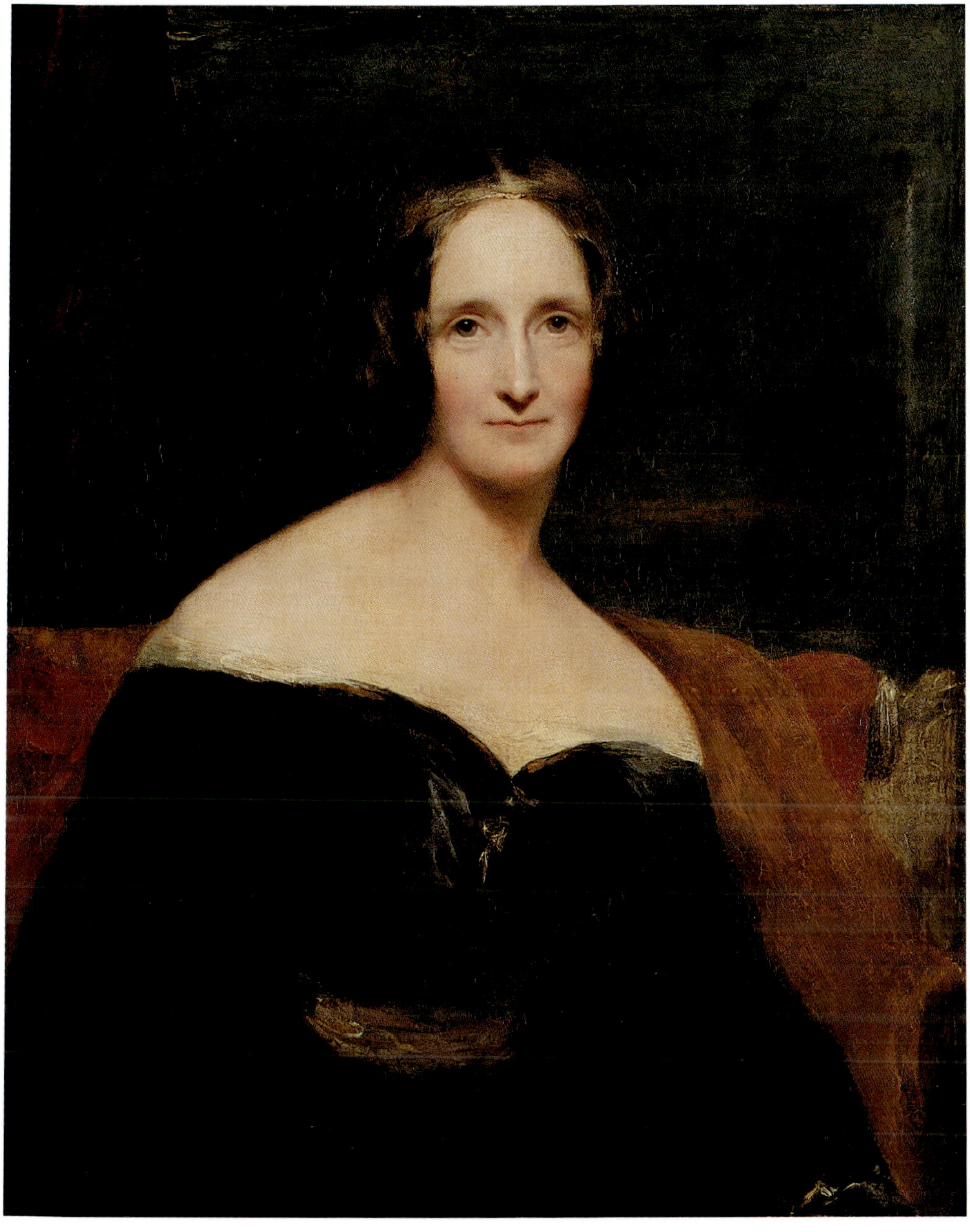

AMELIA CURRAN, 1819

Percy Bysshe Shelley

(1792-1822)

Oil on canvas, 597 × 476 mm (23½ × 18¾ ins)
(NPG 1234)

Born the son of a respectable baronet, Shelley was expelled from Oxford after publishing a pamphlet entitled *The Necessity of Atheism* (1811). He then eloped with the sixteen year-old Harriet Westbrook, and engaged in radical activities in York, Dublin, Devon and North Wales. In 1814 he left Harriet for Godwin's daughter Mary, and four years later departed England for Italy. Among his major poems, published and unpublished, were *Alastor* (1816); *Julian and Maddalo* (1818), an analysis of his friendship with Byron; *Mont Blanc* (1817); and the first three acts of *Prometheus Unbound*.

From Rome Shelley moved to Florence, then Pisa, and finally to Lerici, where he lived until he was drowned in a storm, aged 29. Among his later poetry is the last part of *Prometheus Unbound* (1820); *The Cenci* (1819); *Epipsychidion* (1821), a semi-autobiographical poem on love; and his great elegy on the death of John Keats *Adonais* (1821). He was also, throughout his life, a prolific writer in prose, and made a number of fine translations, including one of Plato's *Symposium* (1818).

Curran's portrait, painted in Rome when the poet was 26 or 27, is the only authentic likeness of Shelley. The artist considered it unsuccessful, and at one point almost consigned it to the flames, but it has the elements of Shelley's appearance as described by Leigh Hunt: 'when fronting and looking at you attentively his aspect had a certain seraphical character that would have suited a portrait of John the Baptist, or the angel whom Milton describes as holding a reed "tipt" with fire'. Often engraved, it became the popular image of Shelley, who in the years after his death became less and less the complex poet and radical intellectual that he was, and more and more, in Matthew Arnold's words, a 'beautiful and ineffectual angel, beating in the void his luminous wings in vain'.

RW & SH

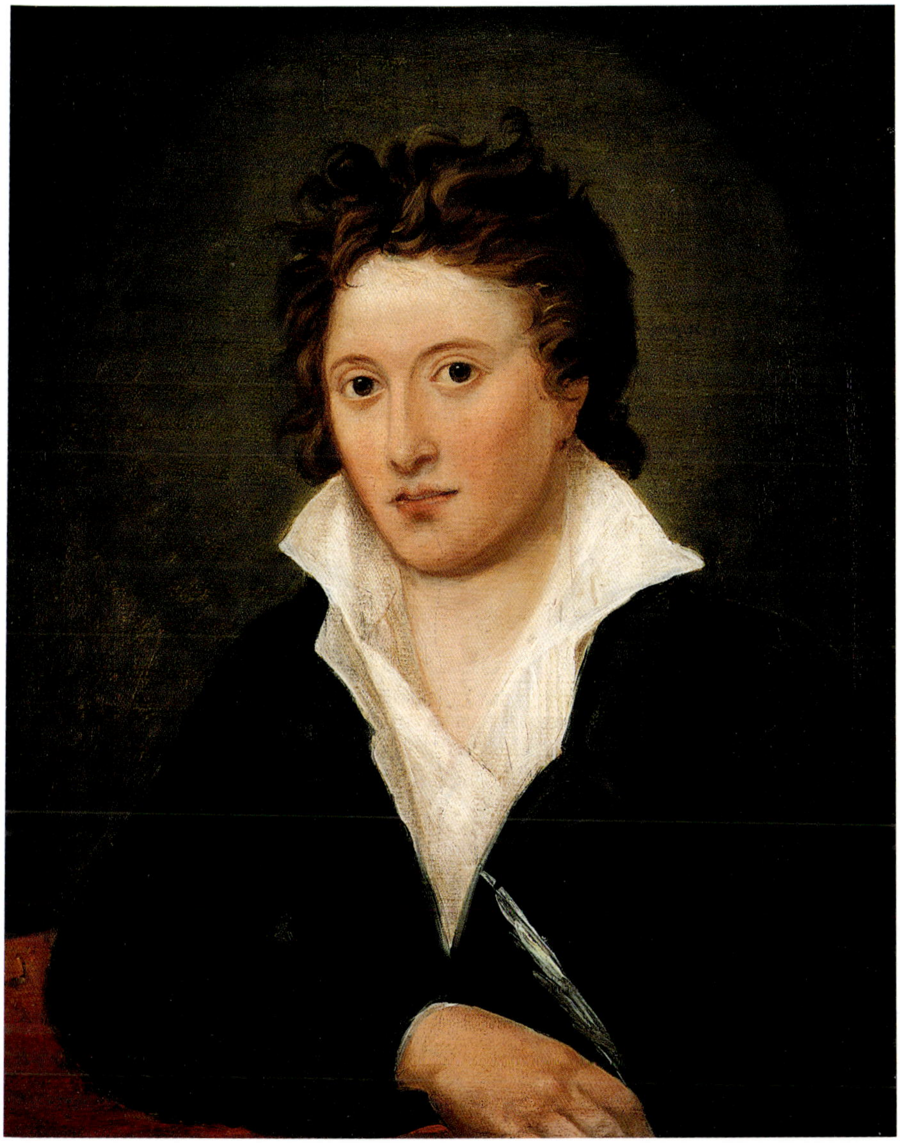

THOMAS PHILLIPS, *c.*1835

George Gordon Byron, 6th Baron Byron

(1788-1824)

Oil on canvas, 765 × 639 mm (30⅛ × 25⅛ ins)
(NPG 142)

'So beautiful a countenance I scarcely ever saw,' wrote Coleridge of Byron, 'his teeth so many stationary smiles – his eyes the open portals of the sun – things of light, and for light – and his forehead so ample, and yet so flexible, passing from marble smoothness into a hundred wreathes and lines and dimples correspondent to the feelings and sentiments he is uttering'. With his aristocratic demeanour, personal charm and beauty, Lord Byron was the very image of what a poet should be. In 1809, he published the satirical *English Bards and Scotch Reviewers*, but it was not until 1812, after he had spent two years travelling through Spain, Malta, Albania, Greece and the Aegean, that he achieved real popularity. That year he published the first two Cantos of *Childe Harold's Pilgrimage*, and, he said, 'awoke to find myself famous'.

Over the next three years he published a succession of oriental tales and was the toast of London society. He had a scandalous affair with Lady Caroline Lamb, and in 1815 married Anabella Millbank. But a year later the marriage collapsed, and he left England for Switzerland, where he befriended Percy Bysshe Shelley, and then settled in Italy, first in Venice, and then in Pisa, with his Venetian mistress Teresa Guiccioli. In 1823 he joined the Greek revolutionaries fighting the Turks, and died in Missolonghi. During his final years he wrote his greatest poetry: *Beppo* (1818), *The Vision of Judgement* (1822), and, particularly, *Don Juan* (1819-24).

Painted after an original of 1813, this portrait by Phillips shows Byron in the costume he had obtained in Albania in 1809, and was commissioned by the poet himself. 'I have some very "magnifique" Albanian dresses', he wrote to his mother Catherine Byron in November 1809, 'the only expensive articles in this country they cost 50 guineas each & have so much gold they would cost in England two hundred'.

RW & SH

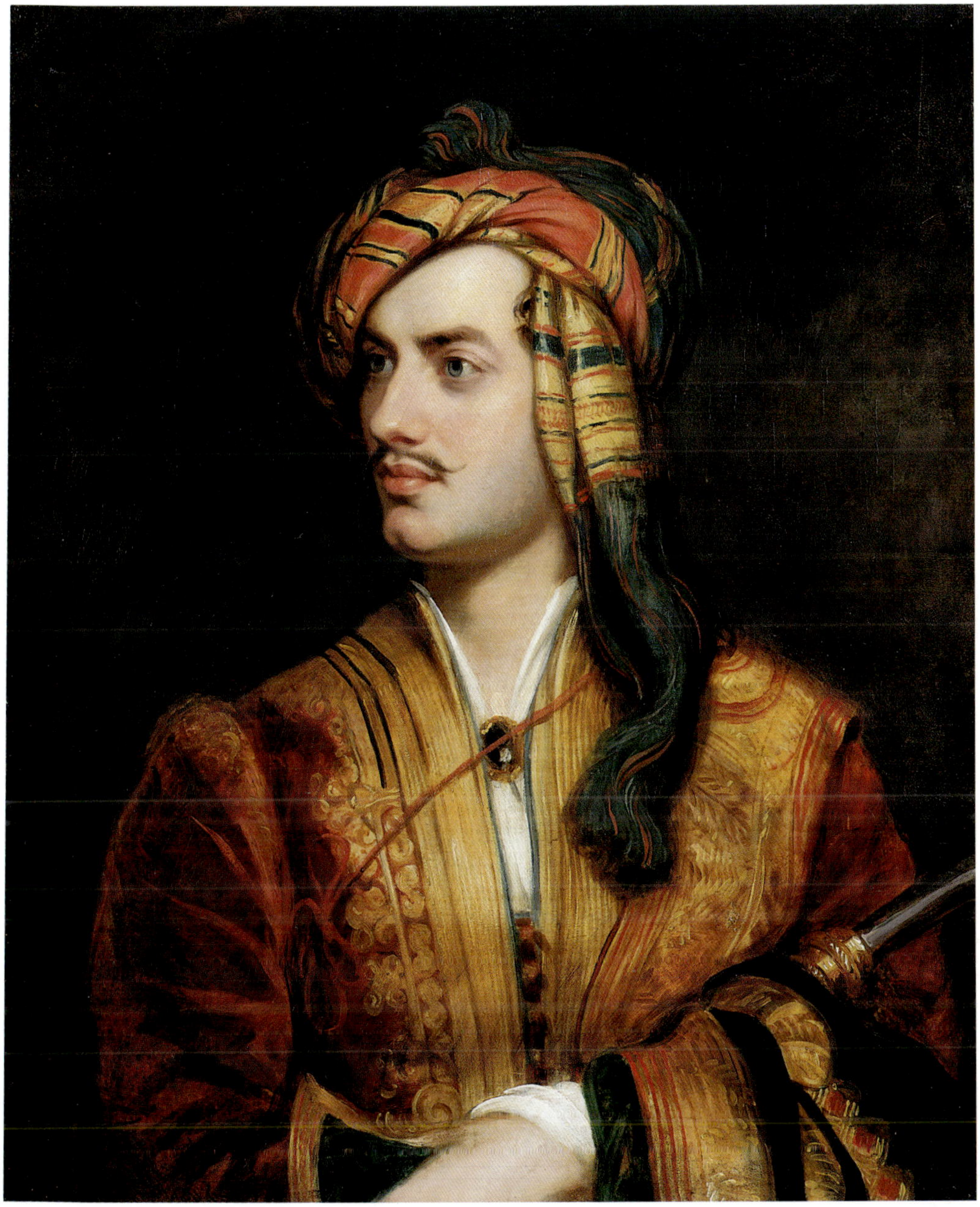

JOSEPH SEVERN, 1821-23

John Keats

(1795-1821)

Oil on canvas, 565 × 419 mm (22¼ × 16½ ins)
(NPG 58)

Keats's life was short, intense, and for a brief period, miraculously creative. In his lifetime he achieved little public renown, but made an unforgettable impact among his circle of friends. His first volume of poetry was published in 1816. This was followed two years later by *Endymion*, which was mercilessly attacked by the reviewers. In the summer of 1818 he made a walking tour of the Lake District and Scotland, and in the eighteen months after his return wrote the poetry by which he is now known: 'Hyperion', 'La Belle Dame sans Merci', 'The Eve of St. Agnes', 'Lamia', and the great odes – 'To a Nightingale', 'On a Grecian Urn', 'On Melancholy', and 'To Autumn'. They were published in 1820, but Keats's poetic career was tragically cut short by consumption, and he died in Rome in 1821, aged only 25.

Joseph Severn looked after the poet during his final days in Rome. After Keats's death he made a number of portraits of him from memory. In them he attempted to combine many of the things he remembered about his friend into a single, sentimental composition, evoking the inherent sadness and unworldly delicacy that coloured later images of Keats. In 1859 he wrote:

> After the death of Keats the impression was so painfull on my mind that I made an effort to call up the most pleasant remembrance in this picture which is posthumous. This was the time he first fell ill & had written the Ode to the Nightingale (1819) on the mor. of my visit to Hampstead I found him sitting with the two chairs as I have painted him & was struck with the first real symptoms of sadness in Keats so finely expressed in that Poem.

RW & SH

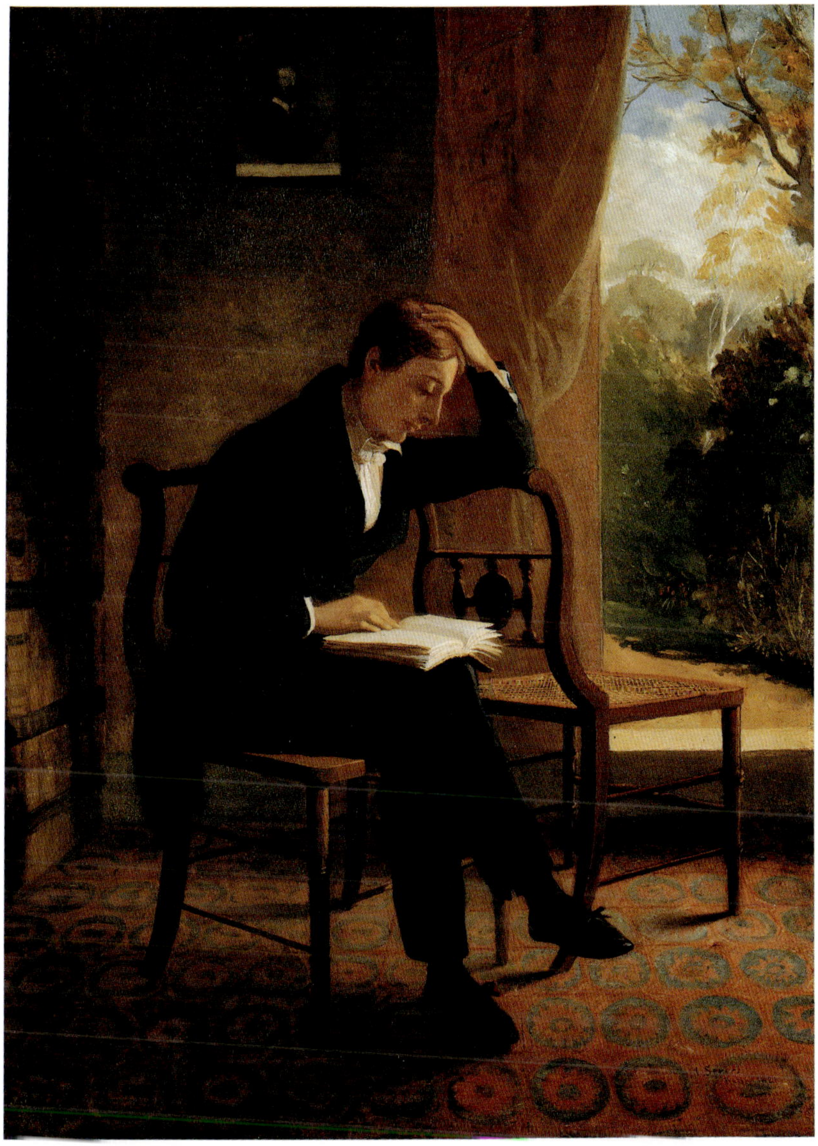

WILLIAM HILTON, 1820

John Clare

(1793-1864)

Oil on canvas, 762 × 635 mm (30 × 25 ins)
(NPG 1469)

John Clare was a poet who, like Robert Burns, was born into poverty and spent much of his life as an agricultural labourer, and who, after a period of self-education became one of the so-called 'ploughman' poets. His native landscape, to which he was intensely attached, was the countryside of Northamptonshire, and specifically the small village of Helpston. In 1820 he published Poems Descriptive of Rural Life, which had a closeness of description of the natural world that could only come from someone who lived and worked in the countryside. It also movingly evoked the hardships suffered by the rural poor, and was an elegy for the old open landscape that was being destroyed by enclosure. It was followed in 1821 by *The Village Minstrel*, a long poem in Spenserian stanzas and then by *The Shepherd's Calendar* in 1827 and *The Rural Muse* in 1835.

In 1837 he became mentally ill, and was committed to an asylum in Epping. He escaped in 1841, under the delusion that he was married to his childhood love. He was to spend the remainder of his life at Northampton General Asylum. He continued to write, but the poems celebrating the vanishing landscape around Helpston are now considered more representative of his genius.

For a while Clare's poetry enjoyed a considerable vogue, and his publisher, John Taylor, probably commissioned this portrait by Hilton at the time of the publication of *Poems Descriptive of Rural Life*. 'What life in the eyes!' T. G. Wainewright wrote of an engraving after Hilton's painting, 'What ardent thirst for excellence, and what flexibility and susceptibility to outward impression in the quivering lips! Observe the thigh caught up unconsciously by the hand! It does Hilton's penetration credit to have arrested that most sophisticated and speaking action'.

RW & SH

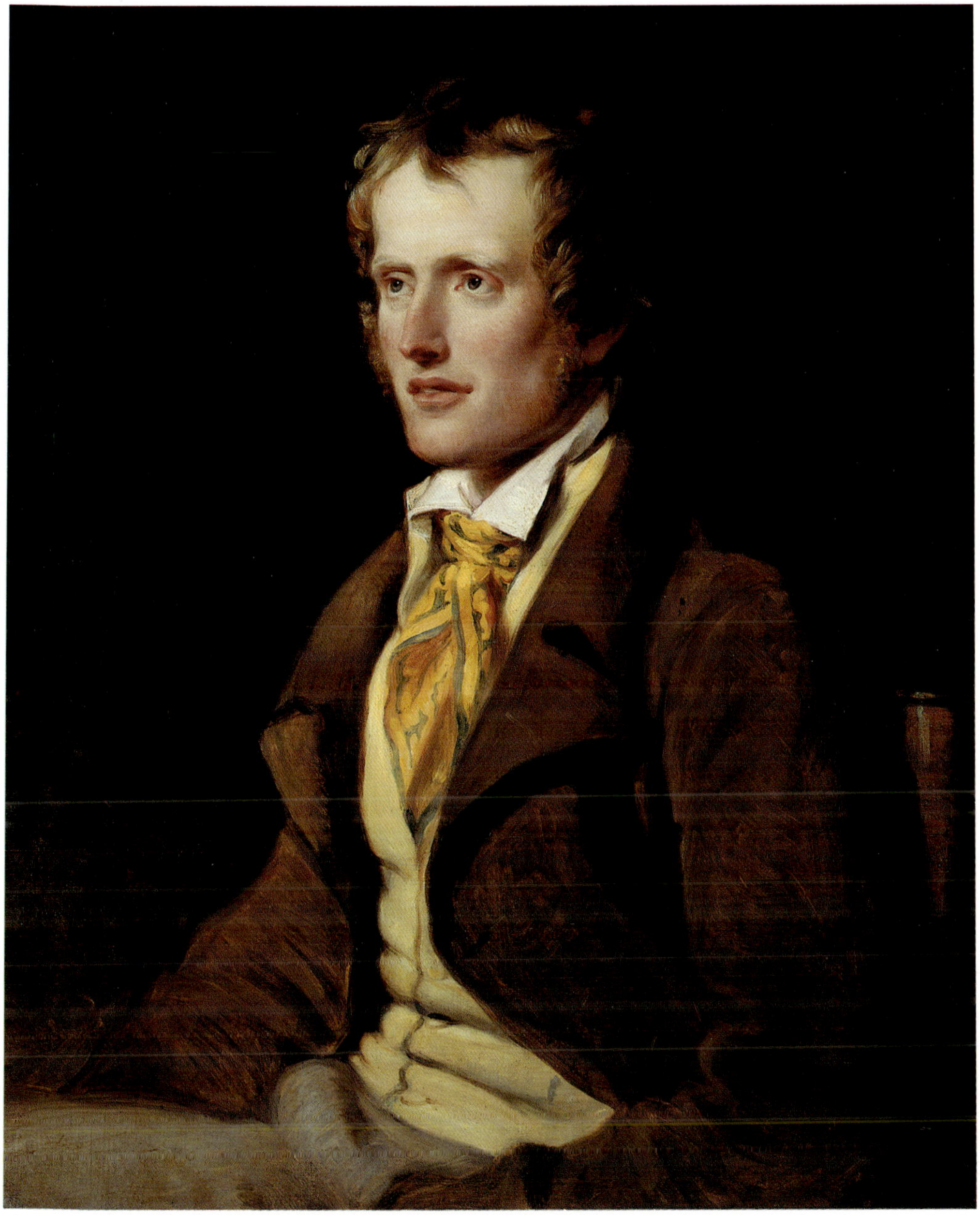

ALEXANDER NASMYTH, *c.*1821

Robert Burns

(1759-1796)

Oil on canvas, 406 × 292 mm (16 × 11½ ins)
(NPG 46)

'What an antithetical mind!' wrote Byron of Robert Burns, 'tenderness, roughness – delicacy, coarseness – sentiment, sensuality – soaring and grovelling, dirt and deity – all mixed up in that one compound of inspired clay!'

Burns was born in Alloway, the son of a poor farmer. Much of his early life was spent working in the fields, and on his father's death in 1784, he and his brother started a farm of their own. The next two years saw the failure of the farm, and Burns's emotional entanglements with a number of women.

In 1786 Burns contemplated emigrating to Jamaica. He had been writing poems for some years, and in an attempt to raise money for the trip he published a collection of them, *Poems, Chiefly in the Scottish Dialect* (1786). Its unexpected success persuaded Burns to remain in Scotland, and a second, expanded, edition was published in Edinburgh the following year. Nasmyth's famous portrait was commissioned for this edition.

In 1788 Burns married Jean Armour, and the following year he took a job as an excise officer. He also began to work with James Johnson on the *Scots Musical Museum* (1787-1803), a collaboration that was to result in some of his best-known songs, including 'Auld Lang Syne'. In 1791 he published a long poem, *Tam o' Shanter* (1795). Also at this time he became a fervent supporter of the French Revolution, although he later turned against it when it grew increasingly violent. He died of rheumatic heart disease in 1796.

Burns's use of native traditions of folk tale and popular song, and the circumstances of his early life, had a great influence on the Romantic poets. In Wordsworth's *Resolution and Independence*, for example, he is celebrated as 'Him who walked in glory and in joy / Behind his plough, upon the mountain-side'.

RW & SH

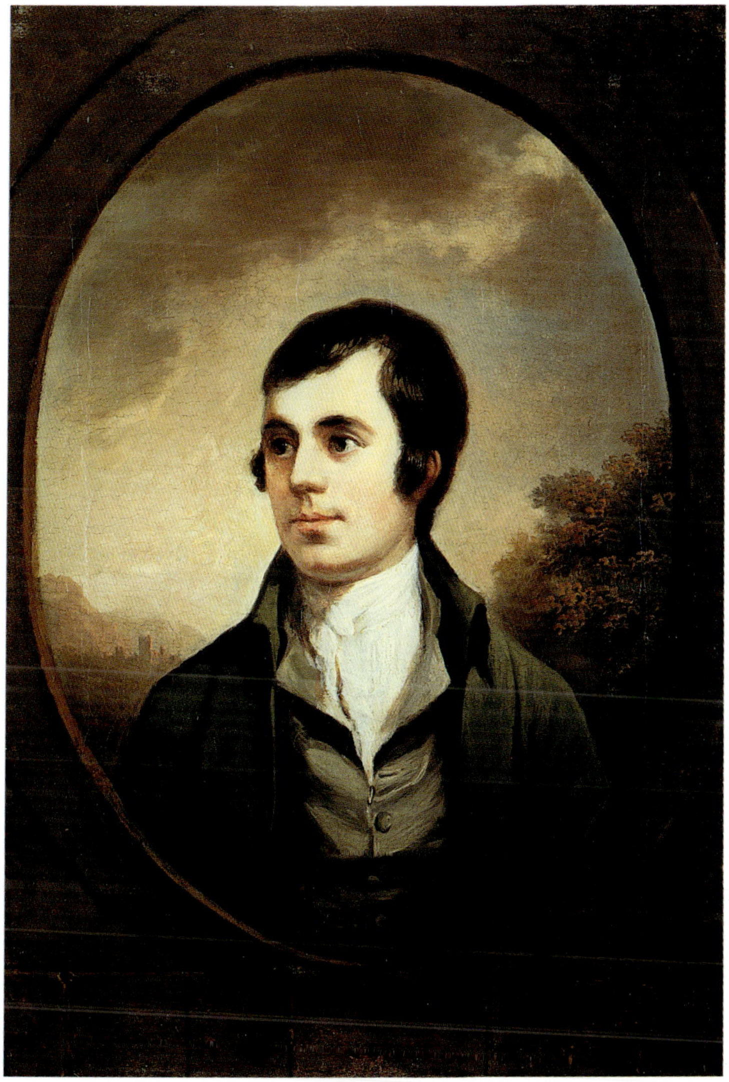

SIR EDWIN HENRY LANDSEER, *c.*1824

Sir Walter Scott

(1771-1832)

Oil on panel, 292 × 241 mm (11½ × 9½ ins)
(NPG 391)

Born in Edinburgh and trained for the law, Scott first showed his gifts as a story-teller in romantic verse tales before turning in his mid forties to his great series of historical novels. In them he invented for Scotland a romantic past from which it has never really escaped.

A passionate Tory, a proud landowner and a co-founder of the *Quarterly Review*, Scott's generosity of nature gave him a popularity that transcended party lines. 'With all his unrivalled power of invention and judgment', Francis Jeffrey wrote of him in a revealing comparison with the more savage Byron, whose advent had turned Scott from poetry to prose,

> the tenor of his sentiments is uniformly generous, indulgent, and good-humoured ... inculcating, at every turn, and as the true end and result of all his trials and experiments, the love of our kind, and the duty and delight of a cordial and genuine sympathy, with the joys and sorrows of every condition of men.

Scott's popularity is underscored by the number of times he was painted, and although with his 'irreducible egg-head' and 'unpoetical physiognomy' he was no easy subject, Landseer's portrait is among the best. There is some uncertainty over its date, but it was probably done in 1824 when the 22-year-old artist – whose later work was so clearly indebted to Scott's fiction – was paying his first visit to Abbotsford, the novelist's estate near Melrose. 'He has painted every dog in the house', Scott reported, 'and ended up with the owner.'

The setting is probably imaginary, and the quill in Scott's hand a poetic licence, but there is a fluency and sense of rapidity in the handling that is well suited to one of the most prolific and professional of British novelists.

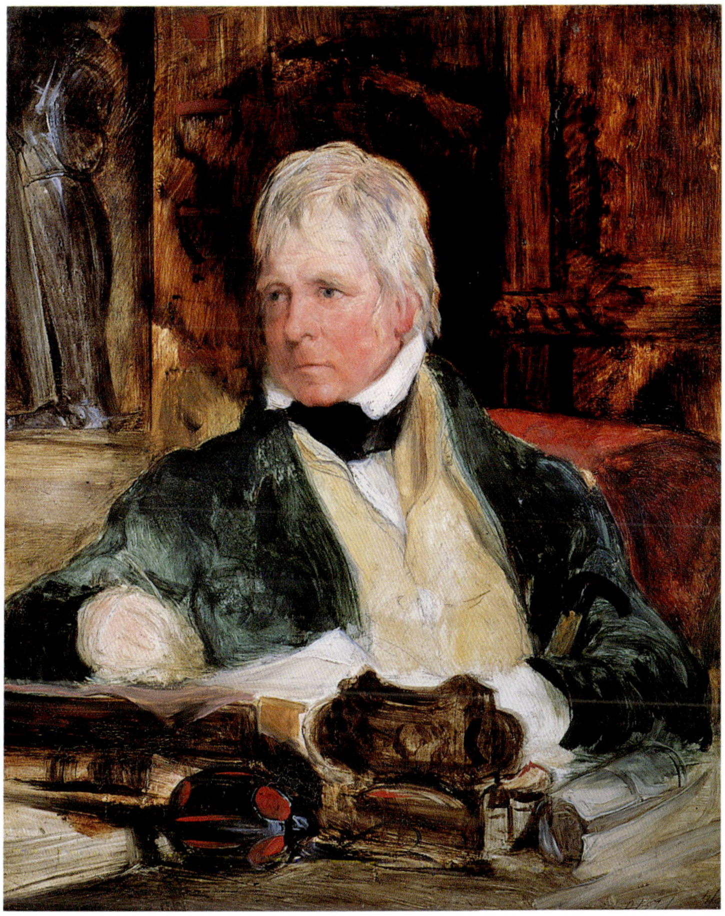

Joseph Mallord William Turner

(1775-1851)

Oil on canvas, 460 × 384 mm (18⅛ × 15⅛ ins)
(NPG 6344)

J.M.W. Turner is perhaps the greatest of all English artists. Born in London, he entered the Royal Academy schools when he was fourteen, and learned more of his craft by copying old master prints and the drawings of John Robert Cozens at the informal 'academy' of Thomas Monro. As a topographical watercolourist he toured extensively through England and Wales and, with his contemporary Thomas Girtin, enormously expanded the expressive range and effect of the watercolour medium.

In painting, too, Turner's achievement was immense and his work grew ever more inventive and visionary in form and colour. Later paintings such as *The Fighting Temeraire* (1839), *The Evening of the Deluge* (1843) and *Rain, Steam and Speed – The Great Western Railway* (1844), are now among the most vivid images of Romanticism, though at the time they bewildered many of Turner's contemporaries.

Extraordinarily prolific, on his death Turner bequeathed 300 paintings and nearly 20,000 watercolours and drawings to the nation. His early champion and most perceptive critic was John Ruskin, who wrote in *Modern Painters* (1843):

> There is no test of our acquaintance with nature so absolute and unfailing, as the degree of admiration we feel for Turner's painting. Precisely as we are shallow in our knowledge, vulgar in our feeling, and contracted in our views of principles, will the works of this artist be stumbling-blocks to us: precisely in the degree to which we are familiar with nature, constant in our understanding of her, will they expand before our eyes into glory and beauty.

Linnell recorded that this portrait was painted on 29 June 1838, 'from recollection … at the request of a friend of his at whose table we frequently met [the Rev. J. Daniell]. I made no memorandum at the time of meeting but painted from memory entirely at the first opportunity.'

RW & SH

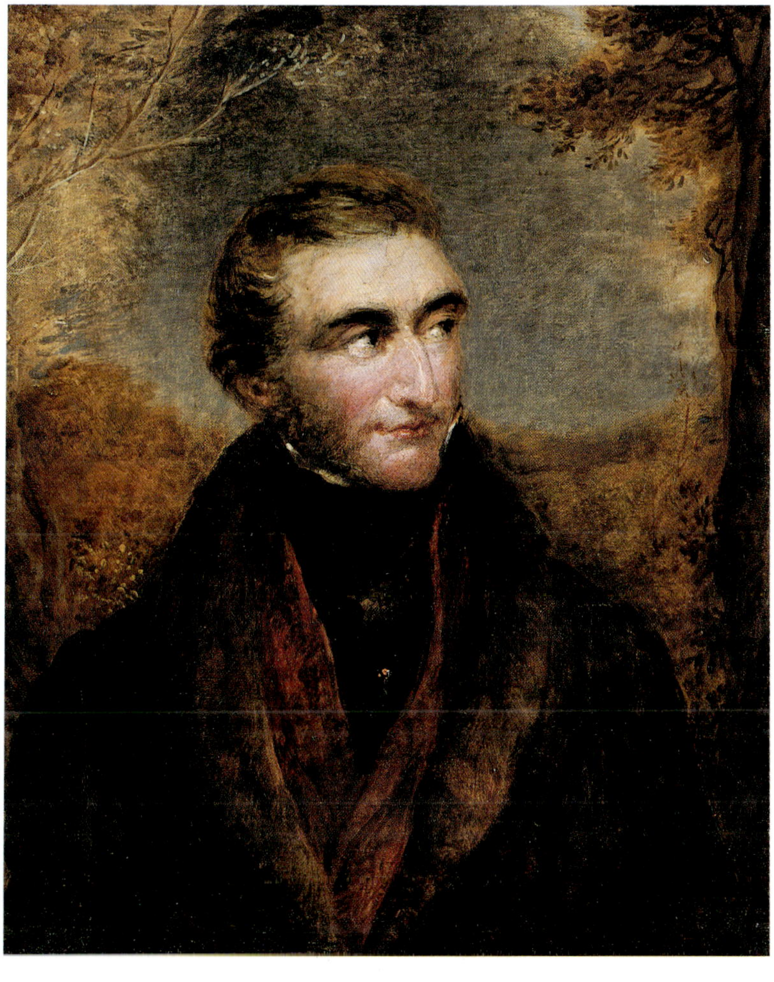

JOHN OPIE, *c.*1800

Thomas Girtin

(1775-1802)

Oil on canvas, 762 × 635 mm (30 × 25 ins)
(NPG 882)

'If Tom Girtin had lived', Turner generously declared, 'I should have starved' and even in his short life Girtin demonstrated a power and originality that make him one of the great English watercolourists. Born in Southwark of Huguenot extraction, Girtin began to paint in a conventional topographical tradition but by his early twenties he had already developed the style and palette that, along with Turner's work, would revolutionize watercolour painting at the end of the eighteenth century.

Girtin never stopped developing as an artist, and in the last years of his life began to work on a larger scale, producing an oil panorama of London now only known from preliminary studies. In 1801-2 he visited Paris, and although he died either of asthma or consumption before he could complete a second projected panorama, the visit resulted in some of his most accomplished work.

It is appropriate that so original an artist should be seen here in a portrait by John Opie. The 'Cornish Wonder' was the son of a West Country carpenter, and, taken up by Dr Wolcot (the notorious satirist Peter Pindar), proved a sensation in London, where his untaught talent and country background won him a fashionable éclat and commissions. 'What is he like?' Northcote asked. 'Like?' he was told, 'Why! like Caravaggio and Velázquez in one.' 'The total absence of artificial manners', Mrs Inchbald wrote of him, 'was the most remarkable characteristic, and at the same time, the adornment and deformity, of Mr. Opie.'

Among others artists and writers, Opie painted Dr Johnson, Fuseli, Southey, Mary Wollstonecraft, and his wife, Amelia Opie. His portrait of Girtin, brush in hand, with its alert and concentrated expression and ruddy colouring, gives no hint of the weakness that within two years would cause his death.

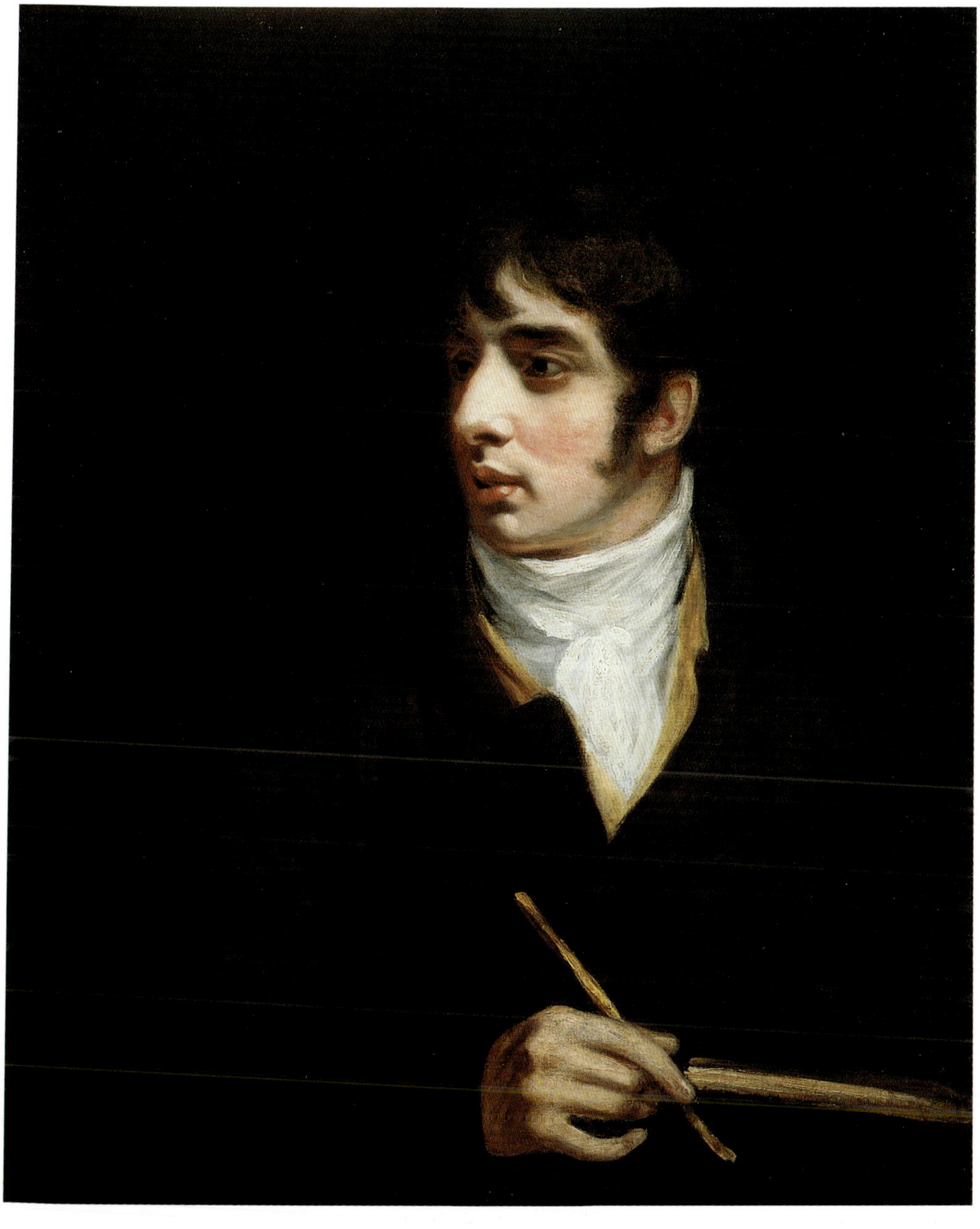

RAMSAY RICHARD REINAGLE, *c.*1799

John Constable

(1776-1837)

Oil on canvas, 762 × 638 mm (30 × 25⅛ ins)
(NPG 1786)

Though John Constable was never a great popular success, in his lifetime he achieved a revolution in landscape painting. His ambition, he said in 1802, was to 'stop running after pictures and seeking the truth at second hand' and 'to get a pure and unaffected representation of the scenes that may employ me'. In his work, humble, familiar scenes of nature are recorded with a new directness and immediacy.

He was born in East Bergholt in Suffolk, and the neighbouring valley of the River Stour was the single biggest inspiration for his work: 'I associate "my careless boyhood" with all that lies on the banks of the Stour', he said in later life, 'Those scenes made me a painter, and I am grateful'. He began his working life in his father's mill, but in 1799, following advice from Sir George Beaumont and Joseph Farington, he enrolled to study at the Royal Academy schools. Over more than thirty years he composed a large number of landscapes, from numerous private watercolours to exhibited oil paintings. His favourite subject was the scenery of Suffolk and Essex, but he also drew and painted scenes from Salisbury, Brighton, Hampstead, Derbyshire and the Lake District.

Quintessentially an English artist, Constable's greatest recognition in his own lifetime came, nevertheless, in France. In 1821 *The Hay Wain* was singled out by the French critics at the Royal Academy, and admired especially by Théodore Géricault. As a result it was borrowed, together with *View on the River Stour*, for the Paris Salon of 1824, and awarded a gold medal by the French king.

The portrait here is by Constable's friend Ramsay Richard Reinagle, with whom Constable stayed when he first came to London, and was made during or soon after Reinagle's visit to Bergholt.

RW & SH

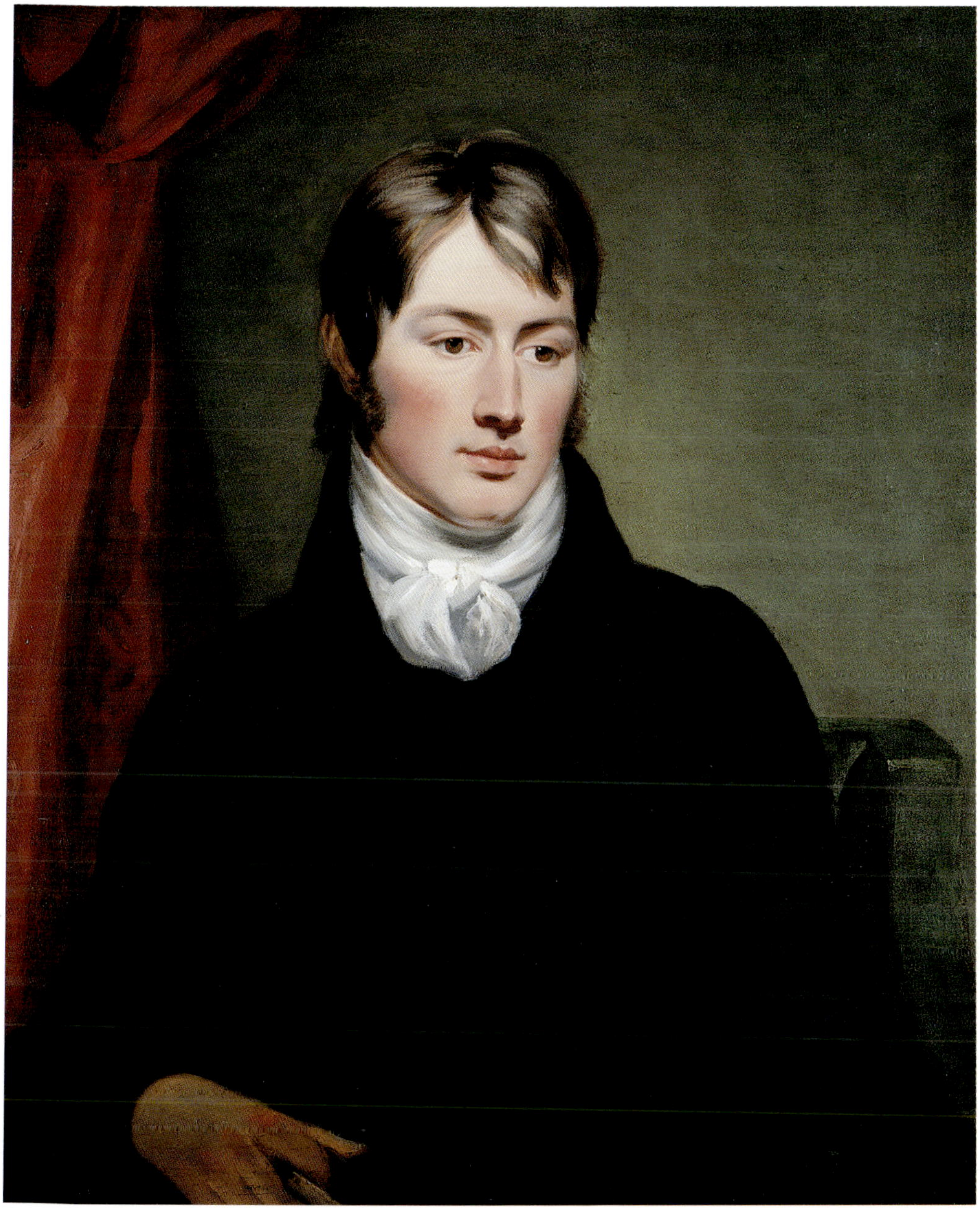

GEORGE ROMNEY, 1795

John Flaxman

(1755-1826)

Oil on canvas, 762 × 635 mm (30 × 25 ins)
(NPG 101)

The precociously talented son of a plaster cast maker, John Flaxman began his career designing classical cameos, friezes and medallions for Wedgwood. In 1787 he left for Rome where he lived for the next seven years. He won himself a European reputation with his illustrations of Homer, Aeschylus and Dante, that he never quite lived up to on his return to England.

His natural sensitivity to Greek vase painting, and his elegant simplicity of line, make him one of England's most distinctive sculptors. He was never at his best in large scale or public commissions, but his talent for archaizing design together with a kind of sexless purity that anticipated the tastes of the mid-century made him a prolific and successful sculptor of private memorials.

A kind and simple man, with an over-large head, pronounced forehead, eyes full of enthusiasm, a 'plebeian' jut of the jaw, and high-shouldered to the point of deformity, he appears here in a painting that is above all a celebration of friendship. There is an uneveness of quality about it that has called its authenticity into question, but this detail is almost certainly by Romney, who in a larger version added himself. At the centre, theatrically posed, stands Flaxman; on the right, the bust of Hayley, the biographer and poet of whom Southey said 'Everything about this man is good except his poetry'; and in the foreground, Hayley's son and Flaxman's much loved pupil, Thomas, whose brief career as an artist was ended by his early death. 'For in my looks what sorrow couldst thou see', William Cowper asked Romney in lines celebrating the warmth of hospitality at Hayley's Eartham home, 'When I was Hayley's guest, and sat to thee?'

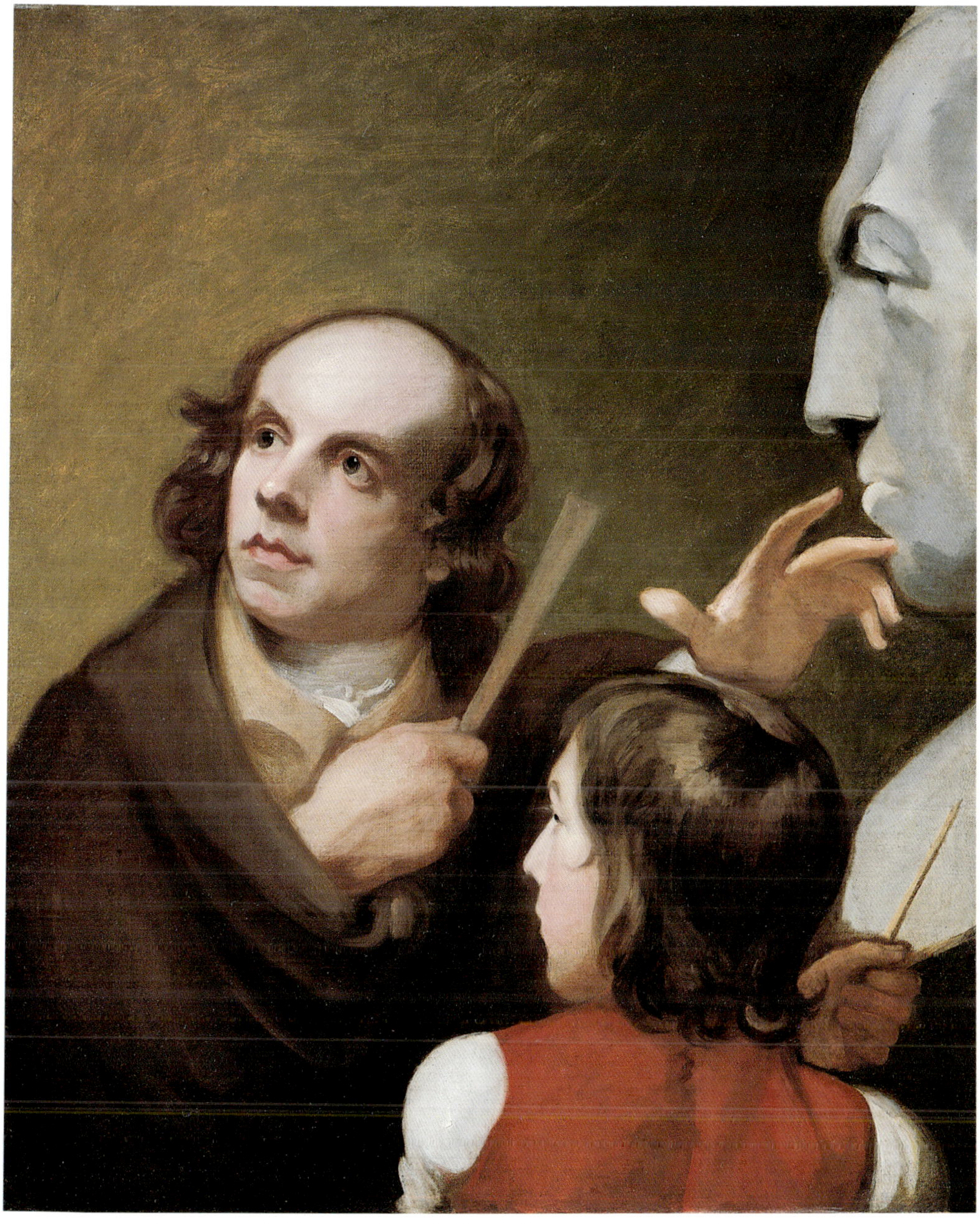

CHARLES WEST COPE, *c.*1828

Joseph Mallord William Turner

(1775-1851)

Oil on card, 159 × 130 mm (6¼ × 5⅛ ins)
(NPG 2943)

WILLIAM MULREADY, 1814

John Varley

(1778-1842)

Oil on panel, 95 × 79 mm (3¾ × 3⅛ ins)
(NPG 1529)

ROGER JEAN, *c.*1805

Thomas Love Peacock

(1785-1866)

Watercolour on ivory, 76 × 60 mm (3 × 2⅜ ins)
(NPG 3994)

CASSANDRA AUSTEN, *c.*1810

Jane Austen

(1775-1817)

Pencil and watercolour, 114 × 80 mm (4½ × 3⅛ ins)
(NPG 3630)

GEORGE LETHBRIDGE SAUNDERS AFTER UNKNOWN ARTIST, *c.*1800

Matthew Gregory Lewis

(1775-1818)

Watercolour on ivory, 114 × 92 mm (4½ × 3⅝ ins)
(NPG 2171)

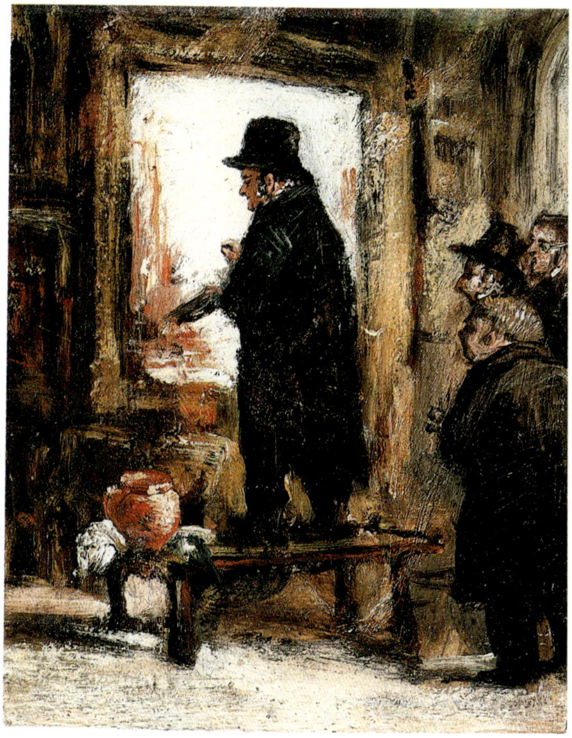

Joseph Mallord William Turner

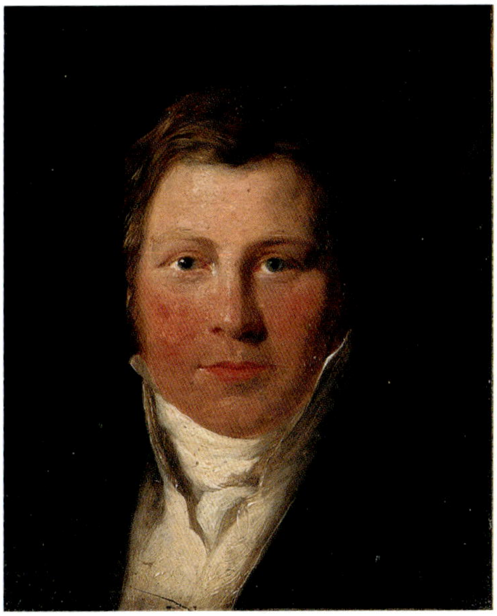

John Varley

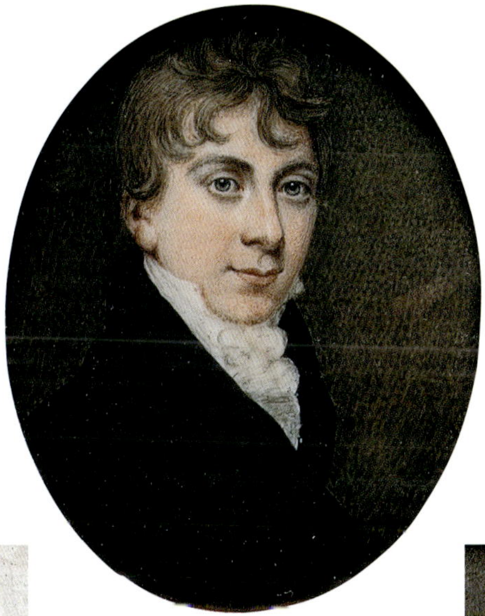

Thomas Love Peacock

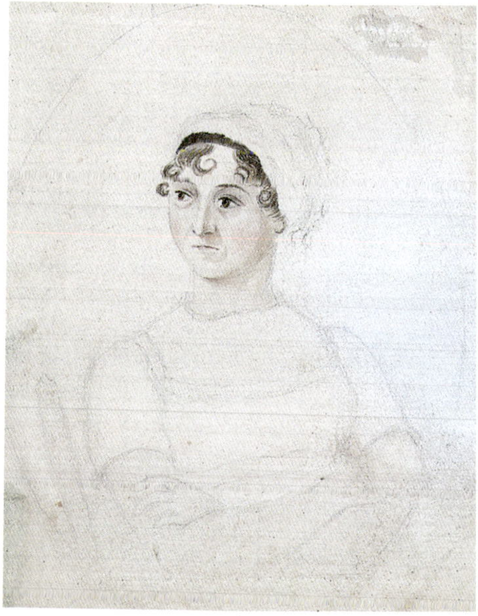

Jane Austen

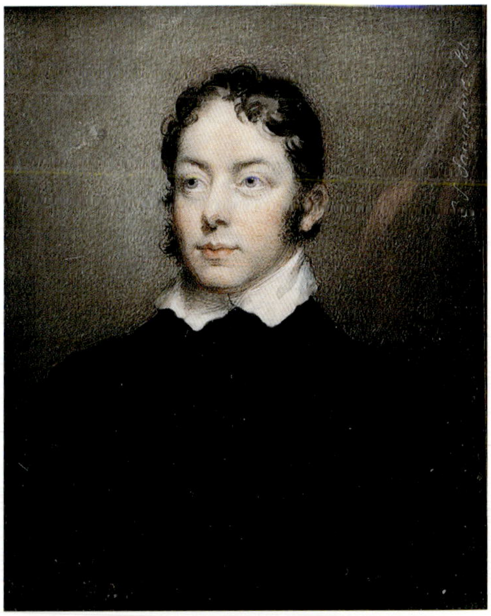

Matthew Gregory Lewis

EDWARD NASH, 1820

Sara Coleridge and Edith May Water

(1802-52)

Watercolour on ivory, 143 × 102 mm (5⅝ × 4 ins)
(NPG 4029)

JOSEPH SEVERN, 1819

John Keats

(1795-1821)

Oil on ivory, 108 × 79 mm (4¼ × 3⅛ ins)
(NPG 1605)

SELF-PORTRAIT, 1830

George Richmond

(1809-96)

Gouache on ivory, 89 × 68 mm (3½ × 2⅝ ins)
(NPG 6586)

GEORGE RICHMOND, 1829

Samuel Palmer

(1805-81)

Watercolour and bodycolour on ivory, 83 × 70 mm (3¼ × 2¾ ins)
(NPG 2223)

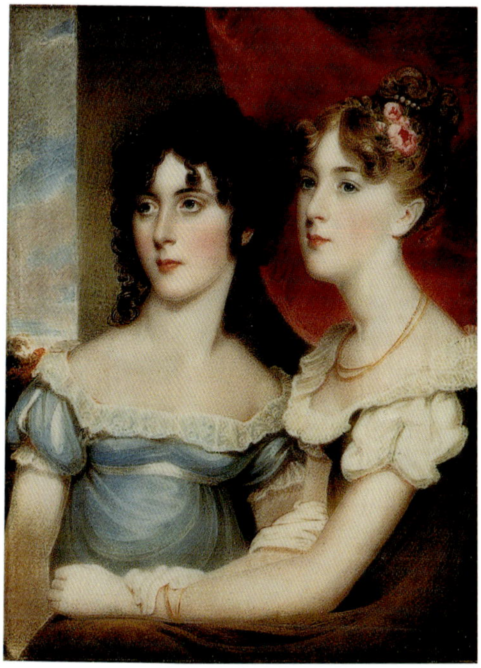

Sara Coleridge and Edith May Water

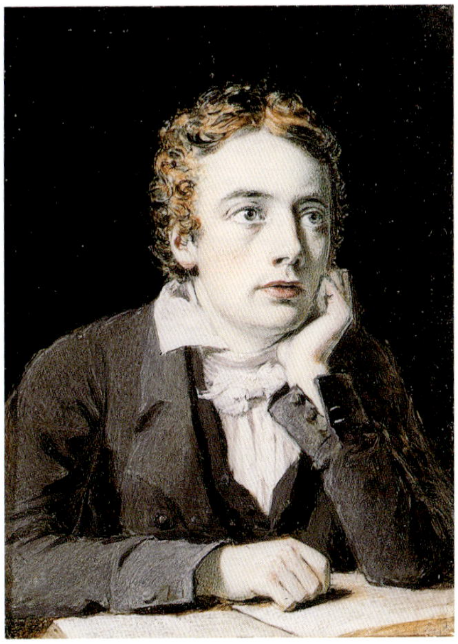

John Keats

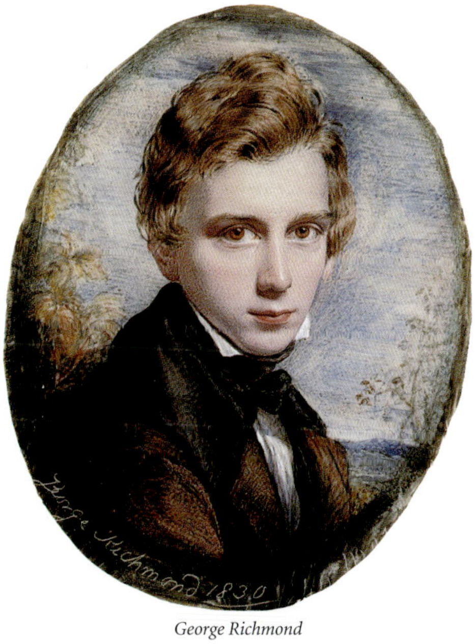

George Richmond

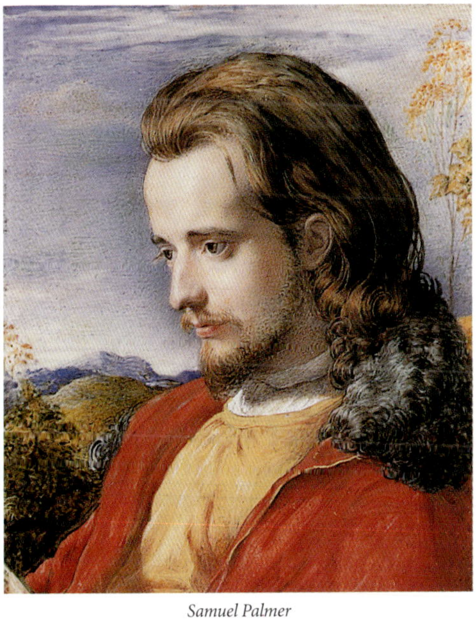

Samuel Palmer

If there is one aspect of this period that an exhibition of this kind reveals above all others, it is the sheer range and variety of talent that it contains, and this small group of miniatures powerfully reinforces the point. Because, if this was supremely the age of Lawrence in portraiture and Gillray in caricature, it was also the great age of English watercolour and landscape, of John Constable, **J. M. W. Turner**, Thomas Girtin, and of Girtin's influential admirer and interpreter, the elephantine **John Varley**.

Varley's unwieldy size (barely contained here within the frame of this affectionate miniature by his brother-in-law, William Mulready) might have made him the butt of jokes, but no one questioned his talent or importance as a teacher to a whole generation of artists. He had first come under Girtin's influence at the end of the eighteenth century, and as a practitioner and theorist passed on his skills in turn to such disparate painters as David Cox, W.H. Hunt, John Linnell and William Mulready himself.

And if the art of the period is marked by its variety, the same is true of its literature. While this was the age of Romantic excess on the one hand, it was also the age of that enemy of excess in all forms, **Thomas Love Peacock**, East India Company employee, comic novelist and satirist. In the preface to a collected edition of his novels Peacock listed 'perfectabilians, deteriorationists, status quo-ites, and transcendentalists' among his targets, but he did himself an injustice. From Byron to Bentham, Coleridge to Robert Owen there was scarcely a theorist, exhibitionist, enthusiast, visionary or historical balladeer who did not feel the edge of his amused and sceptical intelligence. His wry, clever face is seen here in Roger Jean's 1805 portrait.

Like Bentham, Godwin or Peacock, **Jane Austen** is another reminder that the Romantic period did not put an end to those sensibilities that are usually associated with the eighteenth century, any more than it died with Shelley and Byron. The portraits of Byron might catch the Romantic ideal of what the poet *ought* to look like, but if you will not find the author of *Persuasion* (1818) in the rather prim expression of Cassandra Austen's portrait, it is all too easy to recognize the novelist who in *Northanger Abbey* (1818) provided the cool, rational antidote to the Gothic frenzies so successfully peddled by **Matthew 'Monk' Lewis**.

The portrait of Jane Austen is neither a good likeness, nor a good watercolour (David Piper's main regret about it was that Cassandra did not tear it up) but that has never seemed to matter, because there is something in the quiet ordinariness of this sister's 'tribute of affection' that posterity has been keen to identify with the author of *Emma* (1816) and *Pride and Prejudice* (1813). The life and fiction of Jane Austen was actually more varied and disturbed than tradition or this portrait might suggest, but in the doll-like figure of Cassandra's drawing we have the gentle and domestic Jane Austen that her family wished to market to the world and that a Janeite world has been equally keen to buy: 'It is a very pleasing sweet face', one of her family revealingly wrote, 'tho' I confess to not thinking it much like the original – but *that* the public will not be able to detect.' 'There is a *look* which I recognise as *hers*', her niece Caroline Austen wrote of it, 'and though the general resemblance is *not* strong, yet as it represents a pleasing countenance it is *so* far a truth.'

For all the submerged tensions of her life and art, however, it would still be hard to think of two novelists farther removed in experience, temperament or talent than Jane Austen and 'Monk' Lewis. The son of a sugar plantation owner, Lewis was living – bored – in the Hague when at the age of nineteen in the space of ten weeks he wrote the novel that earned him his epithet and gave him his entrée to the social world he craved. In his last years Lewis took up the cause of his plantation workers and made two trips to Jamaica, but it was almost exclusively for *The Monk* (1796) that he was known and for most of his life he seemed happy simply to live off the reputation it brought him as the most successful Gothic novelist of the day. 'A good man', Byron called him, 'a clever man, but a bore.'

There is another aspect of Regency life, of which the intimacy of the miniature, and sometimes even the amateurishness of the form, provides a valuable reminder, and that is the critical importance of friendship. There were of course the great institutions of the country such as the Royal Academy or the Royal Society that brought talent together, but of equal importance in fertilizing and cross-fertilizing the intellectual and creative life of the period were those changing, expanding and dissolving circles of friendship that were such a feature of the age.

The most famous of these will always be the 'Lakers' – **Sara Coleridge**, the author of *Phantasmion* (1837) and daughter of Samuel Taylor Coleridge represents them here – but the group that gathered around Wordsworth and Coleridge is by no means alone. There was the circle centred on Godwin and Mary Wollstonecraft, that could embrace the novelist and beauty Amelia Opie and the radical tailor Francis Place. There was the group that gathered in Switzerland, and spawned in one night, Mary Shelley's *Frankenstein* (1818) and the first story of its kind in English literature, John Polidori's *The Vampyre* (1819). The Pisan circle that formed around Byron and Shelley drew to it Hunt, Medwin, Claire Clairmont, and that exotic figure, who carried the aura if not the substance of Romanticism deep into the nineteenth century, Edward John Trelawny.

The place to feel the importance of these friendships is the Protestant Cemetery in Rome, next to the Pyramid of Caius Sestius. Here lie the ashes of Shelley and, in a grave beside them, those of Trelawny. Less than fifty yards away is the resting place of **John Keats**, and near that the grave of the painter Joseph Severn, best known as the man who nursed Keats through his last illness. He is represented here by the miniature of his friend done in 1819, the year of the great Odes that preceded the first symptoms of Keats's fatal illness.

If friendships played a vital role in the intellectual life of this period, Severn's haunting descriptions of Keats's last terrible days are a reminder that one of the archetypal images of Romanticism is the isolated and misunderstood artist absorbed in his own creative agonies. In the poetry and dramas of Byron this sounded a note that echoes through the literature and art of the nineteenth century. But whether it is in the savage defiance of the Byronic hero, the 'egotistical sublime' of William Wordsworth or the opium-induced nightmares of De Quincey, the Romantic artist fed off himself and his own inner life in ways for which the self-portrait might stand the perfect symbol.

The form is represented here by the delicate gouache on ivory of **George Richmond**, an artist whose later portraits of Ruskin, Charlotte Brontë, Keble, Newman and Gladstone provide a fascinating clue to the subterranean stream of influence that carried the message of Romanticism deep into every aspect of nineteenth century life. His Christ-like and Dureresque portrait of **Samuel Palmer**, landscape artist, visionary and friend of Blake, records an important influence in Richmond's life, but it is the self-portrait that shows him at his best. It was done when he was twenty-one and painted for his wife on their marriage. The son of a miniaturist, Richmond himself was one of the last to work with such distinction in a tradition, stretching back to the Tudor age, that was about to be challenged by the advent of photography. In its penetration and skill this self-portrait is perhaps, of all those here, the work that most obviously justifies the implied compliment to the miniaturists' art in the famous description of Jane Austen working on her little bit of ivory.

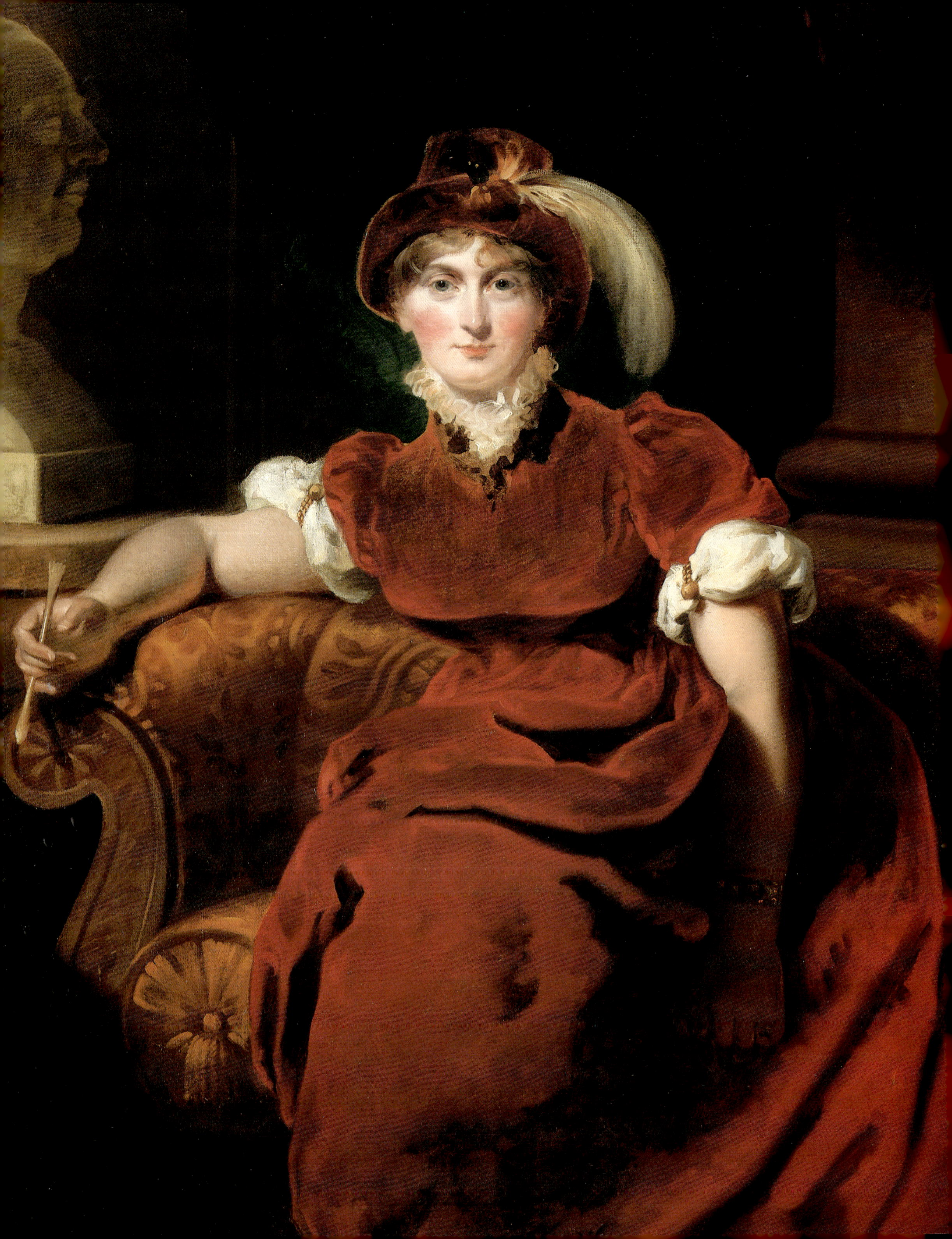

Politics & Society

SIR THOMAS LAWRENCE, 1804

Caroline Amelia Elizabeth of Brunswick (detail)
(1768–1821)

Oil on canvas, 1403 × 1118 mm (55¼ × 44 ins)
(NPG 244)

STUDIO OF SIR WILLIAM BEECHEY, *c.*1809

King George III

(1738-1820)

Oil on canvas, 768 × 648 mm (30¼ × 25½ ins)
(NPG 6250)

It was the sad paradox of George III's life that it was only in madness that he won the affection and admiration of the country that his private qualities had long deserved. The eldest son of Frederick, Prince of Wales, George suffered his first breakdown in 1765 before the serious collapse of 1788 ushered in the twilight decades that finally resulted, after years of political and medical wrangle, in the establishment of the Regency in 1811.

In spite of the loss of the American colonies abroad, and the political agitations of John Wilkes at home, there was a quality of King Lear about George III in his old age, the helpless victim of wretched children and intriguing politicians, that excited the compassion and indignation of almost the whole nation. A certain narrowness and obstinacy continued to characterize his lucid moments, but the threat of republicanism in France and the contrast with the excesses of his growing children finally woke England to the virtues of dignity, simplicity, and personal and public duty that had marked his whole reign.

Indifferent to clothes or fashion, and dressed much the same as an old man as he had been when he was young, he was 'tall and full of dignity, his countenance florid and good-natured', Horace Walpole wrote. Sir William Beechey painted a full-length portrait of him in about 1800, and this bust copy is one of a number of versions. It makes an interesting comparison with the theatrical portraits of George IV by Lawrence. 'I glory in the name of Britain', George III, the first Hanoverian to repudiate his roots, had once declared, and Beechey has painted 'Farmer' George as an English gentleman as much as a sovereign, adorned only with the Star of the Garter.

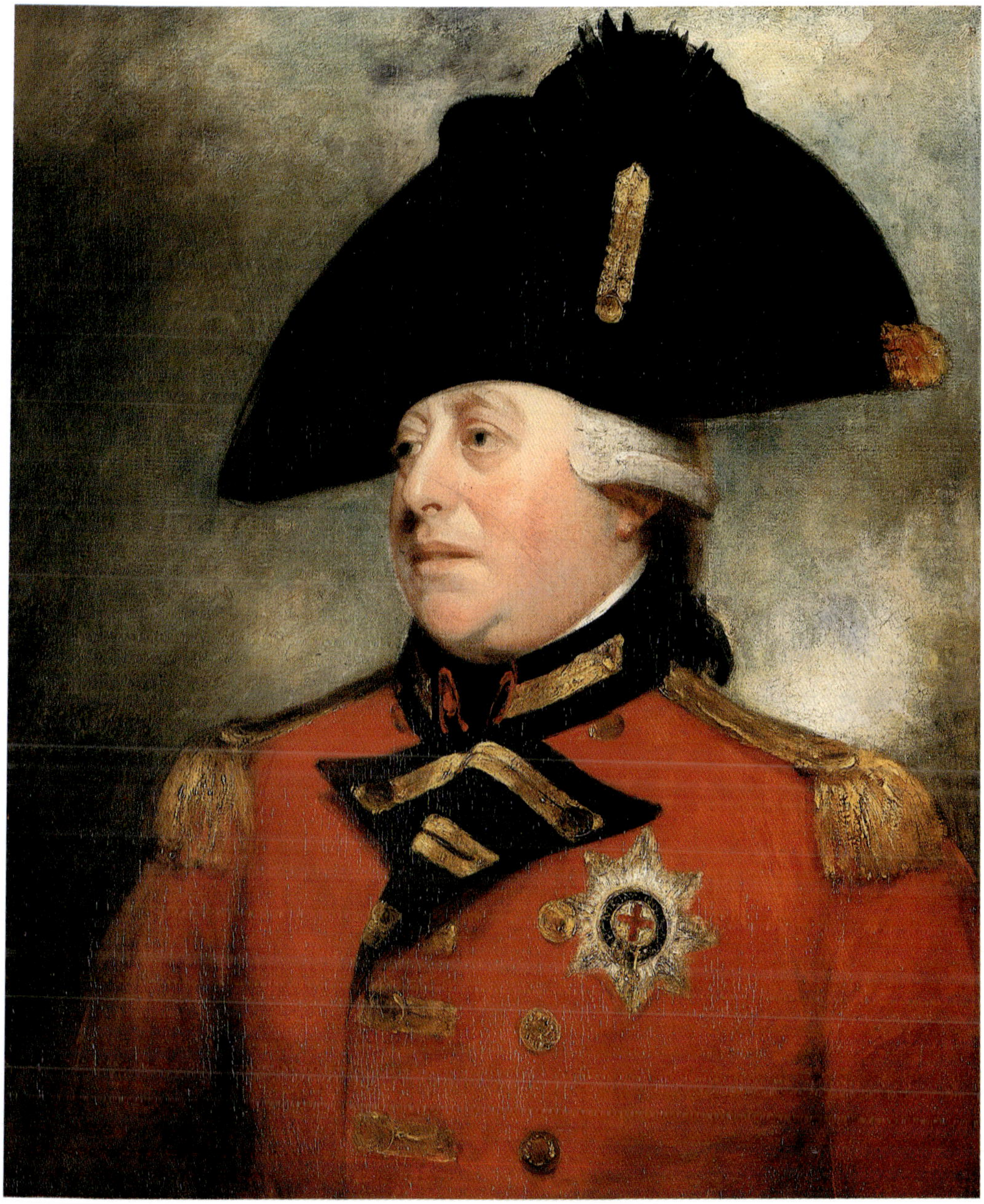

SIR THOMAS LAWRENCE, *c.*1814

King George IV

(1762-1830)

Oil on canvas, 914 × 711 mm (36 × 28 ins)
(NPG 123)

In the age of Gillray and Cruikshank – a golden age of political and social caricature – George IV was fortunate to find in Sir Thomas Lawrence an artist able and willing to make the most of an increasingly difficult job. Northcote had once dismissed Lawrence as 'a sort of man-milliner painter – a meteor of fashion', but if there is a certain truth in the stricture, no painter could have been better suited to capture the stagier aspects of Regency life or to mimic in the texture of his paint the elegance and surface brilliance of the period.

Lawrence's skills were particularly well adapted to the challenges of court art and the problems inherent in painting the ageing but immensely vain Prince Regent. 'Sir Thomas Lawrence has with the magic of his pencil recreated the Prince Regent as a well-fleshed Adonis of thirty-three', Hazlitt wrote of another of Lawrence's portraits of the fifty-two year old Regent; 'we could not, as we stood before this very admirable picture, but derive a high degree of good-natured pleasure from imagining to ourselves the transports with which His Royal Highness must have welcomed this improved version of himself. It goes beyond all that wigs, powders and pomatums have been able to effect for the last twenty years.'

Lawrence received several sittings at his studio for this profile, for which there is a chalk drawing at Windsor Castle. It was done in 1814, and intended for a medal that was never struck. 'I will swear to the exactness of line in His Majesty's portrait at the time I drew it', Lawrence wrote with a defensive note of this image in 1828, 'though the complexion and the coarse texture of skin in the original may make the copy appear flattering and unfaithful.'

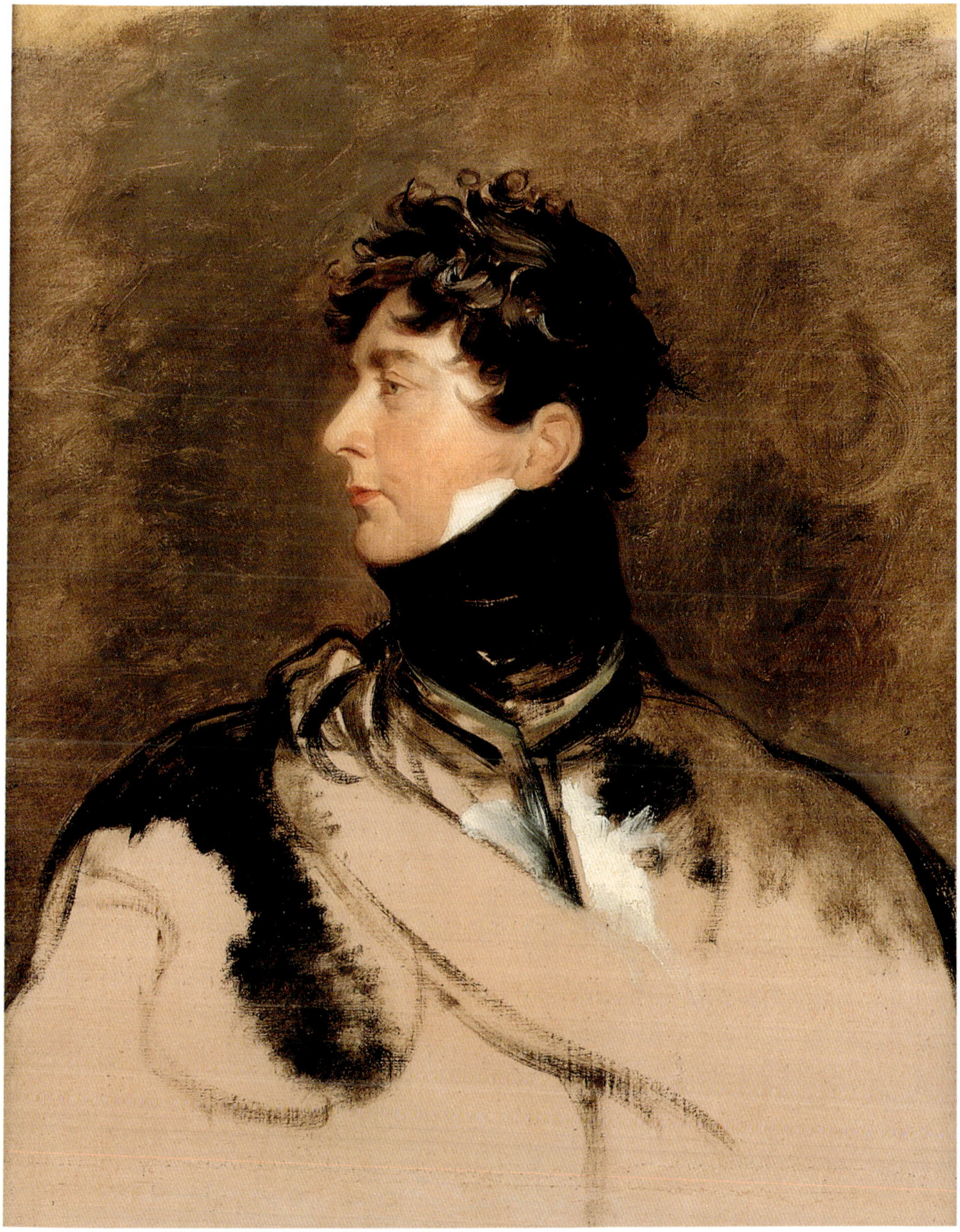

STUDIO OF SIR THOMAS LAWRENCE, 1815

King George IV

(1762-1830)

Oil on canvas, 2413 × 1549 mm (95 × 61 ins)
(NPG 2503)

It seems a perverse irony that the age of Keats, Shelley and Byron in poetry, of Jane Austen in fiction, of Castlereagh in politics and Wellington in arms, should take its name from the title of one of the most fatuous monarchs ever to sit on the British throne.

A man of natural intelligence and charm, the Prince of Wales had been ruined for his role in public life long before his father's illness brought about the Regency in 1811. In the loveless tradition of the Hanoverian dynasty, father and son had fought each other for most of their lives, and a combination of indulgence and constitutional constraint had successfully warped the character of the young Prinny to the petulant and fickle figure (equally disloyal in private and political dealings) who eventually became George IV. 'A violator of his word', Leigh Hunt labelled him, in a description that landed Hunt in gaol for his honesty, 'a libertine, over head and ears in debt, a despiser of domestic ties, the companion of gamblers and demireps, a man who has just closed half a century without one single claim on the gratitude of his country or the respect of posterity.'

'Lawrence's Adonized George IV is disgraceful both to the King and to the Painter; a lie upon canvas', Tom Moore complained, and Lawrence certainly did his smooth best with his subject. By the end of his life George had come to believe that he had fought at Waterloo himself, and Lawrence has shown him here as a soldier, his vast bulk elegantly constrained within one of the Field Marshal's uniforms that he so loved, the equal on canvas at least of those allied sovereigns who had cruelly outshone him in the summer of 1814.

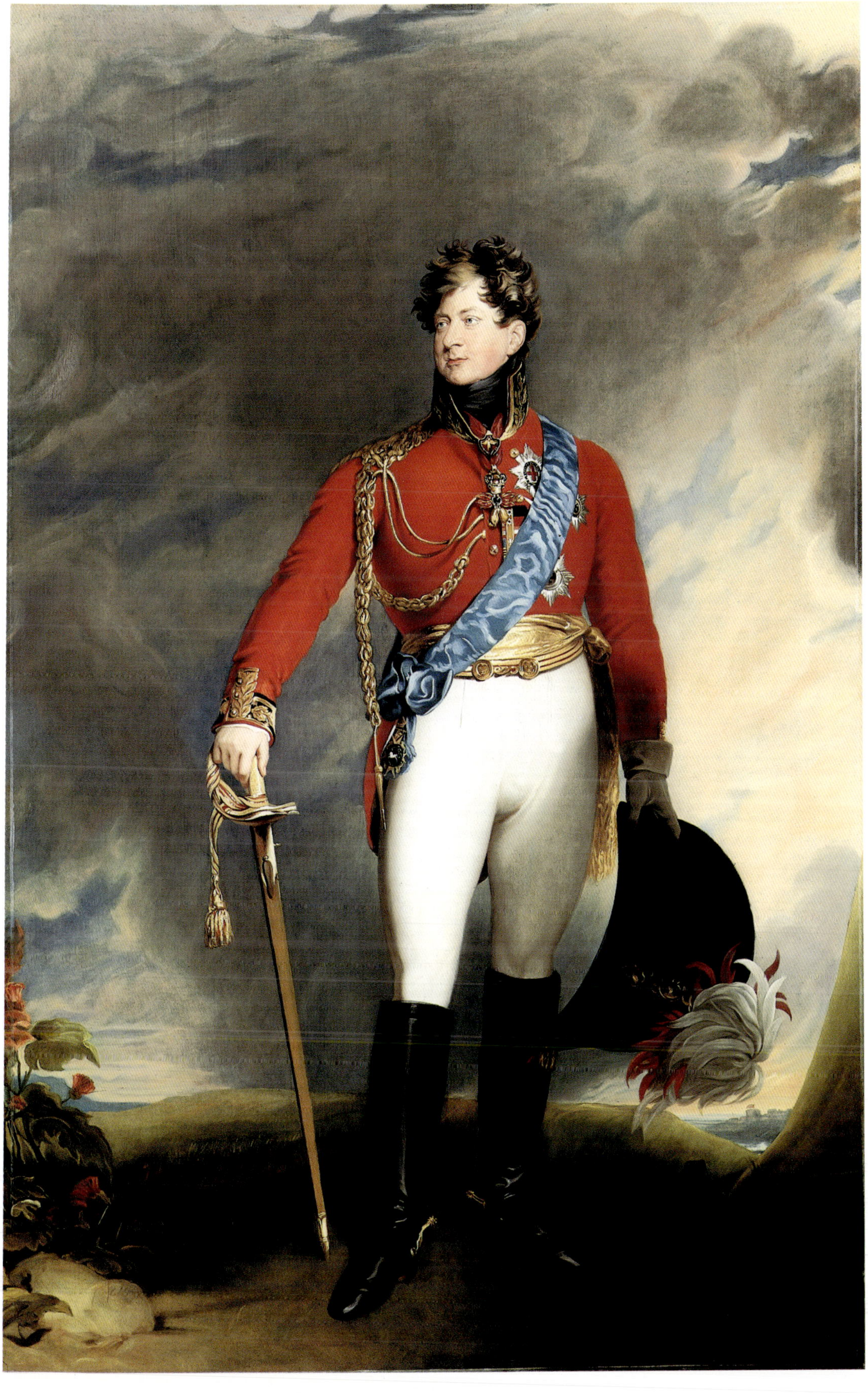

SIR JOSHUA REYNOLDS, *c.*1788

Maria Anne Fitzherbert

(1756-1837)

Oil on canvas, 914 × 711 mm (36 × 28 ins)
(L162)
Reproduced by consent of the owners

Maria Anne Fitzherbert, née Smythe, a Roman Catholic, had already been twice married and twice widowed when the future George IV saw her for the first time at Richmond and fell in love. For two years the reluctant widow drove the Prince to histrionic displays of devotion and despair, but in 1785 she finally accepted his proposal, and was secretly married by a Church of England clergyman in her own drawing room, with her brother and uncle as witnesses.

Widely regarded as the king's mistress (a position she maintained after his marriage to Caroline of Brunswick) Mrs Fitzherbert found herself involved in a deception that had important constitutional implications. Under the Marriage Act of 1772 no member of the royal family beneath the age of twenty-five could marry without the King's permission, and as the Act of Settlement also debarred any heir apparent who married a Roman Catholic from succeeding to the throne, George was forced to deny that the marriage had ever taken place.

In 1787, in a bid to have his debts settled, the denial was formally repeated to Parliament on his behalf by Fox, and whatever the degree of the Prince's complicity in the lie, few relationships in his life show him in a feebler light than his marriage to Mrs Fitzherbert. When he became Regent he demonstrated his capacity for faithlessness in political life, but he was no more loyal in his private affairs and his behaviour to the one woman he genuinely loved – and who deserved his loyalty – finally drove her from the court and into retirement in 1803.

Reynolds's painting – cut down from a full-length portrait – shows her at about the age of thirty-two. One of the beauties of her day, Mrs Fitzherbert's character was such that the ambiguities of her position never seem to have turned the royal family against her, and she was always treated with respect both by George III and Queen Caroline.

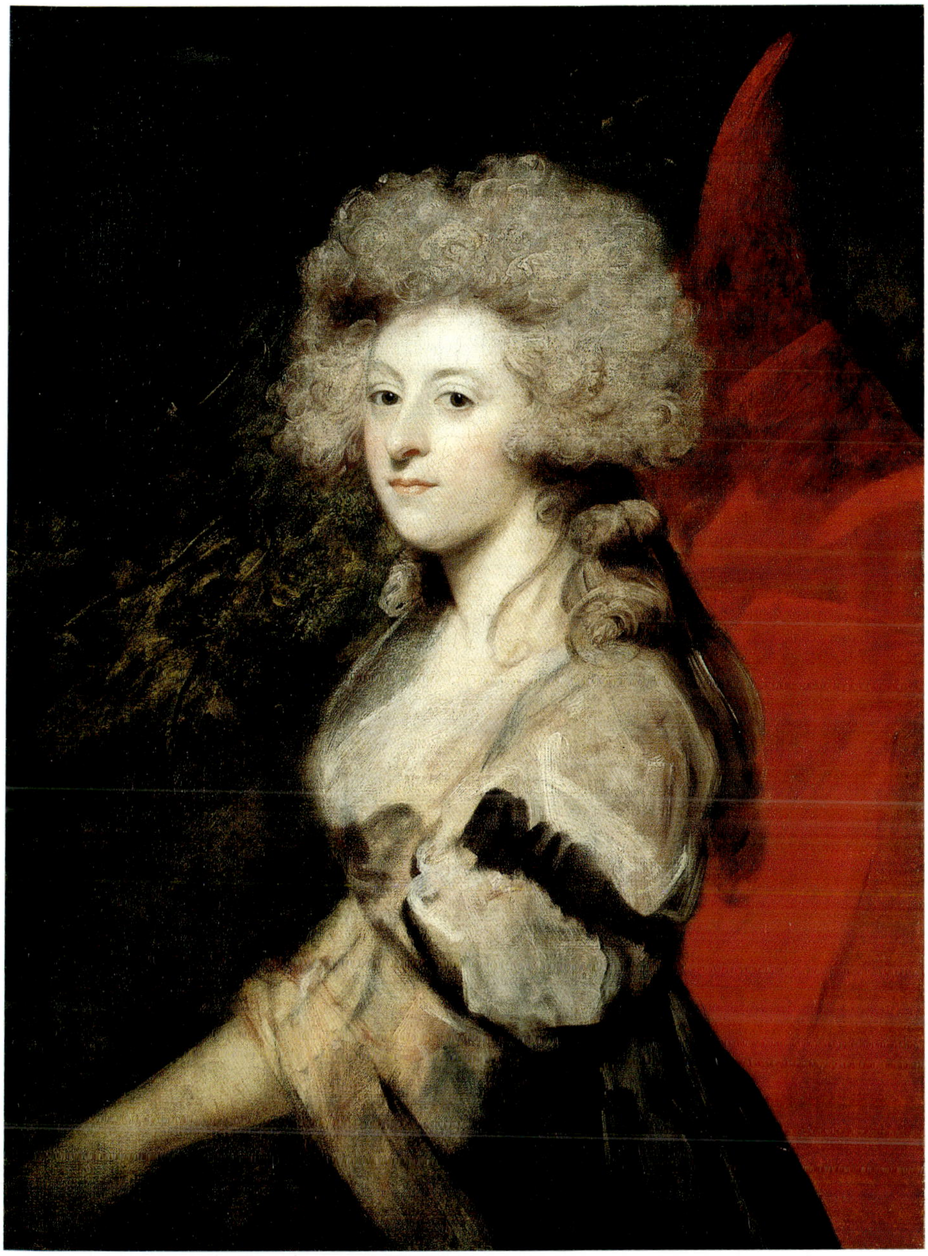

SIR THOMAS LAWRENCE, 1804

Caroline Amelia Elizabeth of Brunswick

(1768-1821)

Oil on canvas, 1403 × 1118 mm (55¼ × 44 ins)
(NPG 244)

In an age of royal extravagance and eccentricities, Caroline Amelia Elizabeth of Brunswick, the second daughter of the Duke of Brunswick and the wife of George IV, yields precedence to no one. Forced by his father on the reluctant and already secretly married Prince of Wales in 1795, Caroline found herself abandoned within the year and left to endure a kind of humiliating internal exile, an object of passionate dislike to her husband and of political opportunism to the warring Whig and Tory factions.

But if Caroline was grossly treated by her husband, with her good-natured vulgarity, her coarseness of tongue and boisterous immorality, she was more than capable of taking her revenge. For more than twenty years she remained a thorn in her husband's side, a rallying point for political opposition to the Regent and his ministers at home, and a further disgrace to the already disgraced Hanoverians when she was allowed to continue her bizarre sexual adventures abroad.

The 'trial' of Queen Caroline on her return from Italy – one of the great constitutional events of the period – is described elsewhere (see p. 92) and Lawrence's portrait shows her at the age of thirty-six. This was the second time he had painted her, the first being in 1798. She holds a modelling tool in her hand, and behind her is a bust of her father, the Duke of Brunswick, who fell at the Battle of Jena and beside whom Caroline would eventually be buried. A 'pretty face', Lord Malmesbury described her, with more charity than most people could muster, 'not expressive of softness – her figure not graceful – fine eyes – good hands – tolerable teeth but going – fair hair and light eyebrows, good bust – short, with what the French call *des épaules impertinentes*.'

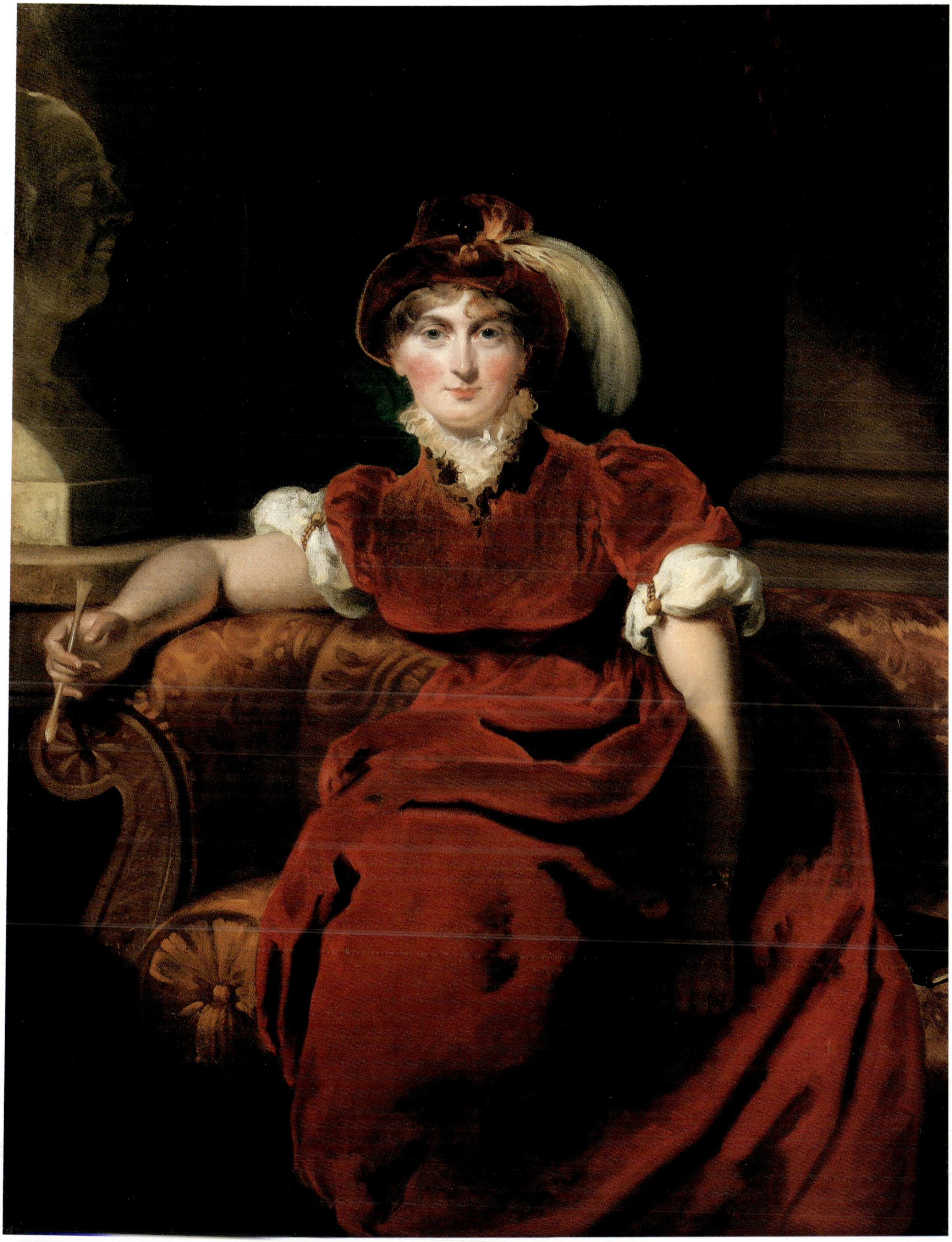

SIR GEORGE HAYTER, 1820-23

The House of Lords, 1820, The Trial of Queen Caroline

Oil on canvas, 2330 × 3562 mm (91¾ × 140¼ ins)
(NPG 999)

During the years that followed the death of George III the forces of change and reform gathered an inevitable momentum, but for three bizarre months in the summer of 1820 the Regency age in all its exuberance, vulgarity, factionalism, and energy gave itself up to one last spectacular display.

The 'trial' was technically not a trial at all, but a debate on a Bill of Pains and Penalties designed to provide George IV with the evidence against Caroline for a divorce. On the accession of George IV Caroline had returned from abroad to a tumultuous welcome, and while the atmosphere in London wavered somewhere between a street party and a revolution – 'no Queen, no King' was the cry – Italian witnesses gave their scandalous evidence and Tories and Whigs fought in the House of Lords a battle they had been waging for a generation around the improbable figure of Caroline.

It ended in compromise and anticlimax. Caroline was subsequently barred from the coronation and dead within a fortnight, but Hayter's painting captures a moment of real constitutional crisis. Hayter realised early that he had a subject worth speculating on and produced a sketch of the proceedings prior to being commissioned by George Ellis, a young Whig politician. Ellis nominated the sitters, and the list was finally expanded to almost three hundred, with 161 sitting to Hayter. The moment depicted is on the sixth day of the trial, with an Italian witness giving evidence. Prominent are the figures of Queen Caroline, counsel for both sides, Lord Grey, with his arm outstretched, and Wellington. Portraits of Ellis and Hayter are visible in the bottom right-hand corner.

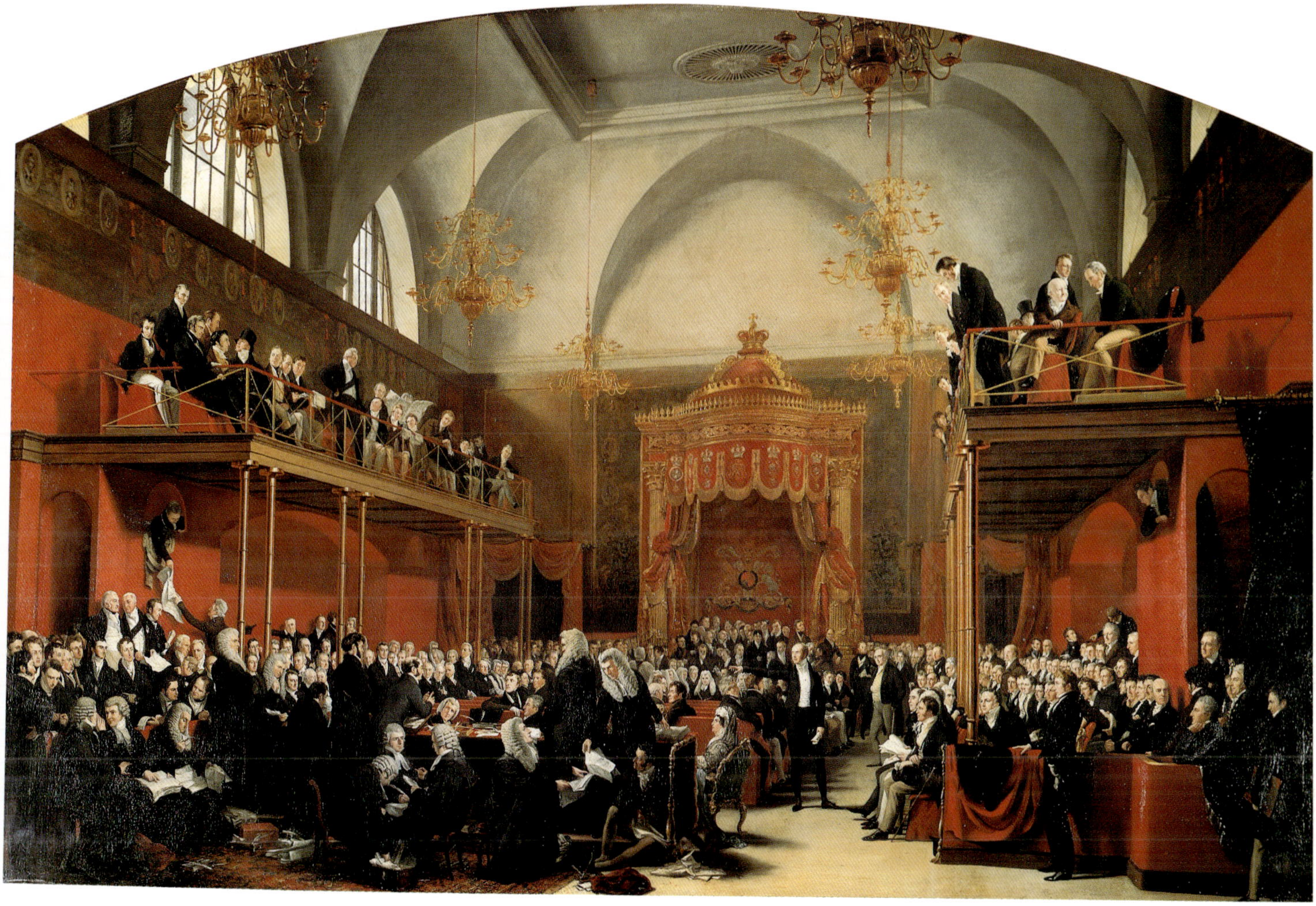

STUDIO OF JOHN HOPPNER, 1804-5

William Pitt

(1759-1806)

Oil on canvas, 1410 × 1080 mm (55½ × 42½ ins)
(NPG 697)

In private a lonely, isolated figure, William Pitt 'the Younger' was the most prominent British politician of his day. His bitter rivalry with Charles James Fox immortalised by Gillray's cartoons, dominated Parliament for more than twenty years.

The second son of the former Prime Minister, the Earl of Chatham, Pitt entered the House of Commons in 1781. At the age of twenty-three he became Chancellor of the Exchequer, and, at the age of only twenty-four, Prime Minister, an office he was to hold until 1801.

As Prime Minister, Pitt sought to reduce the national debt; he reformed the government of Canada and reorganized the East India Company. His attempts to extend its franchise failed, and the French Revolution made the project seem unwise. In 1800 he achieved his objective of union with Ireland, but in 1801 he resigned in protest after George III blocked his Bill for Catholic emancipation. He was persuaded to return as Prime Minister in 1804.

Abroad, Pitt's main preoccupation was the long war with France. With Britain fearing invasion, he organized the coalition with Russia, Austria and Sweden, and greatly strengthened the British Navy. With the victory over the French at Trafalgar he was hailed as 'the Saviour of Europe', to which he famously replied: 'Europe is not to be saved by any single man: England has saved herself by her exertions, and, will, I trust, save Europe by her example'.

Hoppner was commissioned by Lord Mulgrave to paint Pitt's portrait in 1804. It was completed in 1805, a year before Pitt's death. Opinions of the portrait varied. Some thought it a good likeness, but William Wilberforce thought it painted 'at a period too late to give an adequate representation of him'. Pitt's right hand is resting on the gown of the First Lord of the Treasury.

RW & SH

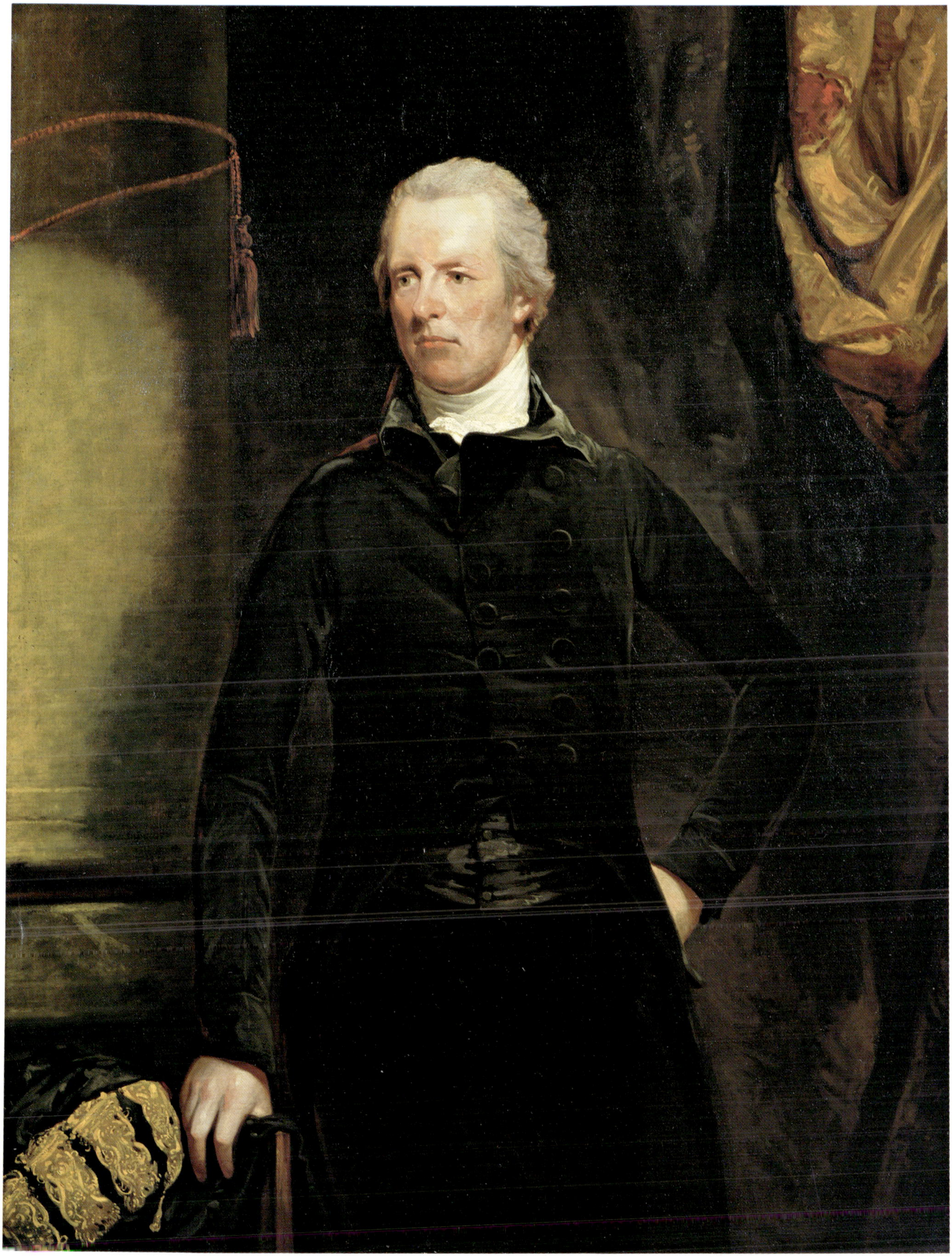

Robert Stewart, 2nd Marquess of Londonderry (Lord Castlereagh)

(1769-1822)

Oil on canvas, 743 × 616 mm (29¼ × 24¼ ins)
(NPG 891)

The 2nd Marquess of Londonderry – or Lord Castlereagh as he is more commonly known – began his political career in the Irish Parliament in the last troubled years of the eighteeenth century.

A moderate in Irish matters by inclination, and an apostate by necessity, Castlereagh resigned over the Catholic question, but returned to politics after the Union to begin his lifelong interest in foreign affairs. In 1804 he became Secretary of State for War, and for the next eighteen years, with a brief period out of office, was a dominant figure in successive cabinets. In his role as Foreign Secretary he skilfully and doggedly deployed British subsidies and influence to bind Europe into a united opposition to Napoleon.

Few British statesmen can ever have done more for their country and received less thanks for it. With the defeat of Napoleon and the Congress of Vienna, Castlereagh's best years were behind him and, indifferent to the claims of nationalism abroad and reform at home, he became the hated butt of liberal rage. 'I met murder on the way,' wrote Shelley, capturing that 'mixture of suavity and obstinacy', that characterized Castlereagh's public life and made his ultimate suicide in 1822 so startling,

> He had a mask like Castlereagh,
> Very smooth he looked, yet grim,
> Seven blood-hounds followed him:
> All were fat; and well they might
> Be in admirable plight,
> For one by one, and two by two,
> He tossed them human hearts to chew,
> Which from his wide cloak he drew.

'*Ma foi*', Talleyrand exclaimed on first meeting Castlereagh, '*comme il a l'aire distingué*.' It was that quality that Hazlitt complained was missing from Lawrence's portrait. Instead, he had made Castlereagh look like a footman, 'with the prim smirky aspect of a haberdasher'.

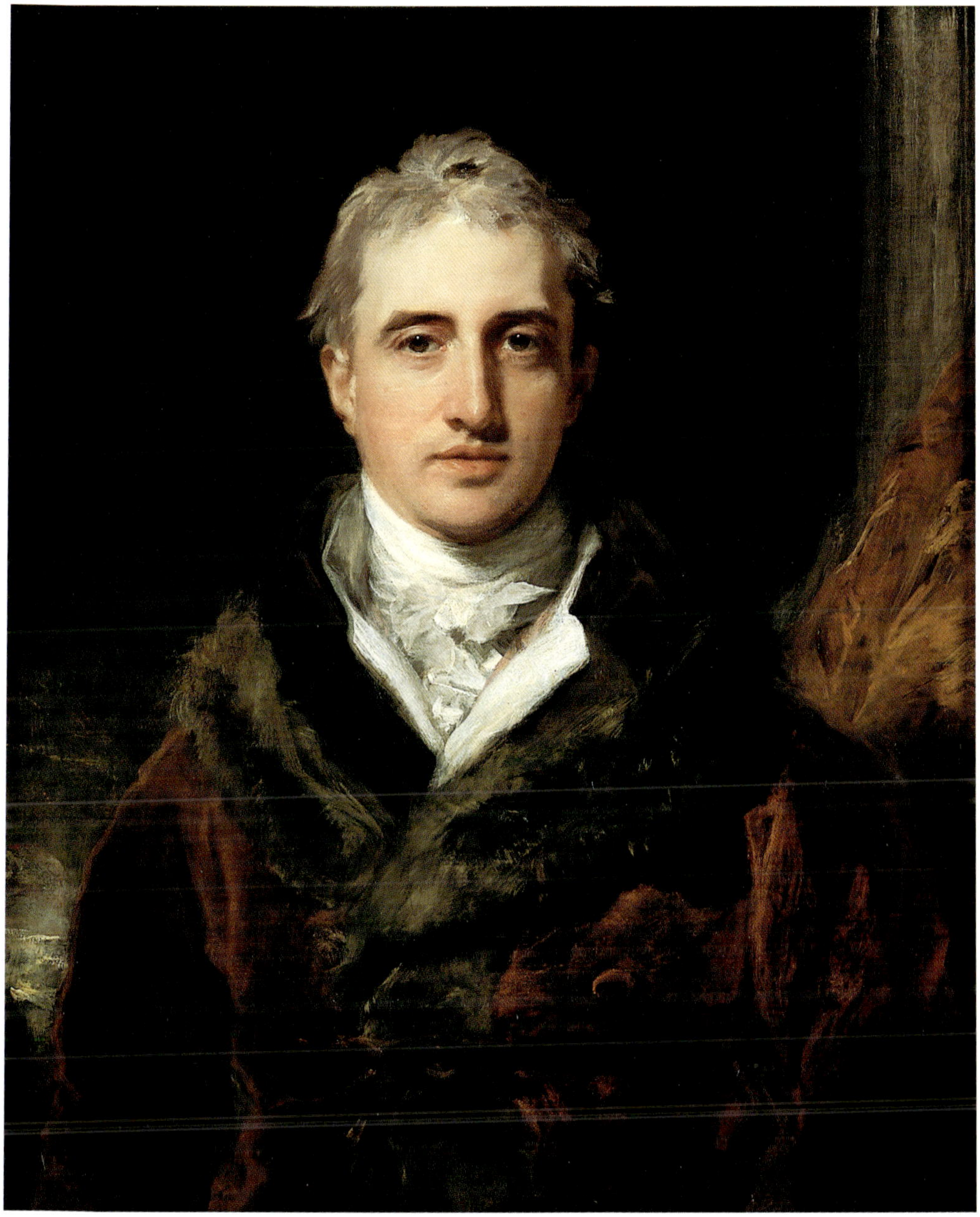

George Canning

(1770-1827)

Oil on canvas, 2381 × 1473 mm (93¾ × 58 ins)
(NPG 1832)

If Castlereagh was the last great eighteenth-century British statesman, George Canning was the first to recognize and exploit the energies of the new age. Canning was loathed by George IV and deeply distrusted by the Tory grandees, but he was a man of far too much talent to keep out of office, and having served in government on and off since the time of Pitt, succeeded his old rival Castlereagh in 1822 at the Foreign Office.

As Foreign Secretary, and then briefly Prime Minister, Canning oversaw the liberalization of British policy towards the forces of nationalism in a Europe increasingly threatened by autocratic repression. He defended the liberal party in Portugal and the Greek cause against the Ottoman Empire, but it is for his recognition of independence for Spain's American colonies that he is best known. He famously declared that he had called the New World into being to redress the balance of the Old, and something of the grandiloquence of that claim is captured in Lawrence's portrait. It was painted in 1825 for Sir Robert Peel's gallery at Drayton Manor, and shows Canning in front of the Treasury Bench in the House of Commons, his right arm raised, the mace to the right. Tom Moore quoted in his diary a criticism that it made Canning look 'like an actor standing before a glass rehearsing a part.' Moore also recorded a conversation between Lawrence and Charles Greville in front of the portrait. Greville said that he 'could imagine him speaking those very words in his great Portuguese speech: "Here I plant my standard and where the standard of Britain is planted no oppressor can ever come!" These *are* the words (said Lawrence) which I had in my mind in painting him.'

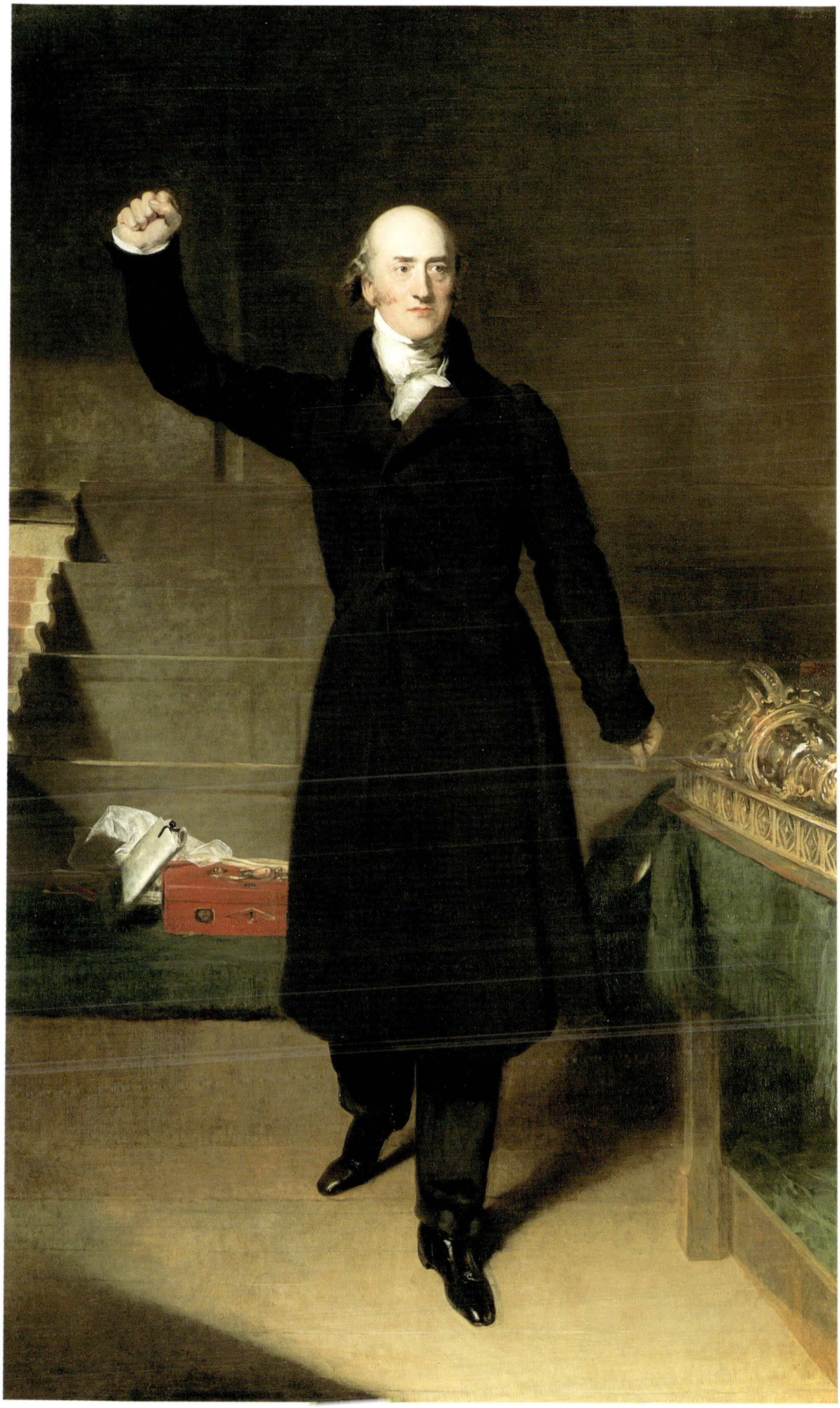

AFTER GILBERT STUART, 1796-1800

George Washington

(1732-1799)

Oil on canvas, 711 × 495 mm (28 × 19½ ins)
(NPG 774)

The Commander in Chief of the United States Army and the first President of the new nation, George Washington was, with Franklin, the first American statesman to make a decisive impact on the consciousness and politics of the Old World. A leader and general of courage and skill, his importance in the context of this exhibition lies less in him as an individual than as the embodiment of an idea of freedom that through the French Revolution did as much to change the course of European history as American.

Stuart's painting – this is a copy of his 'Lansdowne' or 'Teapot' portrait – also provides a valuable visual reminder of the complex origins of nineteenth-century Romanticism and revolt in eighteenth-century enlightenment because it is as an eighteenth-century gentleman and statesman that Washington is depicted. The most important American portrait painter of his day, Stuart had worked in Edinburgh and London (West and Reynolds were among his sitters) before returning to America in 1792, and setting off for Philadelphia two years later with the express intention of painting Washington. 'Imposing in size, noble and well proportioned', Joseph Mandrillon described Washington, in terms well suited to the timelessly classicizing bent of Stuart's portraiture, 'a countenance open, calm and sedate, but without any striking feature, and when you depart from him, the remembrance only of a fine man will remain.' In this version of the portrait the books and papers are not lettered, but in the original the three books on the floor beneath the table are inscribed: GENERAL ORDERS, AMERICAN REVOLUTION AND CONSTITUTION AND LAWS OF THE UNITED STATES; the books on the table THE FEDERALIST and THE JOURNAL OF CONGRESS.

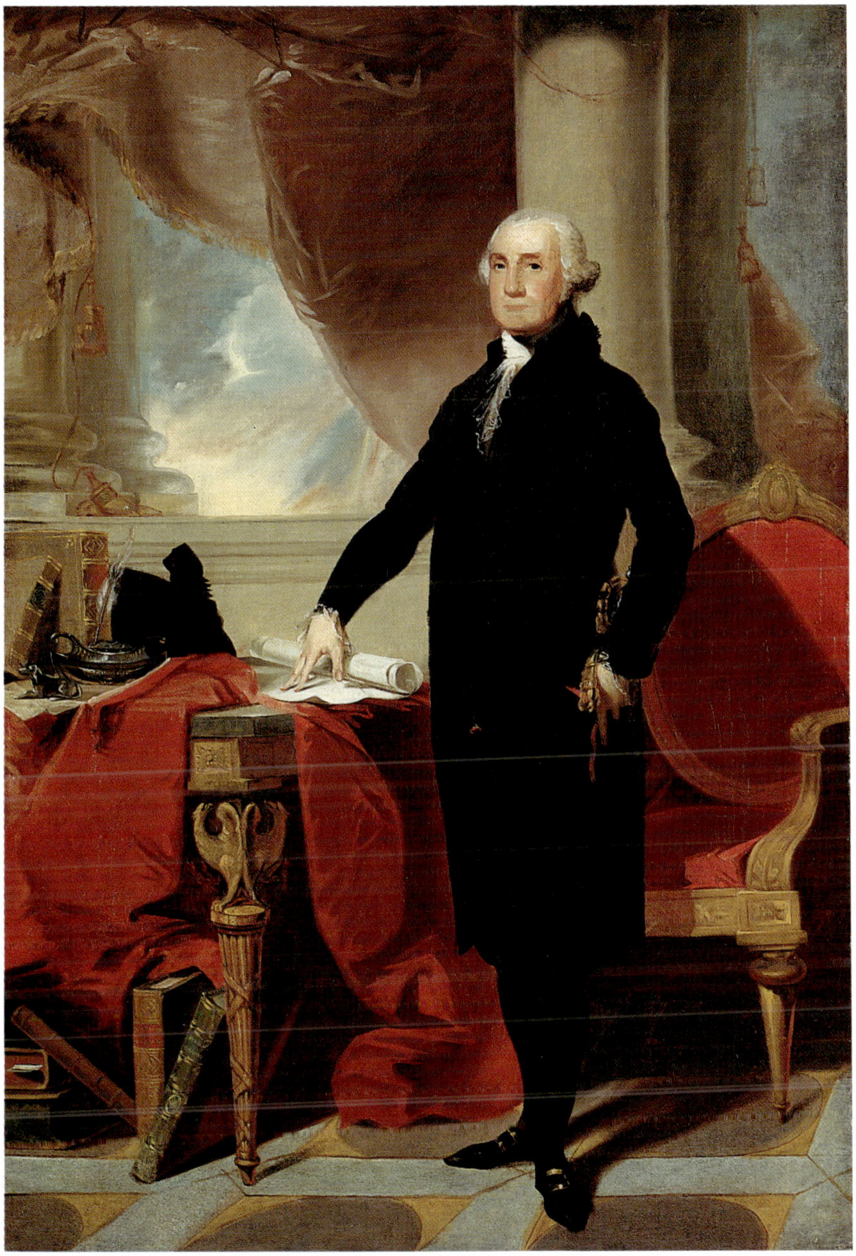

AFTER JOSEPH SIFFRED DUPLESSIS, 1783

Benjamin Franklin

(1706-90)

Oil on canvas, 711 × 572 mm (28 × 22½ ins)
(NPG 327)

One of the most variously talented men of his day, Benjamin Franklin was a polemicist, diplomat, statesman, inventor and scientist of international reputation. Born in Boston and apprenticed as a printer to his brother, he first visited England in 1724-6 and again 1757-62, before settling in London as a colonial agent and self-appointed interpreter of American life to Britain that was increasingly unsympathetic in the crucial years before the outbreak of war.

Attached to his adopted home by conviction and friendships, he was moderate in his counsels and prophetic in his warnings: 'We must all hang together', he once said, 'or assuredly we will all hang separately.' Franklin finally became disillusioned by British intransigence and returned to Philadelphia in 1775 to play a key role in the struggle for Independence.

Back in America, he served as a member of the Second Continental Congress, but his international fame and contacts meant that his greatest use was ambassadorial, and in 1776 he headed the vital American delegation to an *ancien régime* France eager to avenge the humiliations of the Seven Years War.

With victory gained – and the involvement of France a key element – Franklin remained in Europe, where he played an important and conciliatory role as negotiator in the Treaty of Paris that recognized the Independence of the United States. This version of Duplessis's original 1778 pastel conveys a sense of the whole man. Fat, squarely built, his hair thin and grey, his head over-large, he was as much the practical man as the theorist and writer. With its suggestion of solidity and shrewd good sense it captures both the diplomatic negotiator and the inventor of the Franklin stove, bifocal spectacles and the lightning rod.

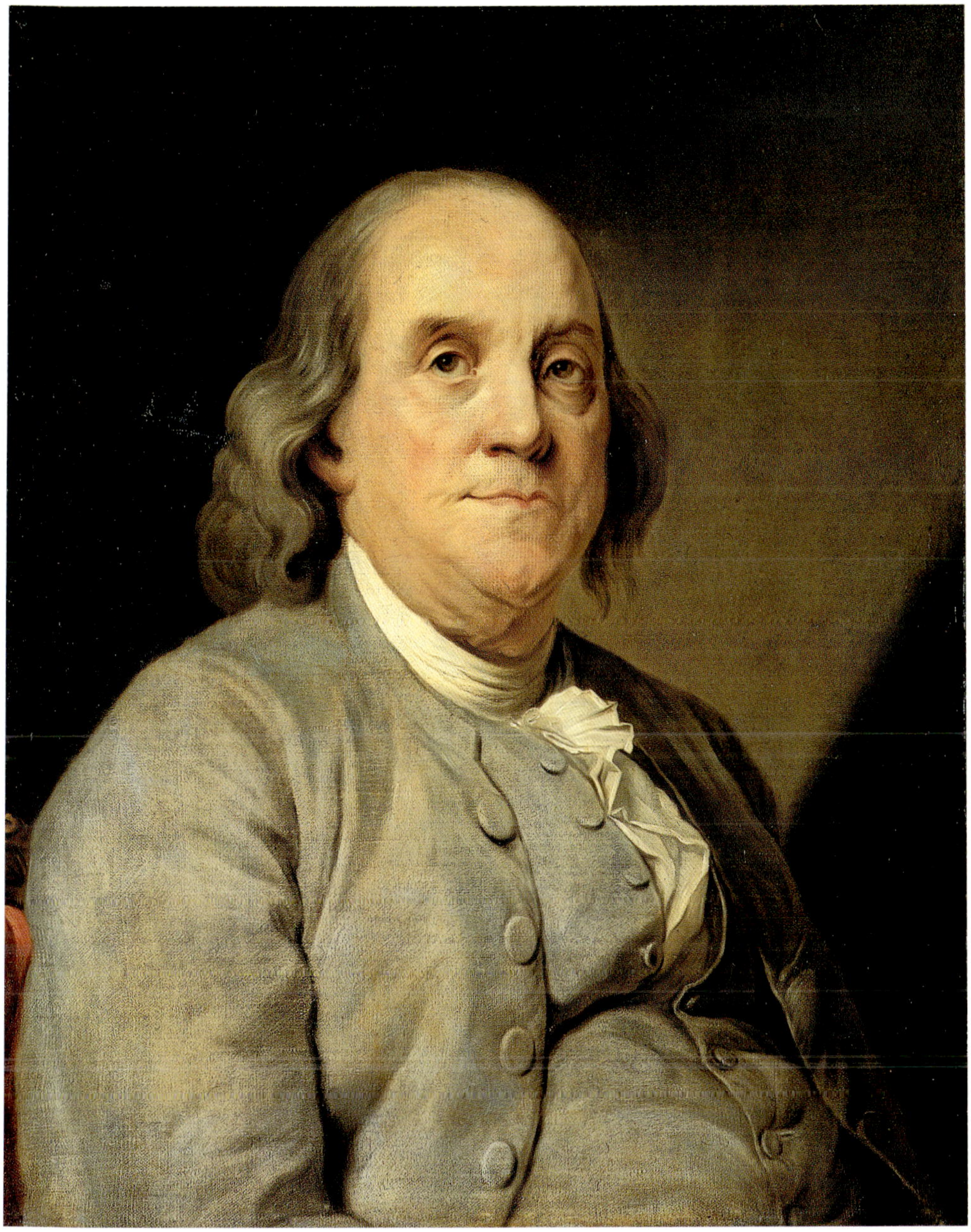

GUY HEAD, 1798-9

Horatio Nelson, Viscount Nelson

(1758-1805)

Oil on canvas, 2229 × 1689 mm (87¾ × 66½ ins)
(NPG 5101)

A tactician of genius, a charismatic and inspirational leader, and a figure who cast his giant shadow across the British Navy for a century after his time, the victor of the battles of Copenhagen, the Nile and Trafalgar, was the most successful British naval commander of the Napoleonic Wars. The son of a Norfolk parson, Nelson first entered the Navy at the age of twelve, and rose rapidly through the ranks on the outbreak of war with France. He had become a viscount and Rear Admiral by the time his death at Trafalgar guaranteed a fame that no disquiet over his personality or private life has ever seriously tarnished.

Nelson was already a decorated Rear Admiral when, in 1798, with only one arm and one eye as a result of previous engagements, he was dispatched to the Mediterranean in search of a French fleet that had eluded the British blockade. Through the early summer he hunted without success, but on 1 August at last came across it lying at anchor in Aboukir Bay. In a brilliant action he manoeuvred himself between the shore and the enemy and destroyed all but two of their ships.

This, the Battle of the Nile, ended Napoleon's eastern ambitions and established Nelson as a popular hero. Head was working in Naples when Nelson arrived there the following month and was probably commissioned by a grateful King Ferdinand to commemorate the victory. There is little attempt at historical accuracy in the painting, but Nelson was pleased enough or vain enough to secure it on the artist's death. Head shows Nelson at the moment of victory, receiving the sword of the French Admiral from an unknown midshipman, the burning wrecks of enemy ships visible in the background.

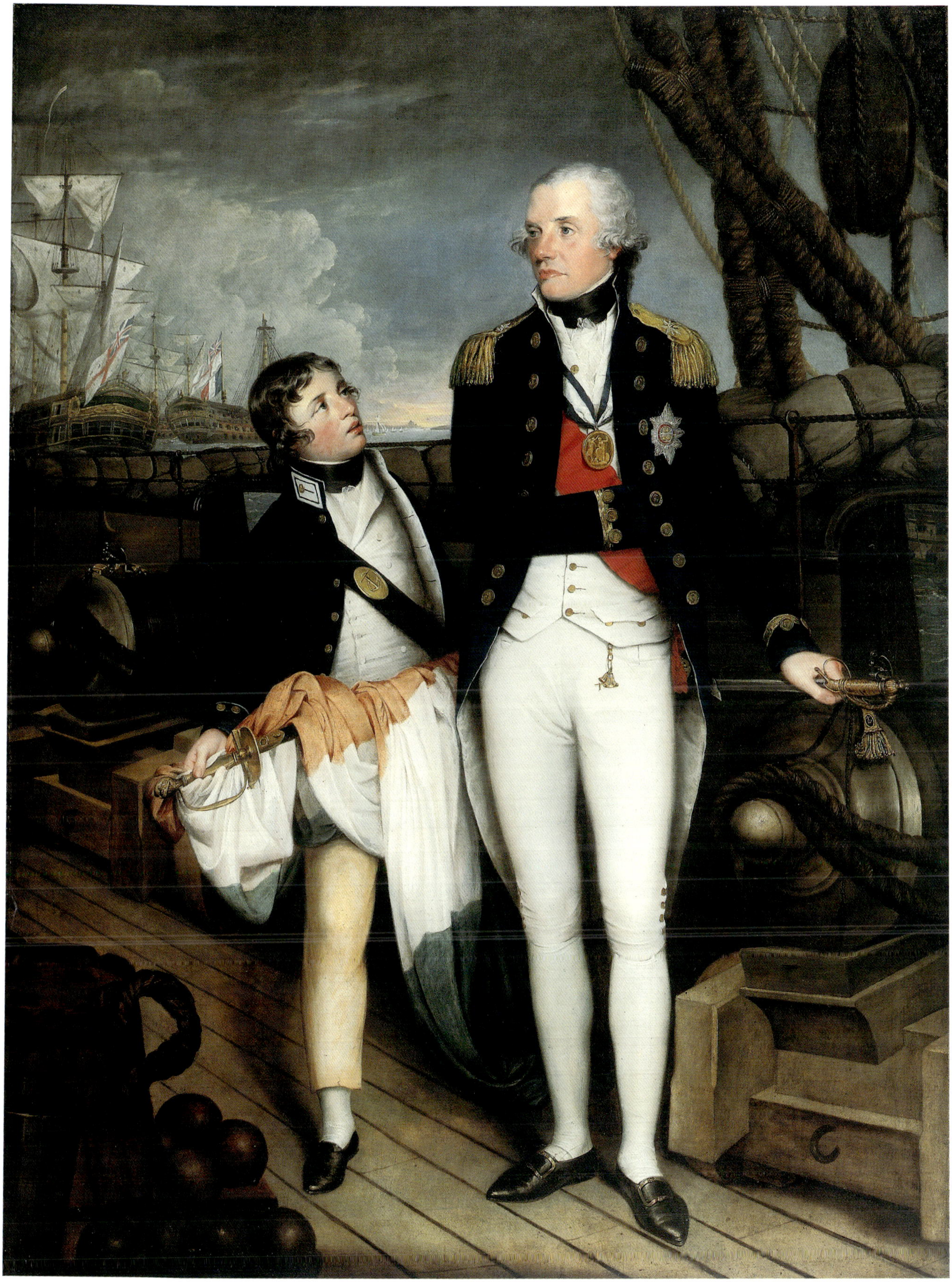

Arthur Wellesley, 1st Duke of Wellington

(1769-1852)

Oil on canvas, 762 × 635 mm (30 × 25 ins)
(NPG 6265)

Soldier, statesman, Prime Minister and national institution, Wellington was, to Benjamin Haydon, 'the greatest man on earth and the noblest.' Wellington had first made his reputation in India, but it was in the Peninsular Campaign that he proved himself more than a mere 'sepoy general', out-thinking and out-fighting Napoleon's marshals at the head of one of the finest armies in British history, before defeating the Emperor himself at Waterloo.

Haydon's relations with Wellington have that comic element that was seldom very distant from any of his artistic ventures. He once described the Duke's appearance as that of a 'helpless infant learning to whistle', but he wished to paint him on the field of Waterloo in a companion piece to his portrait of Napoleon in exile. Wellington was unimpressed. 'The Emperor Napoleon did not consent to be painted', he protested. 'But I am to be supposed to consent; and, moreover, I on the field of the Battle of Waterloo am not exactly in the situation in which Napoleon stood on the rock of St Helena.'

Haydon was not that easily rebuffed, however, borrowing the Duke's clothes from his steward to get the detail correct, and in the end his persistence was rewarded with an invitation to Walmer Castle, Wellington's official residence as Lord Warden of the Cinque Ports. Haydon has left an engaging account of the great man in private, but in paint it was as ever the hero he was interested in. 'I hit his grand, upright, manly expression', he wrote. 'He looked like an eagle of the gods who had put on human shape, and got silvery with age and service.' Count D'Orsay later helped Haydon with the painting of Wellington's horse. 'I thought after he had gone', Haydon recalled, 'this won't do – a Frenchman touch Copenhagen! So out I rubbed all he had touched, and modified his hints myself.'

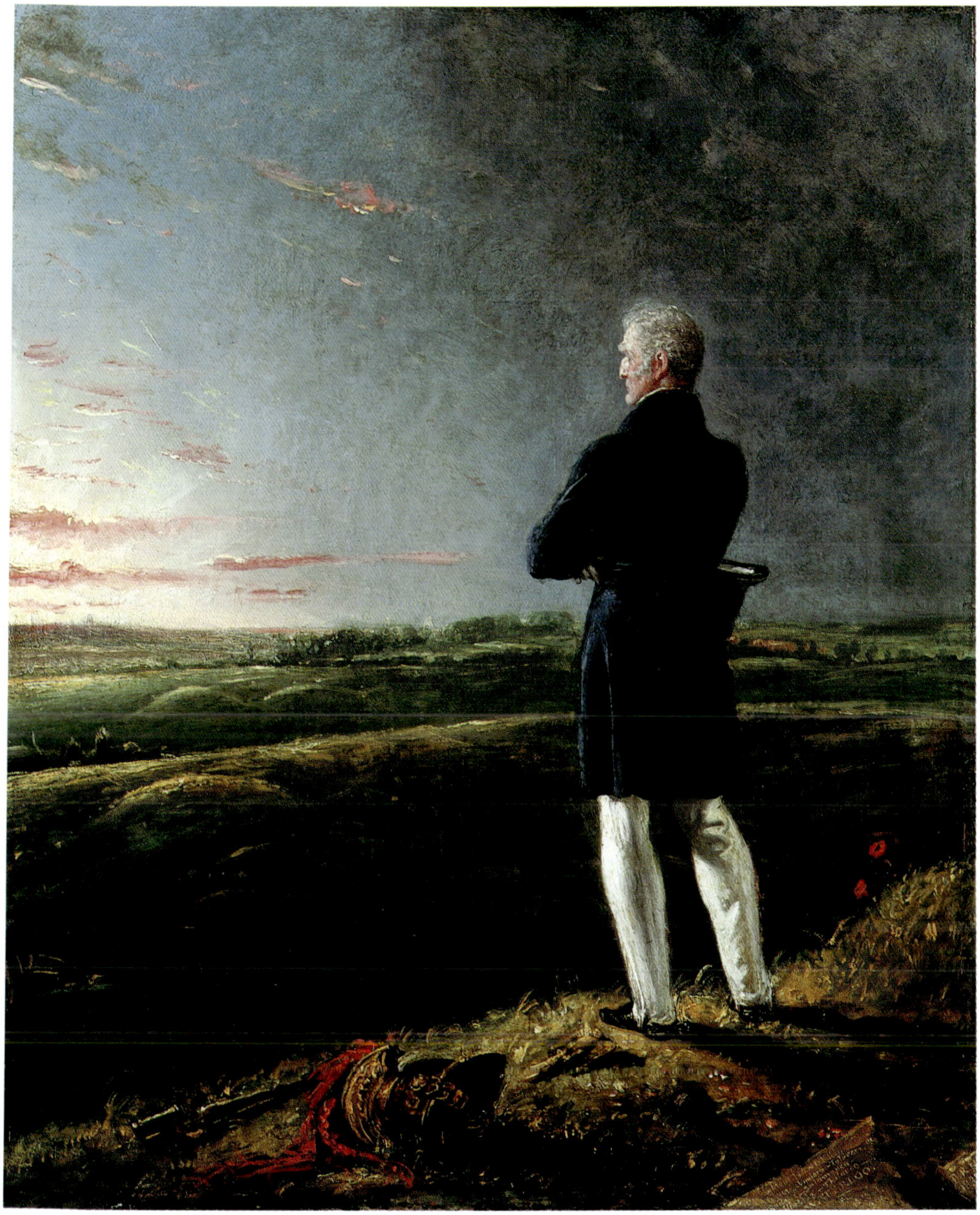

BENJAMIN ROBERT HAYDON, 1830

Napoleon Bonaparte

(1769-1821)

Oil on canvas, 762 × 631 mm (30 × 25 ins)
(NPG 6266)

When Byron went into exile he left England in a coach modelled on Napoleon's campaigning carriage, and with the initials NB (Noel Byron) emblazoned on its side, but what in him was a piece of harmless brag became in Benjamin Haydon a dangerous obsession. Haydon had first painted his hero in 1827, and after buying his death mask and trying on his hat for size (his skull, he noted was 'like Napoleon's 22 inches in circumference') he returned to his subject time and again. In all he painted twenty-three replicas and variants – Napoleon meditating over the Pyramids, Napoleon meditating on the field of Marengo, Napoleon meditating over the sleeping figure of the King of Rome and here (hat, height and uniform all punctiliously exact, Haydon noted in his journal) Napoleon meditating in exile on Elba.

To the Romantics Napoleon was the incarnation of all the energies unleashed by the French Revolution, and 'It was impossible to think of such a genius in captivity', Haydon declared, 'without mysterious associations of the sky, the sea, the rock, and the solitude with which he was enveloped. I never imagined him but as if musing at dawn, or melancholy at sunset, listening at midnight to the beating and roaring of the Atlantic ... in short Napoleon never appeared to me but at those seasons of silence and twilight, when nature seems to sympathize with the fallen, and when if there be moments in this turbulent earth fit for celestial intercourse, one must imagine these would be the times immortal spirits might select to descend within the sphere of mortals, to soothe and comfort, to inspire and support the afflicted.'

On Haydon's suicide, a note was found. 'I fear the glitter of his genius rather dazzled me', he had written under the heading of 'Last Thoughts.'

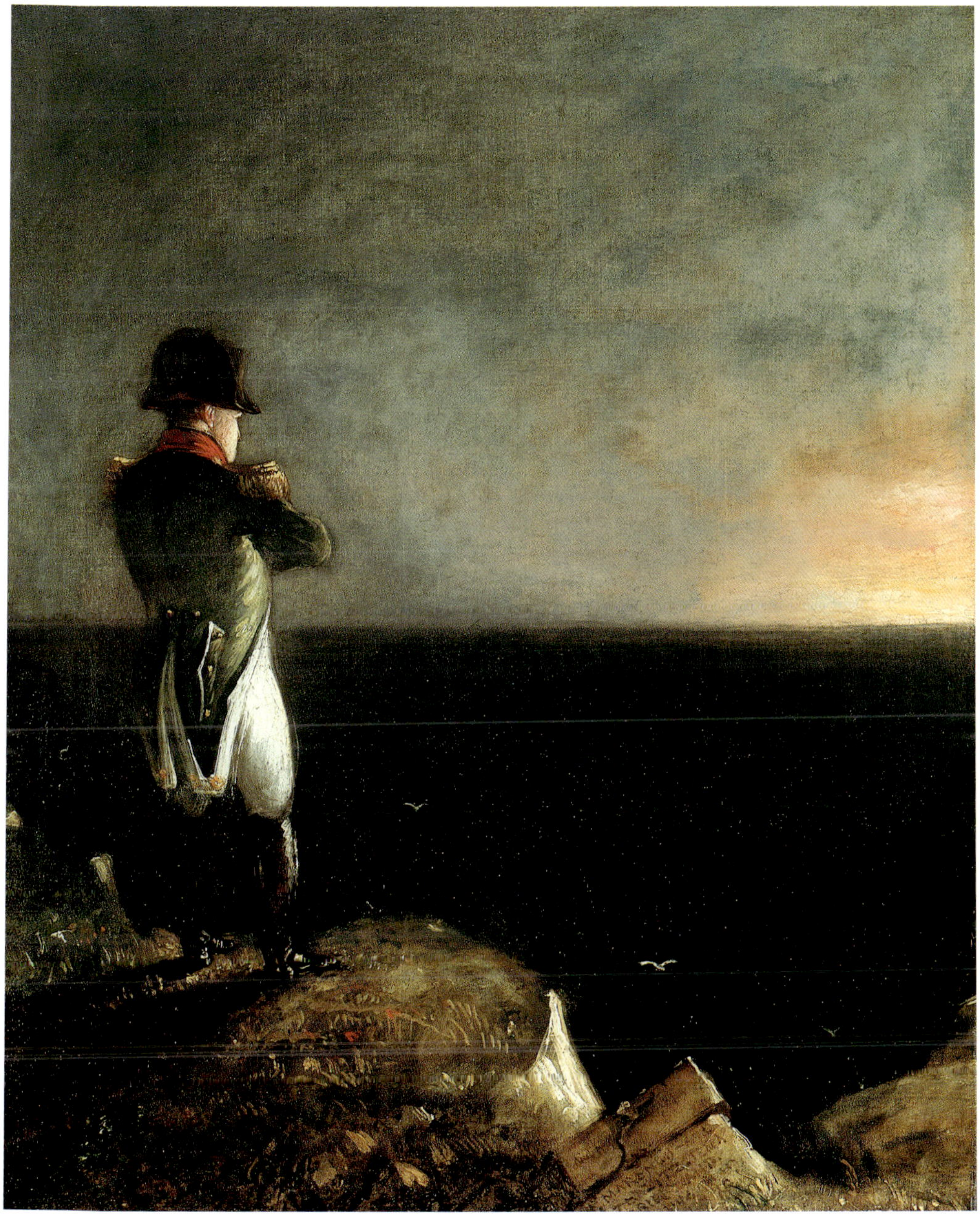

STUDIO OF SIR JOSHUA REYNOLDS, 1767-9

Edmund Burke

(1729-97)

Oil on canvas, 756 × 629 mm (29¾ × 24¾ ins)
(NPG 655)

The statesman and philosopher Edmund Burke, one of Britain's greatest political thinkers, was born and educated in Dublin. He came to London in 1750 when he was twenty-one, and soon abandoned a career in law for literature. In 1756 he published *A Vindication of Natural Society,* and a year later *A Philosophical Enquiry into the Sublime and the Beautiful,* a work which had a profound influence on art, aesthetics, and the appreciation of landscape in the later part of the century.

Increasingly drawn to politics, Burke entered Parliament in 1765. For nearly thirty years, the House of Commons witnessed his brilliant oratory. He strongly opposed George III's influence over Parliament, the subject of his 1770 publication, *Thoughts on the Cause of the Present Discontents.* He argued for the emancipation of Ireland, and was a fierce critic of Britain's policy towards America; his speech, *On Conciliation with America*, was published in 1775: 'Reflect how you are to govern a people, who think they ought to be free, and think they are not'. He was also a force behind the much-needed reform of the corrupt East India Company, and in 1788 he opened the trial of the Governor-General, Warren Hastings, with a speech of inspired eloquence.

In 1790 Burke published his *Reflections on the Revolution in France*, in which, two years before the rise of Robespierre and the Reign of Terror, he expressed his fear that the revolutionary ideals would destroy essential British traditions, and lead to a violent overturning of the ordained order.

Reflections was read throughout Europe, but it cost Burke the support of a number of allies and he was roundly attacked by radical writers like Joseph Priestley, Mary Wollstonecraft and Tom Paine. He retired in 1794, and died three years later.

RW & SH

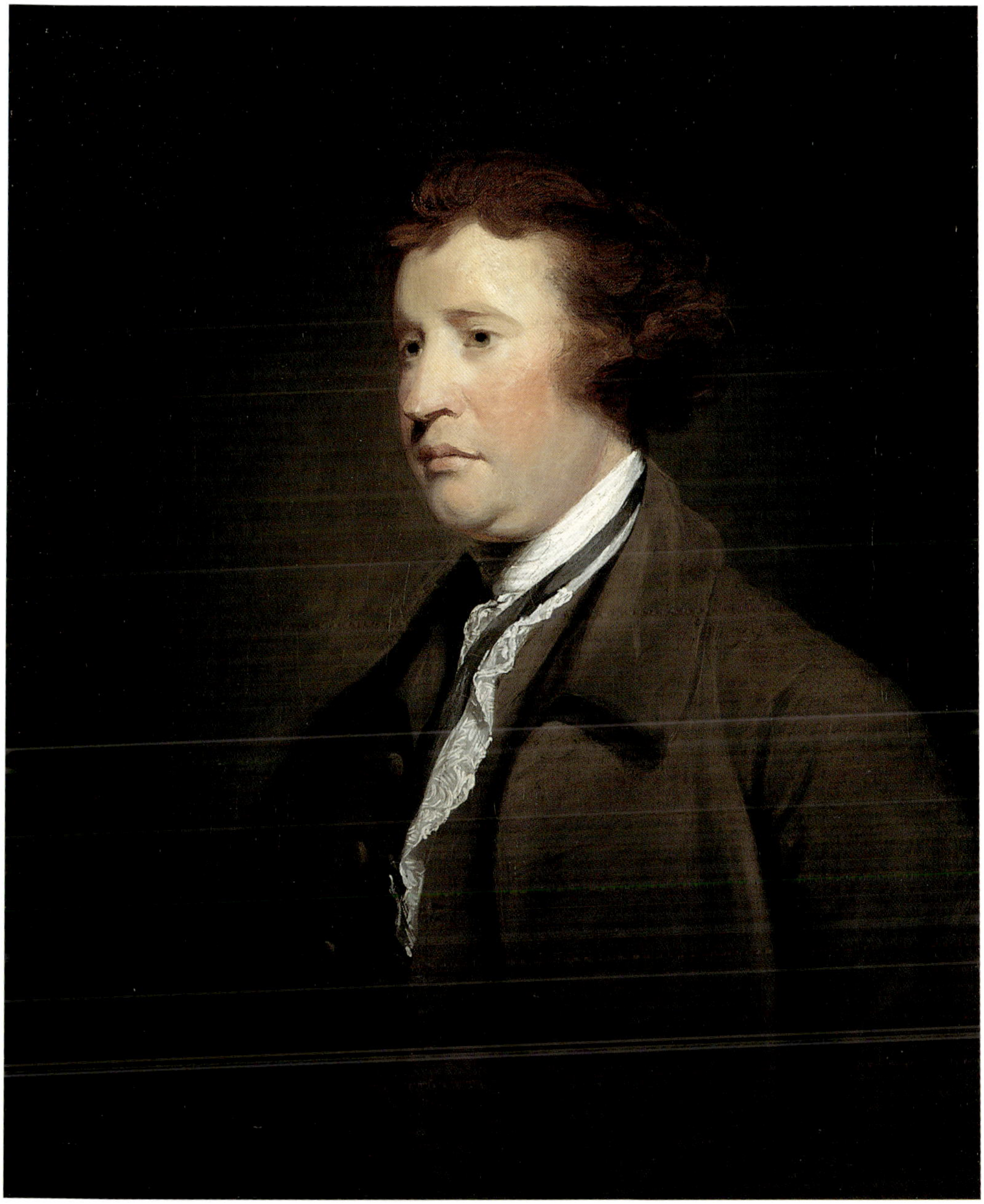

CHARLES WILSON PEALE, 1824

Charles Waterton

(1782-1865)

Oil on canvas, 613 × 514 mm (24⅛ × 20¼ ins)
(NPG 2014)

Landowner, naturalist and writer in the tradition of Gilbert White, Charles Waterton was born at his family seat of Walton Hall in Yorkshire, an eighteenth-century house built on an island in the middle of a large lake within a heavily wooded park. On the death of his father in 1806, Waterton enclosed the estate with a nine-foot wall and, banning guns within its perimeter, turned it into a bird sanctuary and natural history museum.

Most of Waterton's writing was on British birds and wild animals, but from the age of twenty-two he had spent eight years managing family estates in British Guiana. In 1816, 1820 and finally 1824 he made further journeys to South America, the United States, Canada, and the West Indies, recording his experiences, observations and techniques for preserving specimens in his successful book *Wanderings* (1825).

Waterton's explorations had equipped him for an austerely regimented life. He would sleep on a bare floor at Walton Hall with a block of wood for a pillow, before rising at three to light a fire. From four to five he would spend an hour in his chapel, after which he would read chapters from the life of St Francis Xavier and *Don Quixote*, before spending the rest of the day on letters, stuffing birds, or in his park. Almost six foot high, his hair always cut short, he was painted by Charles Peale – a naturalist as well as artist – in Philadelphia while on his North American travels. Waterton had taught Peale's son, Titian, his method for preserving specimens, and he is seen here with two of them, a Guiana Red Cotinga and a cat. Peale wrote that the portrait, 'although done in a short time is an acknowledged likeness.'

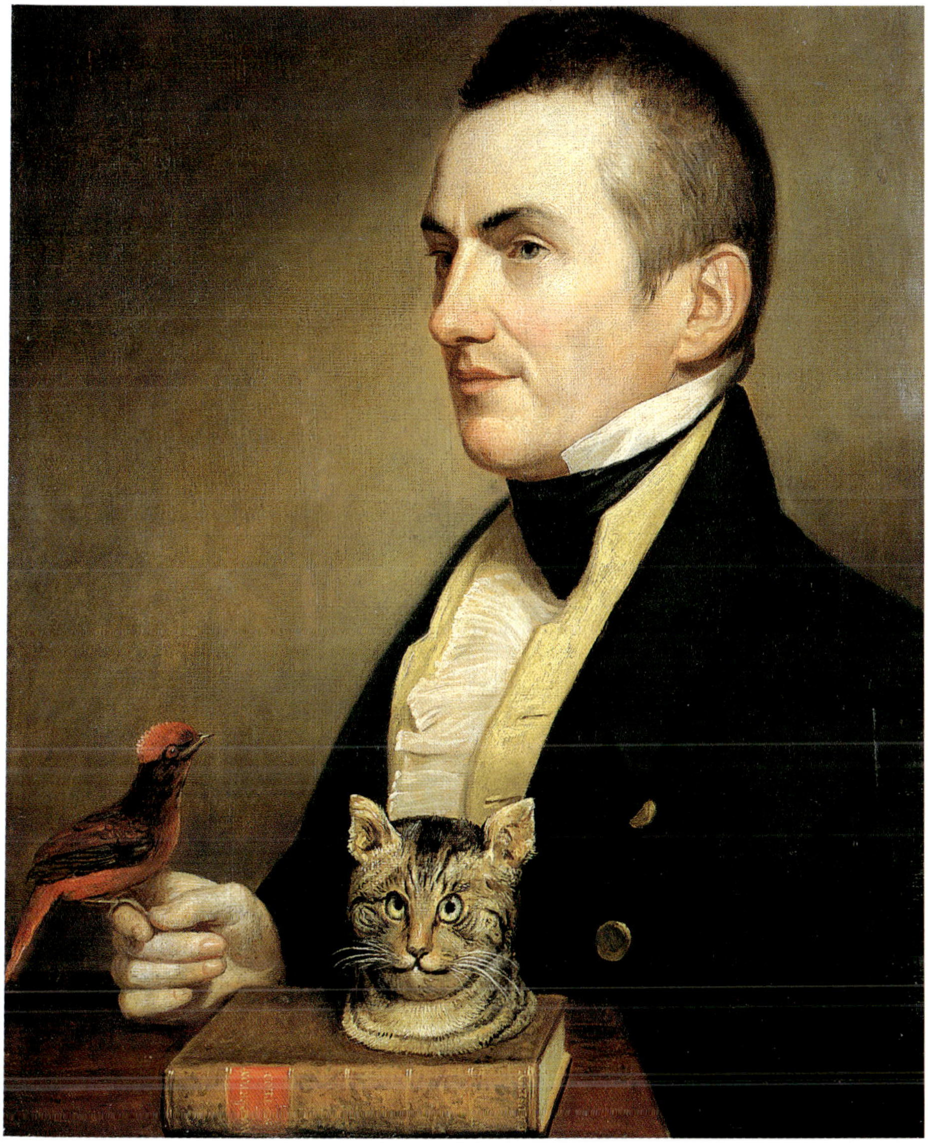

Study for Patrons and Lovers of Art

Oil on canvas, 622 × 470 mm (24½ × 18½ ins)
(NPG 792)

For all the extravagance of George IV's reign, there had been no more cultured court or sovereign in English history since the time of Charles I. In the popular imagination George will always be known for his excesses, but if this was the age in which St Paul's pupped and produced the Brighton Pavilion it also saw the birth of the National Gallery. Wonder's painting is as much a reminder of the cultural philanthropy that would eventually produce the great galleries and museums of Victorian England as it is of private patronage.

This is one of four preliminary studies commissioned by General Sir John Murray for a painting of an imaginary gallery hung with pictures from famous collections. On the left, kneeling in front of Titian's *Bacchus and Ariadne*, purchased by the National Gallery in 1826, is George Watson Taylor, the owner of the Parmigianino hanging on the wall above his head. On the right of the standing group, holding palette and maulstick, is the artist; in the centre, The Revd William Holwell-Carr, a benefactor of the National Gallery. Between them, top hat and cane in hand, stands the dominant figure of Wonder's patron, who in a varied military career had been court-martialled and acquitted but admonished for sacrificing the guns and ignoring Wellington's instructions at Tarragona in the Peninsular War.

In the light of this it is interesting that, although in this version Nollekens's bust of Wellington (belonging to Angerstein, whose collection was bought by Parliament to form the nucleus of the National Gallery) holds a prominent position, in the final imaginary gallery busts of Milton and Locke replace it. Several paintings are also identifiable, including works by Velázquez, Garofalo, Raphael and *The Visitation* by Rembrandt.

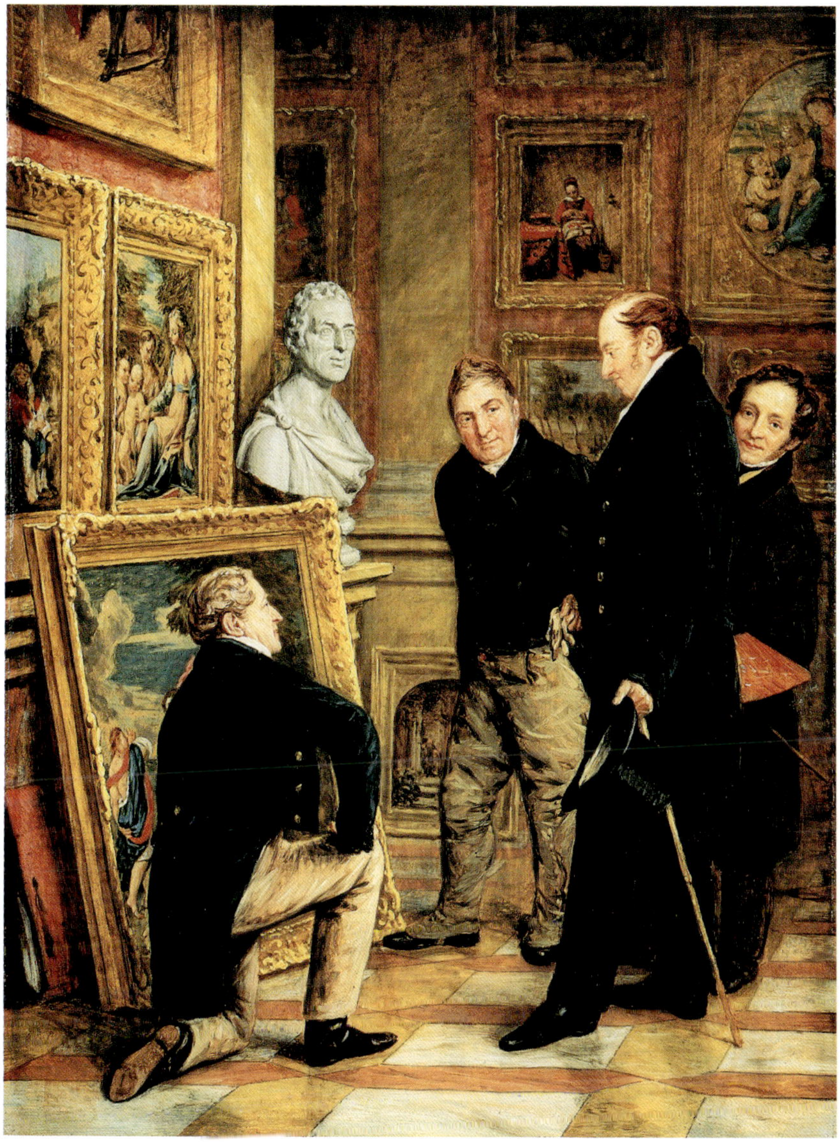

PIETER CHRISTOFFEL WONDER, *c.*1830

Study for Patrons and Lovers of Art

Oil on canvas, 549 × 483 mm (21⅝ × 19 ins)
(NPG 795)

This is another of Pieter Wonder's four studies for his imaginary gallery. Seated is George Wyndham, 3rd Earl of Egremont, a friend of General Sir John Murray and lover of the arts, best known now for his association with Turner at Petworth, but a patron also of Flaxman, Haydon, and Constable. It is likely that his painting by Teniers, *The Archduke Leopold's Gallery* (1651), which hung at Petworth, Egremont's great country house in Sussex, inspired Murray to commission Wonder's imaginary gallery.

Standing on the left in profile is Sir Robert Peel, the Home Secretary of the day and the future Tory Prime Minister. Peel was one of the most important patrons of the period, and in 1871 the National Gallery bought a substantial part of his collection.

The third figure in the group, arms folded behind the Earl of Egremont, is the only artist except Wonder himself included in the final imaginary gallery, the successful genre painter, Sir David Wilkie. There is no work of his represented in Wonder's painting, but Wilkie was a favourite painter of the Marquess of Stafford, another of the patrons represented in the final work, and his *Village Holiday* entered the National Gallery with the Angerstein pictures in 1824. 'I shall be very happy to accede to the request your Ladyship makes to sit for a portrait to Mr Wonder', Wilkie wrote to Sir John Murray's widow (Murray never saw his finished commission) 'and particularly that it was the wish of the late Sir John Murray that I should have a place in the picture he is painting.' In the completed work, this group stands beside an easel with Correggio's *Madonna of the Basket*, bought for the National Gallery in 1825.

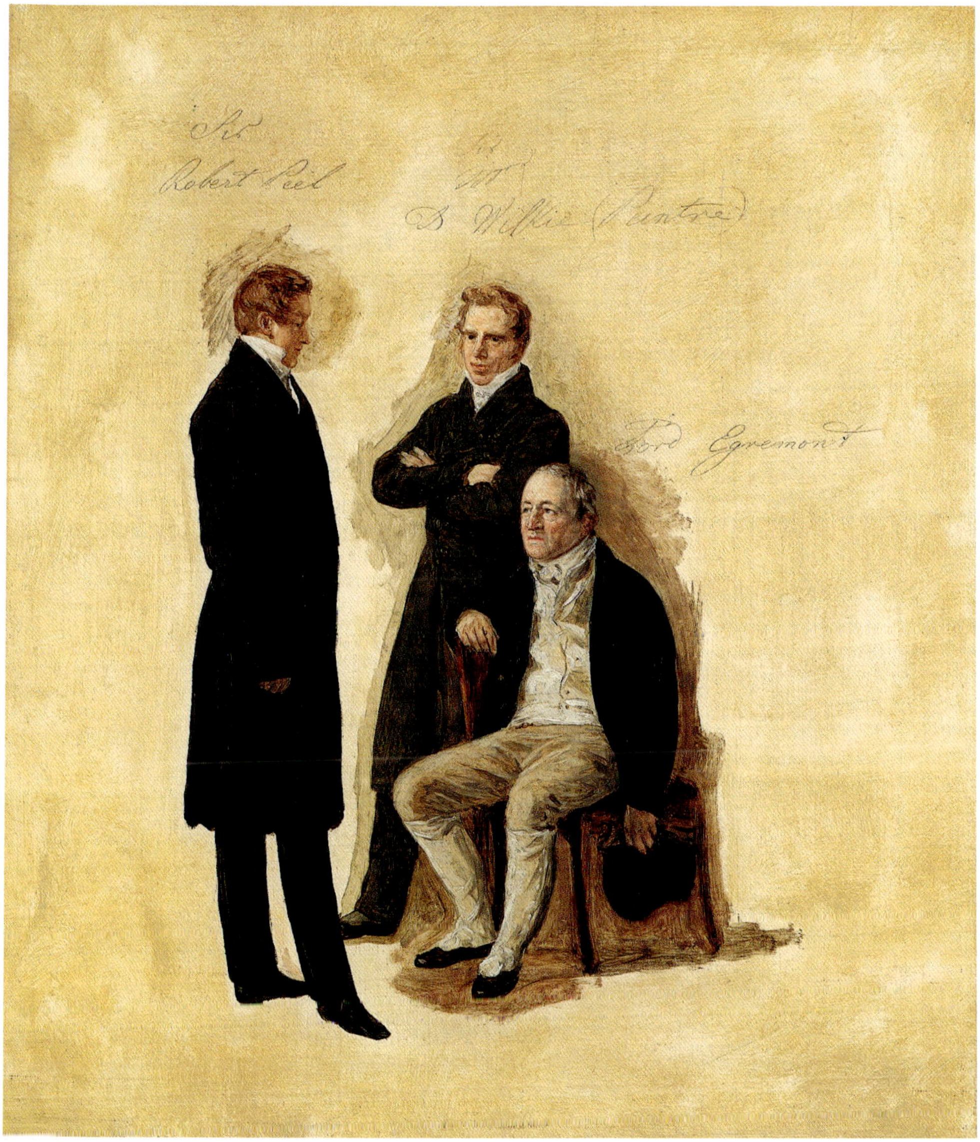
Sir
Robert Peel
Mr
D Wilkie (Painter)
Lord Egremont

GILBERT STUART, *c.*1785

Benjamin West

(1738-1820)

Oil on canvas, 902 × 699 mm (35½ × 27½ ins)
(NPG 349)

The prototype of the New World expatriate artist and the second president of the Royal Academy in succession to Sir Joshua Reynolds, Benjamin West was the first American painter to achieve an international reputation. Born in Pennsylvania on what is now the campus of Swarthmore College, West studied and worked in Italy with considerable success before moving to London at the end of the Seven Years War in 1763.

In an age of Classical revival and interest – the first volume of Stuart and Revetts's *Antiquities of Athens* had appeared the year before, in 1762 – West's large neo-classical history paintings were immediately popular. Throughout his career his style adapted to reflect the changing fashions and influences of his times, but he is still best remembered for the canvases that first attracted the patronage of George III – and in particular for *The Death of Wolfe (1771).* This wedded the conventions of the neo-classical style to contemporary dress and events in a revolutionary way.

Even before he became President of the Royal Academy in 1792, West was a magnet to other visiting American artists, and Gilbert Stuart lodged in his house as a pupil and assistant shortly after arriving in London in 1775. His first portrait of West was exhibited in 1781. This painting shows a slightly older West, and Bayly's Bible in his hand helps date it to *c.* 1785. In the background is West's vast *Moses Receiving the Law*, which was painted for Windsor Castle. In an interesting glimpse of changing tastes and expectations, the *Monthly Magazine* complained in 1804 that Stuart had made the President of the Royal Academy and other artists he had painted look like 'so many mercers or haberdashers.'

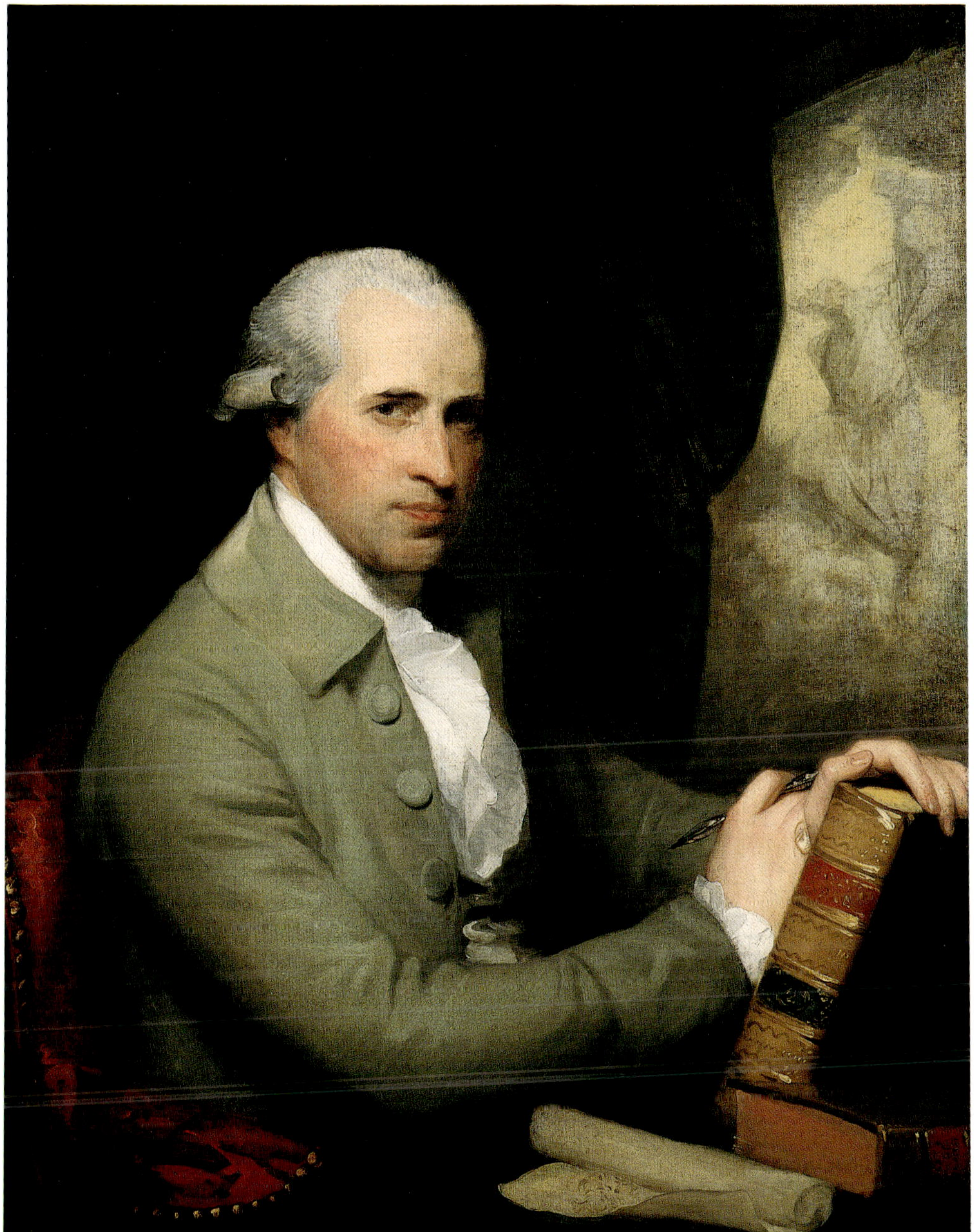

EDWARD FRANCESCO BURNEY *c.* 1784

Frances D'Arblay ('Fanny Burney')

(1752-1840)

Oil on canvas, 762 × 635 mm (30 × 25 ins)
(NPG 2634)

Fanny Burney was a novelist and diarist who, in her sharp, satirical portrayals of English society, anticipated Jane Austen. Her first novel, *Evelina, or the History of a Young Lady's Entrance into the World*, was published anonymously in 1778, when she was twenty-six. It was immediately popular, and in one year went through five editions. One of her greatest supporters, once he had learned her identity, was Dr. Johnson: 'Miss Burney is a real wonder,' he told Mrs. Thrale in 1779, 'What she is, she is intuitively. Dr. Burney told me that she had the fewest advantages of any of his daughters, from some peculiar circumstances. And such had been her timidity, that he himself had not had any suspicion of her powers.' In 1782 she published another novel, *Cecilia*, which, again, was a huge popular success.

In 1786 she became Second Keeper of the Robes to the Queen, but she disliked life at Court and in 1791 was given leave to resign. In 1793 she married a French refugee, General Alexandre d'Arblay and was henceforth known as Madame d'Arblay. She published two more novels after her marriage, *Camilla* in 1796 and *The Wanderer, or Female Difficulties* in 1814 and died in 1840, aged 87. Her *Letters and Journals* were published six years after her death.

Fanny Burney sat to her cousin in 1782, when she was 30. In her diary entry for 12 August we see that deceptive timidity referred to by Johnson: 'The instant dinner was over, to my utter surprise and consternation, I was called into the room appropriated for Edward and his pictures, and informed that I was to sit to him for Mr Crisp! Remonstrances were unavailing, and declarations of aversion to the design were only ridiculed; both daddies interfered and when I ran off, brought me back between them and compelled my obedience; – and from that time to this, nothing has gone forward but picture-sitting!'

RW & SH

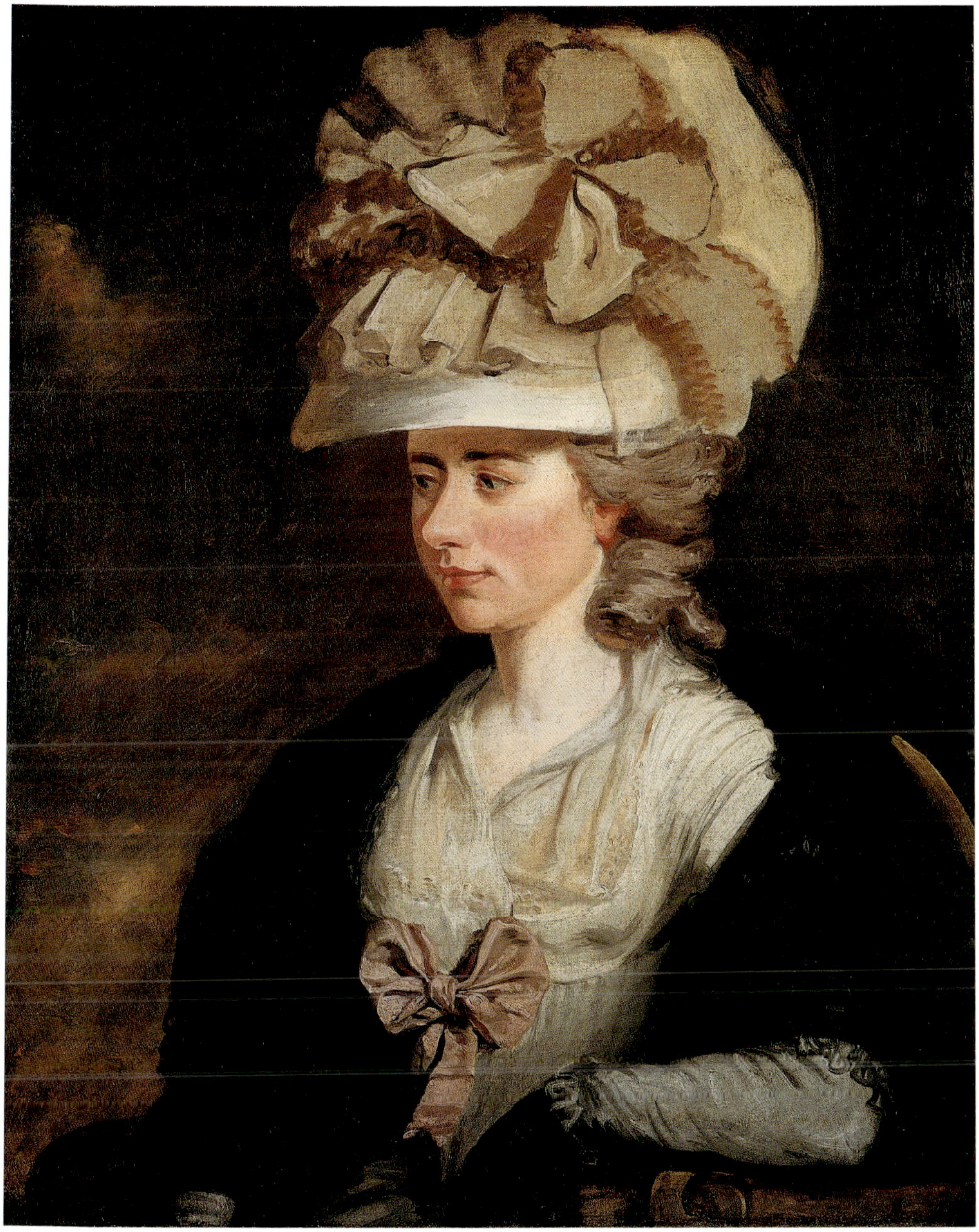

GILBERT STUART, *c.*1785

John Philip Kemble

(1757-1823)

Oil on canvas, 749 × 622 mm (29½ × 24½ ins)
(NPG 49)

The son of the actor Roger Kemble, the brother of Charles and Sarah (Mrs Siddons) and the uncle of Fanny, John Philip Kemble was the leading figure of one of the theatre's most famous dynasties. Educated at his father's wish at Sedgley Park and Douai for the priesthood, Kemble himself felt no vocation and abandoned the church for the stage. After a lengthy apprenticeship in the provinces he made his London debut as Hamlet in 1783.

It was with the London theatre, and its sometimes tempestuous history, that Kemble will always be most closely associated, and as actor and manager he played and mastered a range of roles that no other tragedian could match. In 1809 he was the victim of the notorious 'O. P – old prices – riots' that marred the reopening of Covent Garden after fire. But the reception that greeted his Coriolanus – his greatest part – when he finally retired in 1817 was a testament to his importance and popularity.

Vain enough, in Rogers's phrase, to be jealous of Mont Blanc, ludicrously affected in some of his pronunciations – his 'e's came in for particular mockery – and stiltedly declamatory in his style, Kemble was nevertheless a man of cultivation and decency and an actor of high intelligence and classical grandeur. Byron called him 'the most supernatural of actors'; Pitt, the noblest he had seen. 'There had been no other such countenance on the stage', Sir Thomas Lawrence declared. 'If 1000 men were collected together you would be struck with the face of Kemble.' Stuart's painting shows him at about the age of twenty-eight, the elegant man 'of good sense and gentleman-like feeling' that Scott, one of Kemble's great drinking partners (Kemble would take his wine 'by pailfuls' Scott said), fondly recalled.

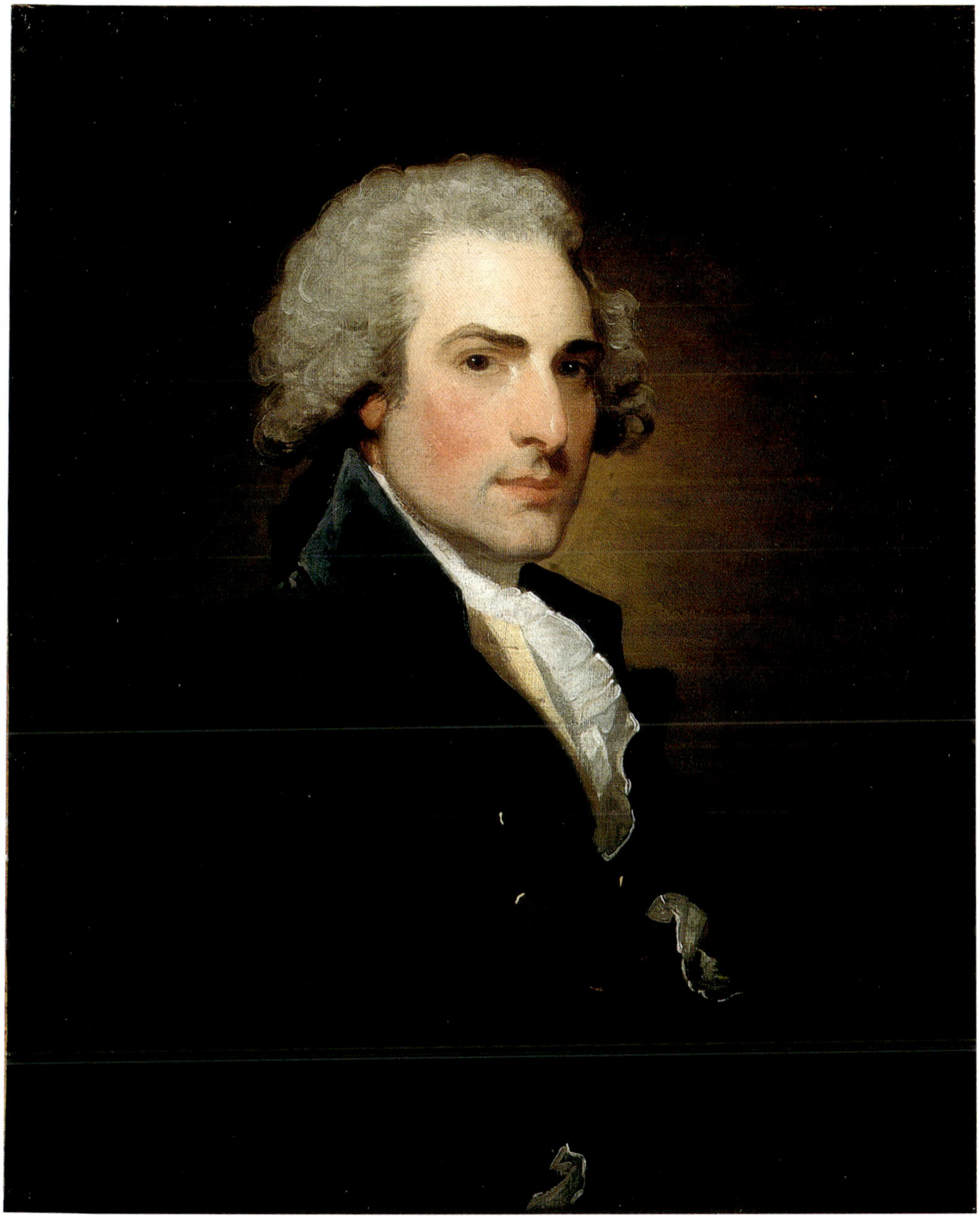

JOHN OPIE, 1804

William Henry West Betty

(1791-1874)

Oil on canvas, 1981 × 1490 mm (78 × 58⅝ ins)
(NPG 1392)

The 'Young Roscius' of the early nineteenth-century stage, William Betty was the most famous child actor of his day, playing Romeo in Dublin and Hamlet in Belfast before he was thirteen. In 1804 he made his London debut and for two seasons was a theatrical sensation, his appearances drawing such numbers that Byron complained his life was at hazard 'from the *affectionate squeezes* of the surrounding crowd.' Betty 'seemed almost like some gay creature of the elements', Hazlitt recalled of him at this time, 'moving about gracefully with all the flexibility of youth and murmuring Aeolian sounds with plaintive tenderness.'

After studying at Cambridge, Betty returned to the stage in 1812, but the charm had gone with the youth. 'Betty is performing here', a disillusioned Byron reported from Cheltenham to Lady Melbourne, one of the great society hostesses of the Regency world. 'I fear, very ill, his figure is that of a hippopotamus, his face like the Bull and *mouth* on the pannels of a heavy coach, his arms are fins flattened out of shape, his voice the gargling of an Alderman with the quinsey, and his acting altogether ought to be natural, for it is certainly like nothing that *Art* has ever yet exhibited on the stage.'

Opie's portrait shows Betty in the part of Young Norval in John Home's *Douglas*, a rôle he first took on at Covent Garden in December 1804. Opie was paid 100 guineas for the work but a row blew up when he attempted to exhibit the portrait at the Royal Academy exhibition of 1805. Betty's father, fearing it would prejudice sales of a print of his son, turned on the artist with all the fury of a Regency tennis father, threatening to cut the portrait to pieces and to sue Opie for £5,000.

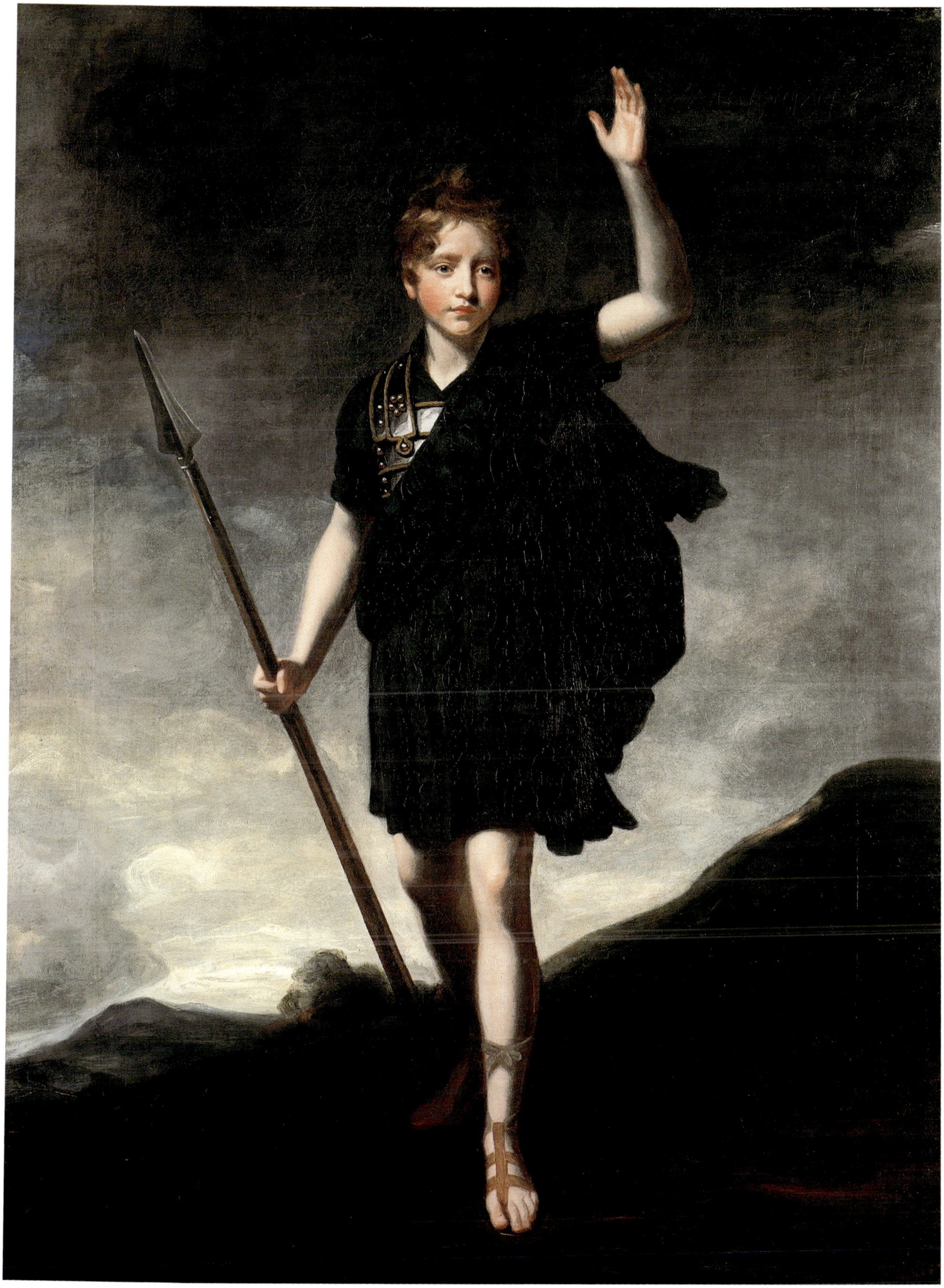

MATHER BROWN, *c.*1790

Henry Angelo

(1756-1835)

Oil on canvas, 775 × 648 mm (30½ × 25½ ins)
(NPG 5310)

Among all the statesmen, poets, scientists, artists and soldiers collected together here, Mather Brown's portrait of the great fencing master, Henry Angelo, is a reminder of another side of life in what Sydney Smith called that 'Golden Parallelogram' of fashionable Regency London. The son of the famous Italian equestrian and swordmaster, Domenico Tremonando, Angelo inherited his father's *académie* and shared rooms, at number 13 Bond Street, with the great pugilist and Champion of England, 'Gentleman' John Jackson.

It was there, in an atmosphere somewhere between that of a private club and a gymnasium, that a generation of 'Bond Street loungers' from Fox to Byron could practice their marksmanship in the shooting gallery or take lessons in fencing and boxing. It was rumoured that Angelo and Jackson were more than business partners, but whether that is true or not, for men like Byron their establishment provided a perfect meeting place of the aristocracy and the demi-monde. Byron first had lessons from Angelo at Harrow School, tried unsuccessfully to bring him to Cambridge as the official fencing master, and for the rest of his life retained an affection for him. 'Do let me know what there will be likely to be done', he wrote from Italy in September 1819, the month after post-war industrial and political discontent in England had climaxed in the Peterloo Massacre. 'A revolutionary commission into Leicestershire would just suit me ... I shall rub up my broad-sword exercise – in which I was really a proficient – ask *old Angelo* – if I did not cut his arms and elbows about rarely? during our practice in Albany.' He was equally proud of his record with Jackson, and had his portrait on his collage screen pasted with prints of the notable actors and pugilists of the day.

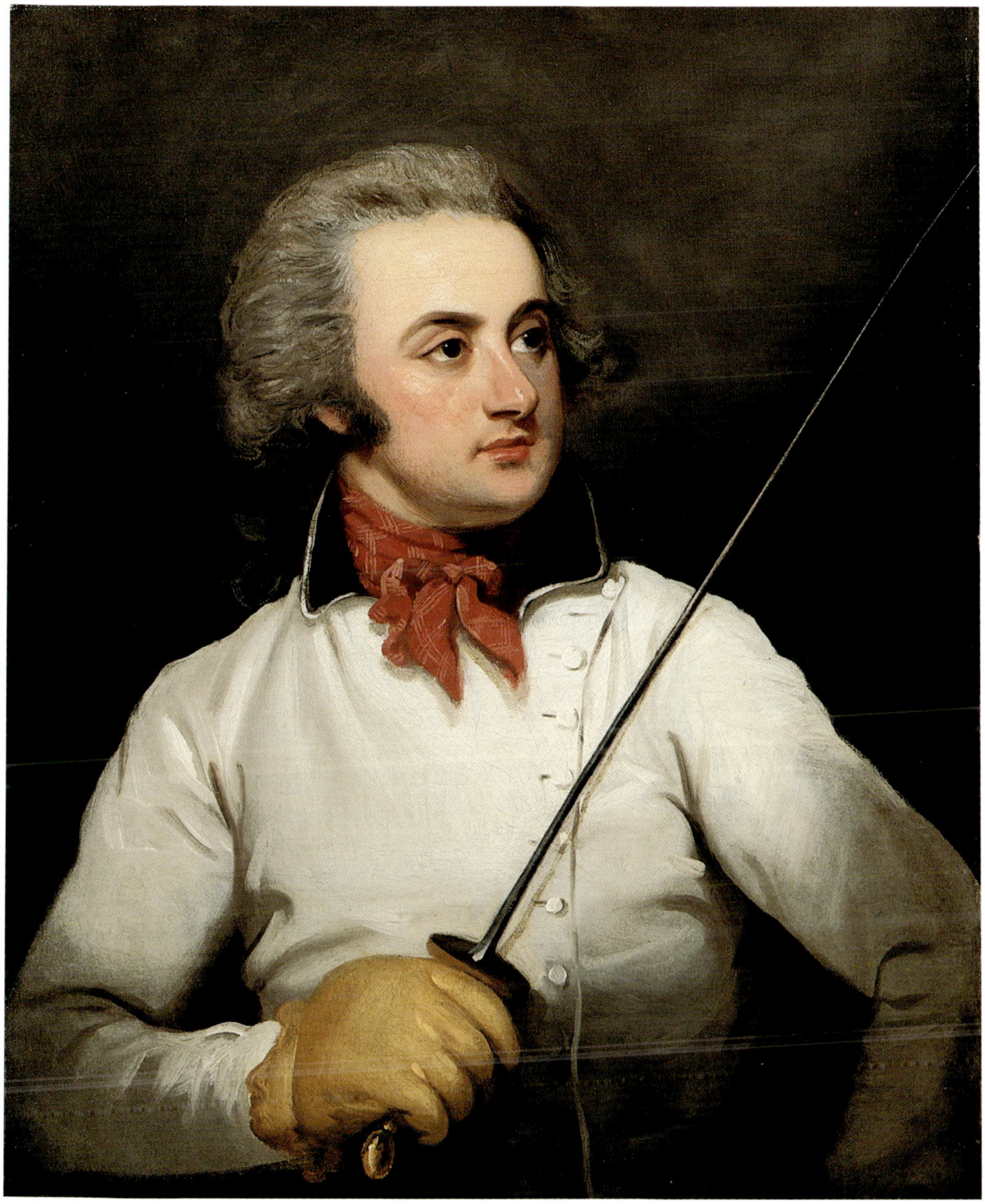

UNKNOWN ARTIST, *c.*1800

James Belcher

(1781-1811)

Oil on canvas, 762 × 638 mm (30 × 25⅛ ins)
(NPG 5214)

Jem Belcher was one of the most elegant and widely admired bare-knuckle prizefighters of the early Regency. He was renowned for his handsome looks, his extraordinary pluck, his eccentric boxing style, and his unshakeable good manners both inside and outside the ring. He was also famous for his unnerving habit of telling jokes to his opponents at the bloodiest moments of combat. 'Belcher's style was original,' wrote Pierce Egan in *Boxiana* (1812) '... his antagonists were terrified by his gaiety and decision ... and fighting-men in general were confounded with his sangfroid and intrepidity.'

Belcher came from a Bristol family of boxers. His brother Tom and apparently even his sister boxed. He found early fame in London before he was twenty, in a gruelling series of thirty-round contests with the bruiser Bourke, each of which he won. However, tragedy struck in July 1803 when he lost an eye playing rackets at the Fives Court, St Martin's Street. He married and took a pub, first the Jolly Brewer in Wardour Street, Soho and later the Coach and Horses, Frith Street.

But Belcher could not bear to abandon the ring. Though he could no longer 'judge the distances', for six years he gallantly went on boxing and losing, finally being beaten by the young Tom Cribb in 1809. According to Egan, the crowds wept for their fallen hero. Belcher died, exhausted and heartbroken, two years later, aged only thirty, a Romantic poet among pugilists. This portrait by an unknown admirer was presented to his widow.

Jem Belcher's cool style made him a favourite among Regency dandies, writers and painters. In 1808 he took part in an exhibition match organized by Lord Elgin, and attended by several members of the Royal Academy, including Sir Thomas Lawrence, Flaxman, and Benjamin West. He was admired by Byron, and worshipped by William Hazlitt who fondly recalls him in his famous essay *The Fight* (1821). Belcher always wore immaculate dark clothes, set off by a vivid and extravagant neckcloth (usually blue with white spots). This became known as a 'belcher', and is still remembered wistfully among the tailors of Savile Row.

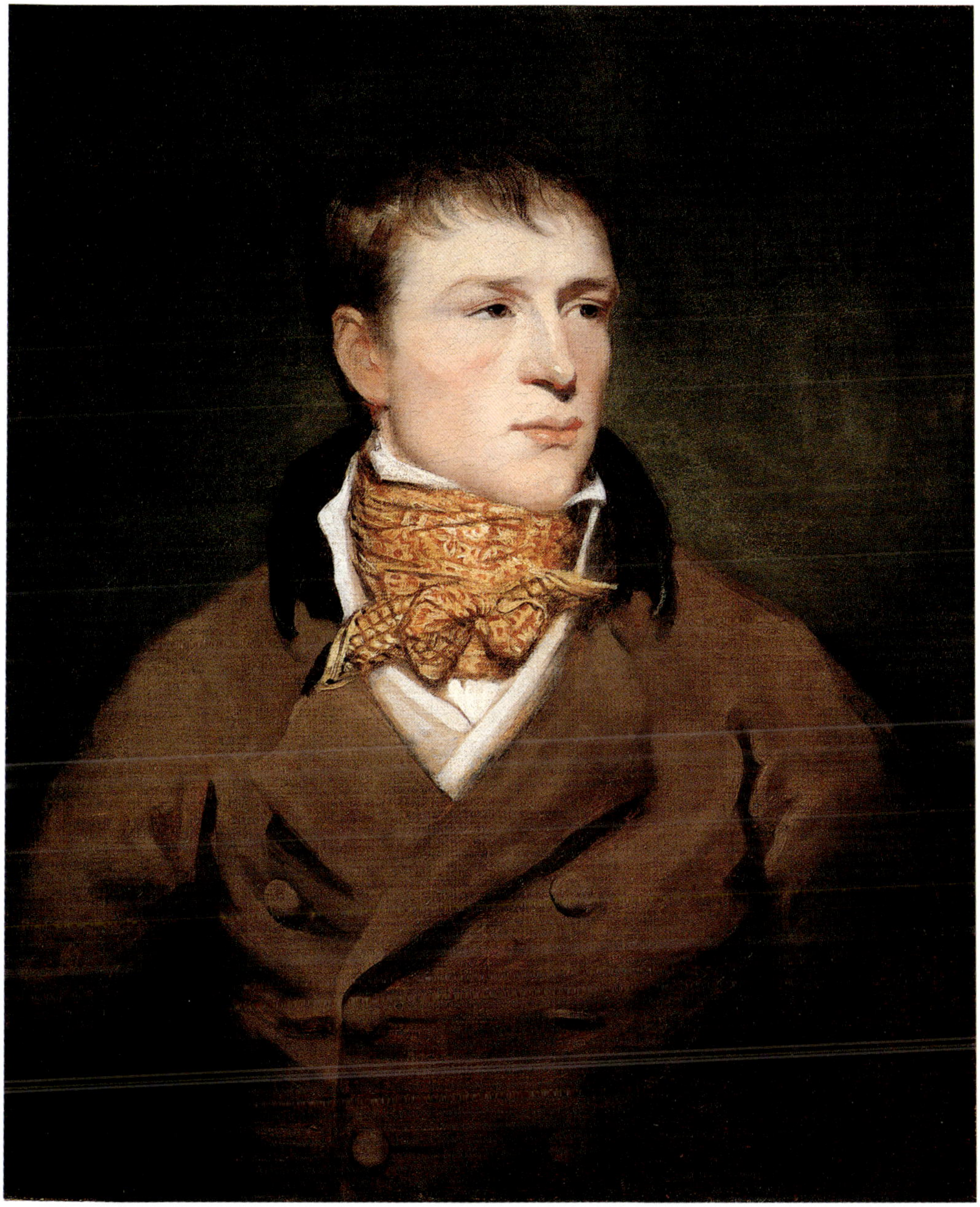

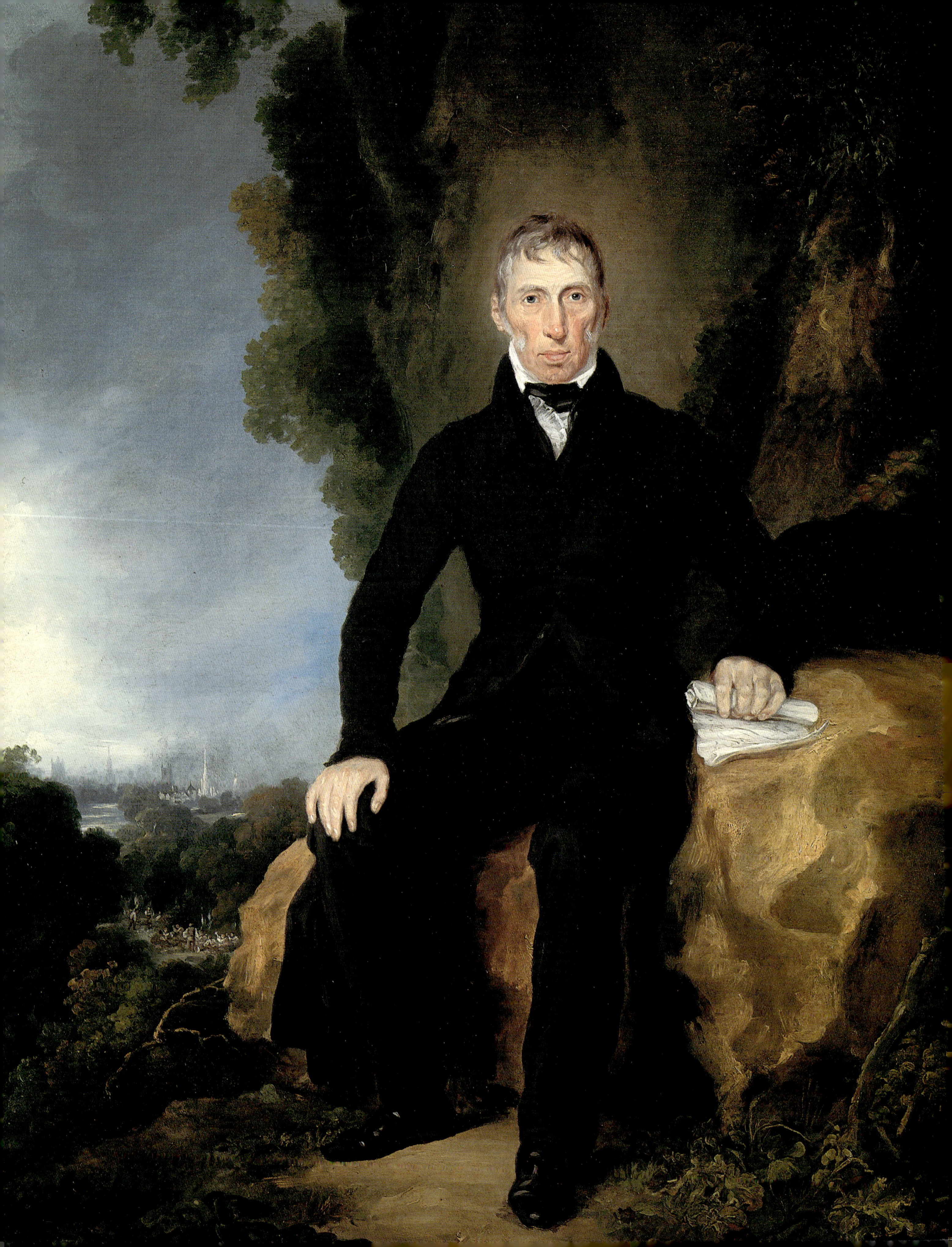

Science & Reform

UNKNOWN ARTIST, *c.*1830

John Loudon McAdam (detail)
(1756–1836)

Oil on canvas, 895 × 692 mm (35¼ × 27¼ ins)
(NPG 3686)

HENRY WILLIAM PICKERSGILL, exh.1829

Jeremy Bentham

(1748-1832)

Oil on canvas, 2044 × 1384 mm (80½ × 54½ ins)
(NPG 413)

Jeremy Bentham was one of the great reforming philosophers of the late eighteenth and early nineteenth centuries. 'The father of English innovation', wrote John Stuart Mill in 1838, 'both in doctrines and in institutions, is Bentham: he is the great *subversive*, or, in the language of continental philosophers, the great *critical*, thinker of his age and country'.

After an education at Westminster and Oxford, Bentham was called to the Bar, but he never went into practice. In 1776 he published, anonymously, a *Fragment on Government*, an attack on the existing laws of England, and in 1791, after a three-year stay in Russia, *Panopticon*, a proposal for prison reform. His most important work, *Introduction to the Principles of Morals and Legislation,* had been published in 1789.

Bentham was the leader of a group known as the 'Philosophic Radicals', and the central maxim of his philosophy, generally termed Utilitarianism, was that 'it is the greatest happiness of the greatest number that is the measure of right and wrong'. Happiness could, Bentham believed, be quantitatively measured, something to which Hazlitt, in *The Spirit of the Age* (1825), objected: in so thinking 'he had "bound volatile Hermes", and reduced the theory and practice of human life to a *caput mortuum* of reason, and dull, plodding, technical calculation'.

In time Bentham's beliefs were translated into practical reform. He inspired a number of important changes in English jurisprudence, and a reformation of the Poor Law. Liberal economists saw Utilitarianism as a justification for laissez-faire and free trade. On his death in 1832, he directed that his skeleton, masked in wax and dressed in his own clothes, should be kept at University College, London, which he had helped to found, where it is still on display.

RW & SH

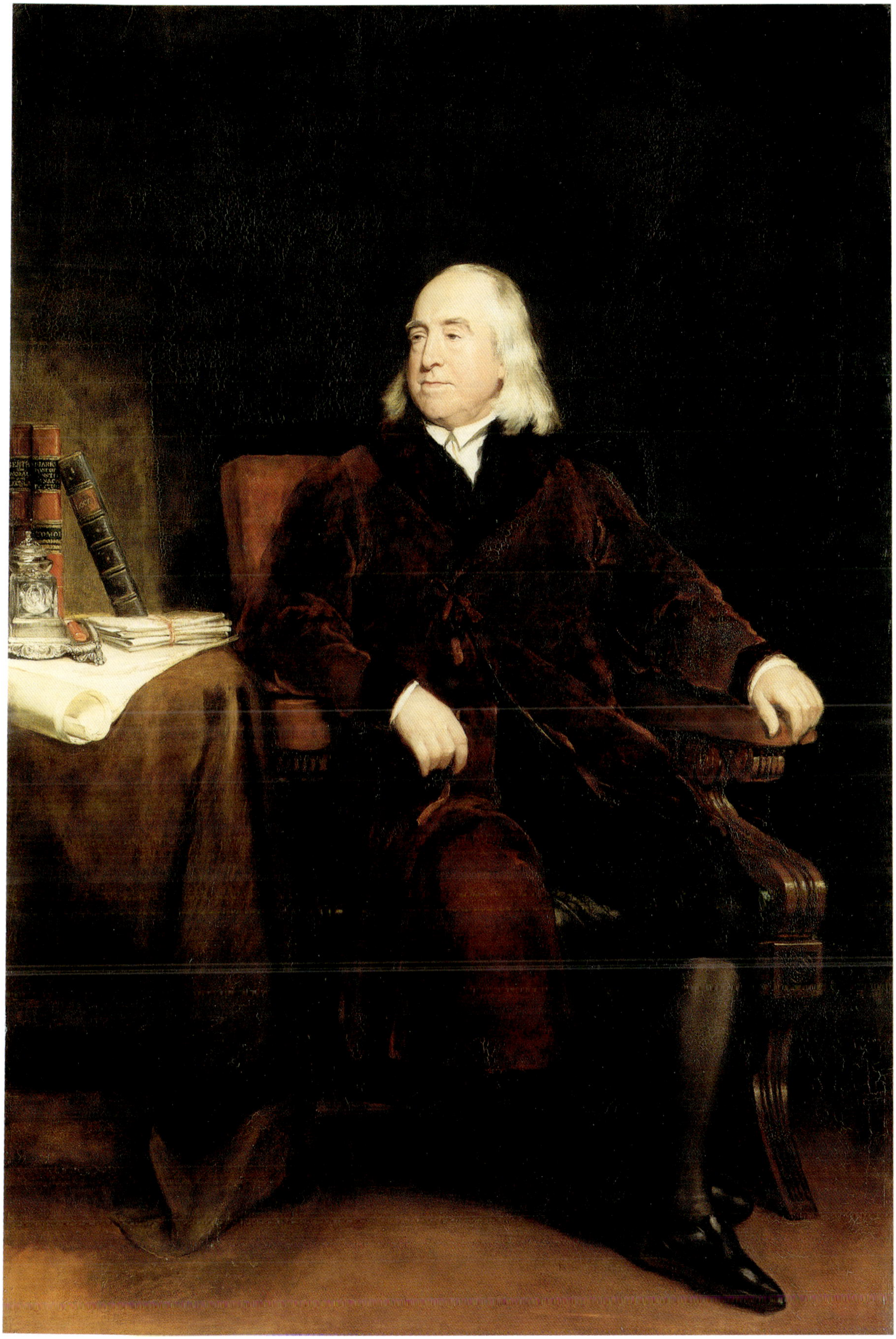

SIR GEORGE HAYTER, 1834

Daniel O'Connell

(1775-1847)

Oil on millboard, 356 × 305 mm (14 × 12 ins)
(NPG 4582)

Politician, barrister, journalist, reformer and architect of mass agitation, 'The Liberator', as Daniel O'Connell was known, was the greatest figure in the emergence of Irish Nationalism as a force in nineteenth-century political life.

After attending the English College at St Omer and Douai, O'Connell entered Lincoln's Inn and was called to the Irish Bar in 1798, rapidly winning himself a reputation for his brilliance in court, as a champion of Catholic emancipation and an enemy of the Union. For the next twenty years O'Connell was at the forefront of the political and religious debate over Ireland, but his most important contribution began in 1823 with the founding of the Catholic Association to champion the rights of the peasantry. The Association was suppressed after only two years, but O'Connell had effectively altered the nature of political activism in Ireland, uniting Nationalist and Catholic aspirations and mobilizing the Irish clergy to the cause in ways that would have profound repercussions for the future of Anglo-Irish politics.

Prosecuted more than once by the English authorities, and barred from taking his seat in Parliament in 1829 for refusing the oath of allegiance, O'Connell was returned by the Dublin voters in 1832. There were other more radical Irish leaders, who thought his relations with his English allies altogether too cosy, but until his death in Genoa he fought tirelessly to promote Irish interests, giving his last impassioned speech to the House as the shadow of the Great Famine fell across Ireland. The portrait is a study for Sir George Hayter's *House of Commons* (1833-43), his group painting of the first MPs elected after the Great Reform Act of 1832. In the finished painting O'Connell is hatless, but the pose and features are otherwise similar.

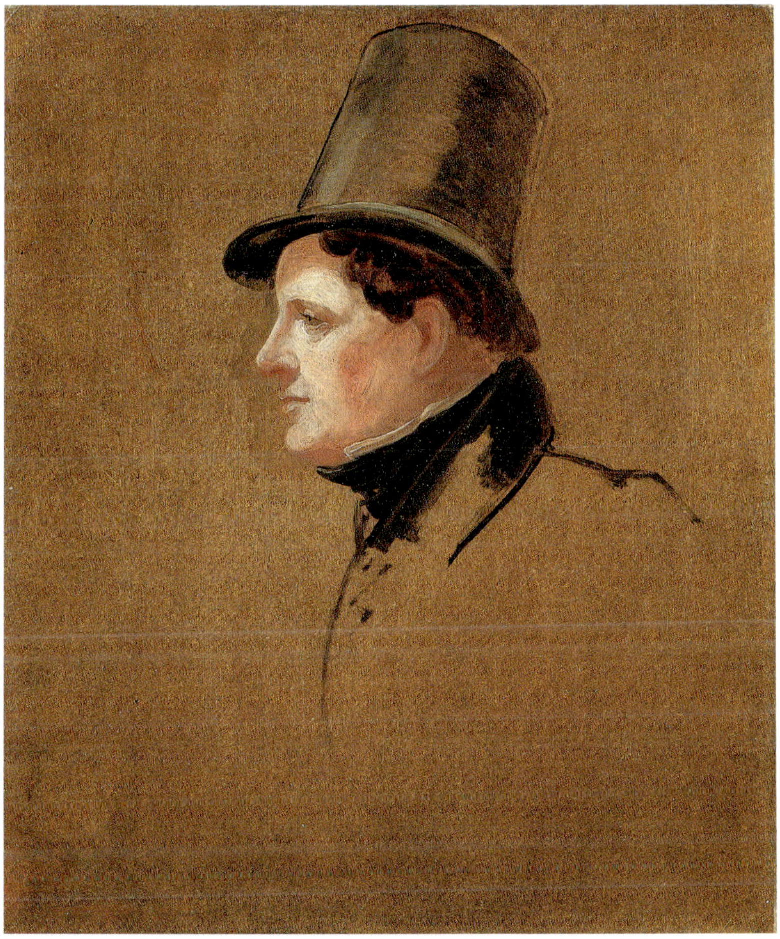

ATTRIBUTED TO THOMAS PHILLIPS, *c.*1820

Charles Grey, 2nd Earl Grey

(1764-1845)

Oil on canvas, 1276 × 1010 mm (50¼ × 39¾ ins)
(NPG 4137)

The name of Charles Grey will always be associated with the Great Reform Act of 1832 that extended the franchise to the middle classes and paved the way to universal suffrage. At the time there was a bitter debate over its likely consequences, but if Grey can take credit for overseeing the most important single act of constitutional reform of the nineteenth century, no man could have had less idea of its ultimate implications. 'If any persons suppose that this Reform will lead to ulterior measures', he confidently told Parliament in November 1831, 'they are mistaken; for there is no one more decided against annual parliaments, universal suffrage, and the ballot, than I am. My object is not to favour, but to put an end to such hopes and projects.'

Charles Grey, the son of the Earl Grey who had fought during the American War of Independence, was educated at Eton and Trinity College, Cambridge and entered Parliament as the MP for Northumberland in 1786. He first came to prominence during the impeachment of Warren Hastings, and made his name as a consistent supporter of reform at home and abroad, opposing repressive legislation throughout the long wars with France and supporting the independence of nationalities in foreign affairs.

Grey was briefly Foreign Secretary in 1806-7, but resigned over Catholic emancipation, and it was as a relic of the Whig party's Foxite past that he finally became Prime Minister in 1831 and forced through the moderate reform he had been advocating for almost forty years. 'Lord Grey's basis of character was excessive amiability, and it was this which attached others to him', Haydon recorded in his diary. Phillips' portrait dates from 1820-1, and shows Grey – for all his reforming zeal – as the elegant, cool aristocrat that he was.

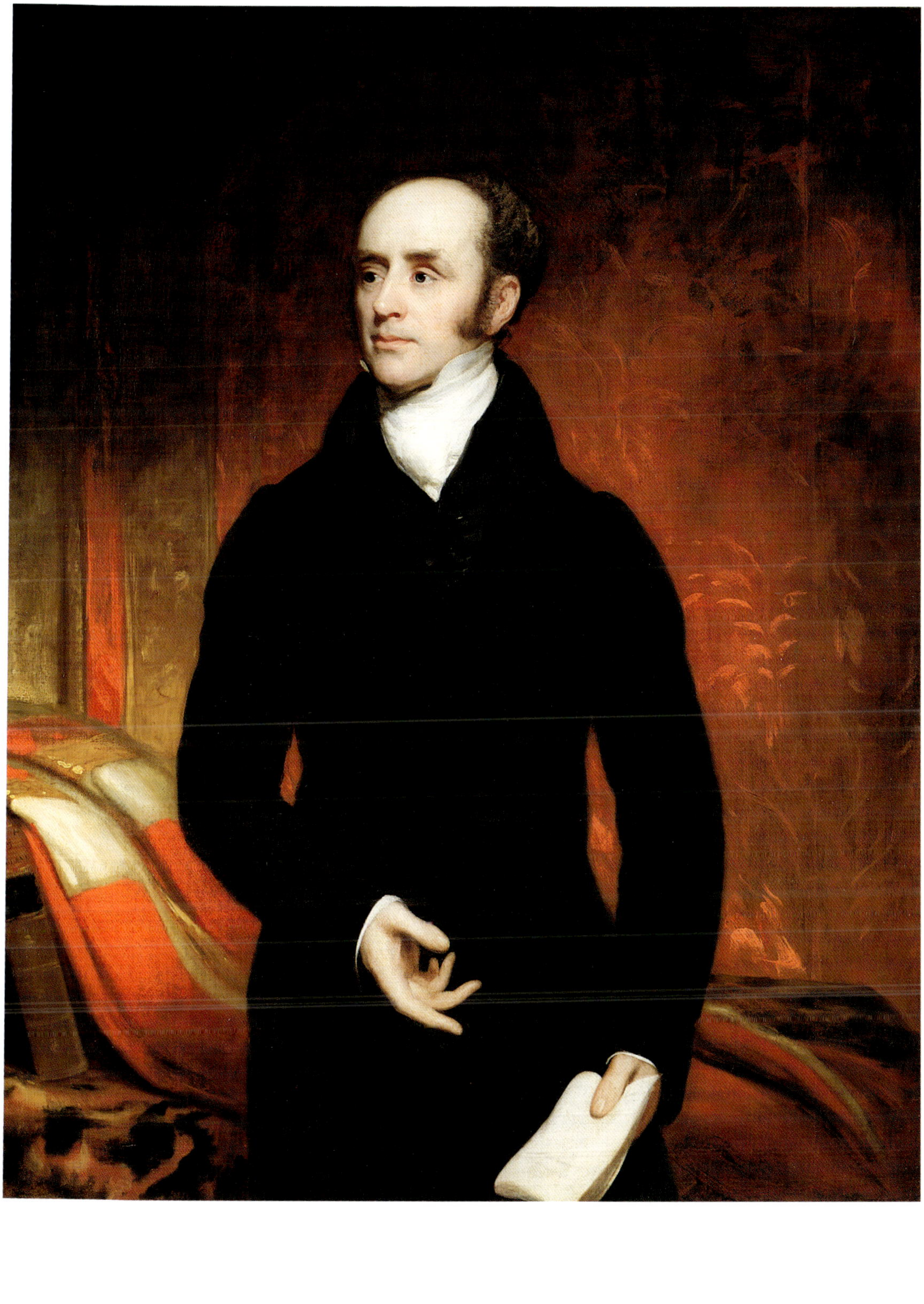

SIR THOMAS LAWRENCE, 1828

William Wilberforce

(1759-1833)

Oil on canvas, 965 × 1092 mm (38 × 43 ins)
(NPG 3)

Writing in his Italian exile, Byron once fondly recalled how the dramatist, Richard Brinsley Sheridan, 'was found drunk one night in the kennel and asked his *Name* by the Watchman he answered – " Wilberforce"'.

The watchman could have had no wittier answer to his question than the name of the man who had dedicated his whole life 'to the suppression of the Slave Trade and the reformation of manners.' There was a touch of sanctimoniousness about Wilberforce that gives Sheridan's response a genuine edge, but if Wilberforce had some of the failings of the Evangelical movement, he embodied all its virtues, and no man worked more tirelessly in the great reforming crusades of his day.

As a leading figure within the influential group of Evangelicals known as the 'Clapham Sect', a Member of Parliament and a friend of Pitt, Wilberforce also had the public standing to give his private beliefs a decisive historical force. He had first been elected to the House of Commons in 1780, and from 1787 onwards was the parliamentary leader of the triumphant Abolitionist movement and a leading figure in causes that ranged from the 'suppression of vice' and duelling, to animal cruelty and the use of children as chimney sweeps.

There is a saccharin quality about Lawrence's unfinished portrait that gives little idea of the energy and commitment of the young Wilberforce, or of the man who the whole House of Commons stood to cheer on the passage of his Abolition Bill in 1807. In his *Recollections* (1864), however, John Harford maintained that 'the intellectual power and winning sweetness of the veteran statesman are happily blended in this portrait.' Slight and frail in old age, Wilberforce's odd pose is explained by the fact that he was forced to wear 'a steel girdle cased in leather and an additional part to support the arms.'

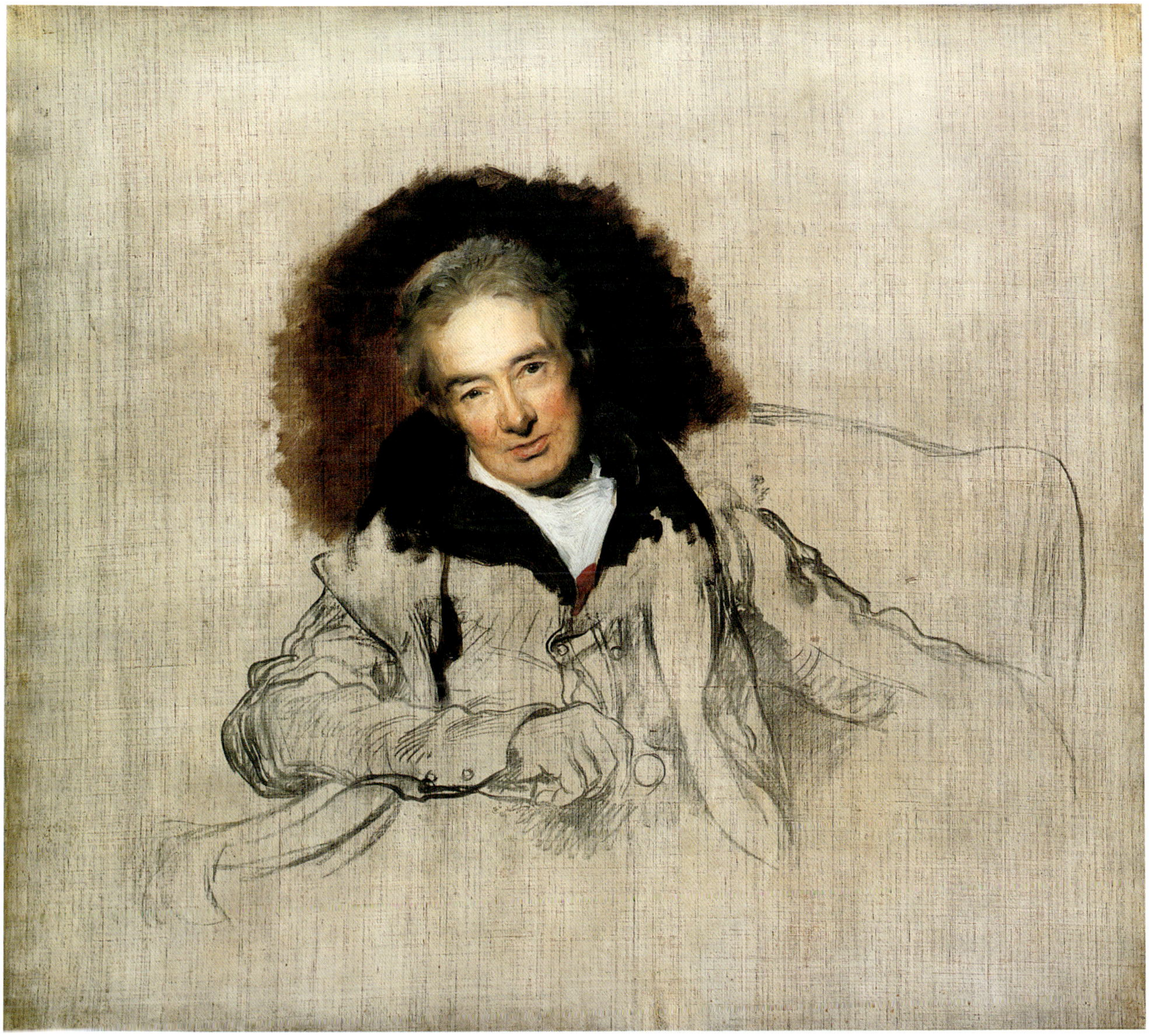

HENRY WILLIAM PICKERSGILL, exh.1822

Hannah More

(1745-1833)

Oil on canvas, 1257 × 895 mm (49½ × 35¼ ins)
(NPG 412)

Hannah More has not enjoyed a good posthumous press, but during a long life her vast output of evangelical writings won her a popular following and private reputation that is now hard to understand. The precocious daughter of a Tory and High Church schoolmaster, she was born near Bristol, and after winning a small local reputation with her writing, visited London where a meeting with the great actor, Garrick, propelled her into the world of blue-stockings, Reynolds, Burke and Johnson.

Garrick called her 'Nine' (all the Muses rolled into one) but any pleasure the young Hannah More had taken in the success of her play *Percy* (1778) was put behind her when the death of Garrick in 1779 and the growing influence of such evangelicals as William Wilberforce turned her mind to more serious issues. In 1788 she published her *Thoughts on the Importance of the Manners of the Great to General Society*, and for the next forty years was a leading figure in the Evangelical movement, an early proponent of the Sunday School system, a friend of the 'Clapham Sect' and the author of improving tracts, ballads and tales that are said to have reached a circulation of two million readers.

She was Tory in her political views, antagonistic towards women's rights, and deeply conservative in her social and educational beliefs: hard as the condition of the poor was, she believed it was a good deal better than they deserved at the hands of God. And in Pickersgill's portrait painted in 1822 – the year Shelley died, the year before Byron sailed for Greece – she seems the relic of an earlier age untouched by the forces of Romanticism.

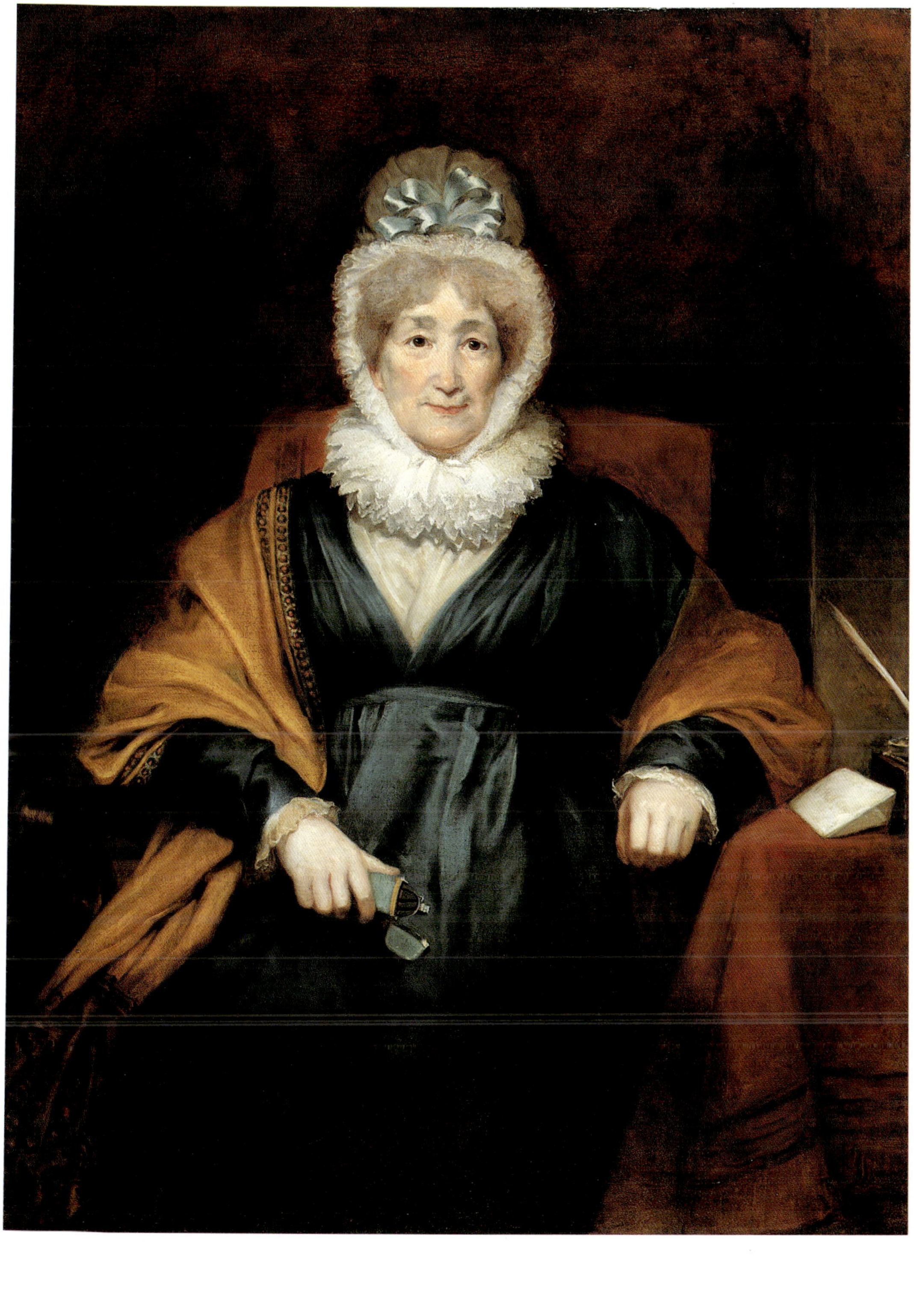

SIR THOMAS LAWRENCE, *c.*1790

Sarah Trimmer

(1741-1810)

Oil on canvas, 762 × 635 mm (30 × 25 ins)
(NPG 5498)

Alongside the evangelical writer Hannah More, Mrs Sarah Trimmer – children's author, founder of Sunday Schools and relic of a previous age – survives here as a reminder of just how many different and contradictory strands make up the cultural history of a period dominated by the great figures of the Romantic movement.

Deeply suspicious of the effects of imaginative literature on children, she provided her own antidote with *A History of the Robins* (1786), a classic of the kind of improving literature that enjoyed an incomprehensible vogue well into the nineteenth century. 'Accept, my dear parent, the first tribute of gratitude which I have been able to offer you', a small bird, bringing its mother a gift of a spider is made to say in one typical passage. 'The eyes of the mother sparkled with delight; and knowing Pecksy's love would be disappointed by a refusal, she ate the spider, which her dutiful nestling had so affectionately brought her; and then said, "How happy would families be, if everyone like you, my dear Pecksy, consulted the welfare of the rest, instead of turning their whole attention to their own interest."'

Completely forgotten now, Sarah Trimmer – like the Grub Street hacks immortalized by Pope in his *Dunciad* (1728) – is preserved together with Hannah More in the amber of Byron's great satire, *Don Juan* (1819-24). 'In short, she was a walking calculation', Byron wrote of Donna Inez, his hero's hypocritically pious mother,

> Miss Edgeworth's novels stepping from their covers,
> Or Mrs Trimmer's books on education,
> Or 'Coelebs Wife' set out in quest of lovers,
> Morality's prim personification,
> In which not Envy self a flaw discovers;
> To others' share let 'female errors fall'
> For she had not even one – the worst of all.'

She is seen here, pen in hand, her arm, appropriately, resting on the Bible.

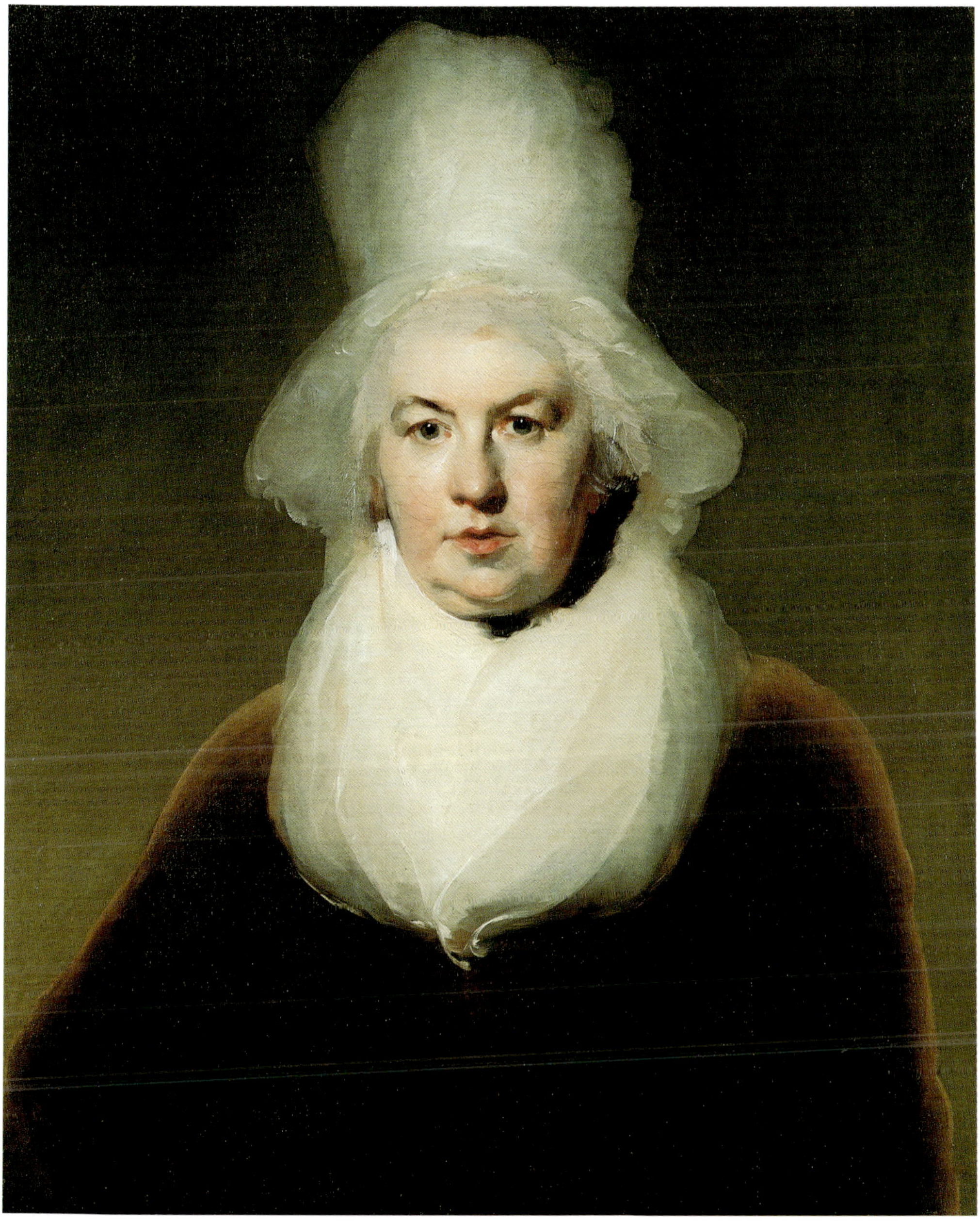

JOHN BOULTBEE, 1788-91

Robert Bakewell

(1725-95)

Oil on canvas, 710 × 910 mm (27¾ × 35¾ ins)
(NPG 5949)

In spite of the growth of commerce, and the beginnings of industrialization, eighteenth-century Britain was still essentially an agricultural nation, with the social and political structures of the country firmly rooted in the land. With the demands of a growing population and the stimuli of new inventions, improvements were required in the techniques and management of farming, and alongside such figures as 'Turnip' Townsend and Coke of Holkham, Robert Bakewell has a distinguished place in the agrarian transformation that made the more dramatic triumphs of the Industrial Revolution possible.

Robert Bakewell was born in the English Midlands, the son of a tenant farmer. When his father's health failed he took over the management of the 440 acres that he eventually inherited. As a young man he had travelled widely to look at different farming methods, and once in control of his own land he succeeded in transforming the quality of cattle, horses and sheep with his breeding experiments. It was said that where England produced 1lb of mutton before Bakewell, after him it produced two.

With his innovative techniques in feeding and housing stock, his improvements in fertilization and irrigation, and his forward-looking kindness to animals (his sheep were 'kept as clean as race-horses') Bakewell turned his land into a model farm that attracted visitors in much the same way as Robert Owen's mill would do later. He is shown here in a portrait by John Boultbee, a local Leicestershire artist who is also recorded as painting 'a favourite horse of Mr Bakewell'. It shows him as he became in later life, a living advertisement for his methods: 'tall, broad set', the *Gentleman's Magazine* recalled him, 'and, in his later years, rather inclined to corpulence. His countenance bespoke intelligence, activity and a high degree of benevolence.'

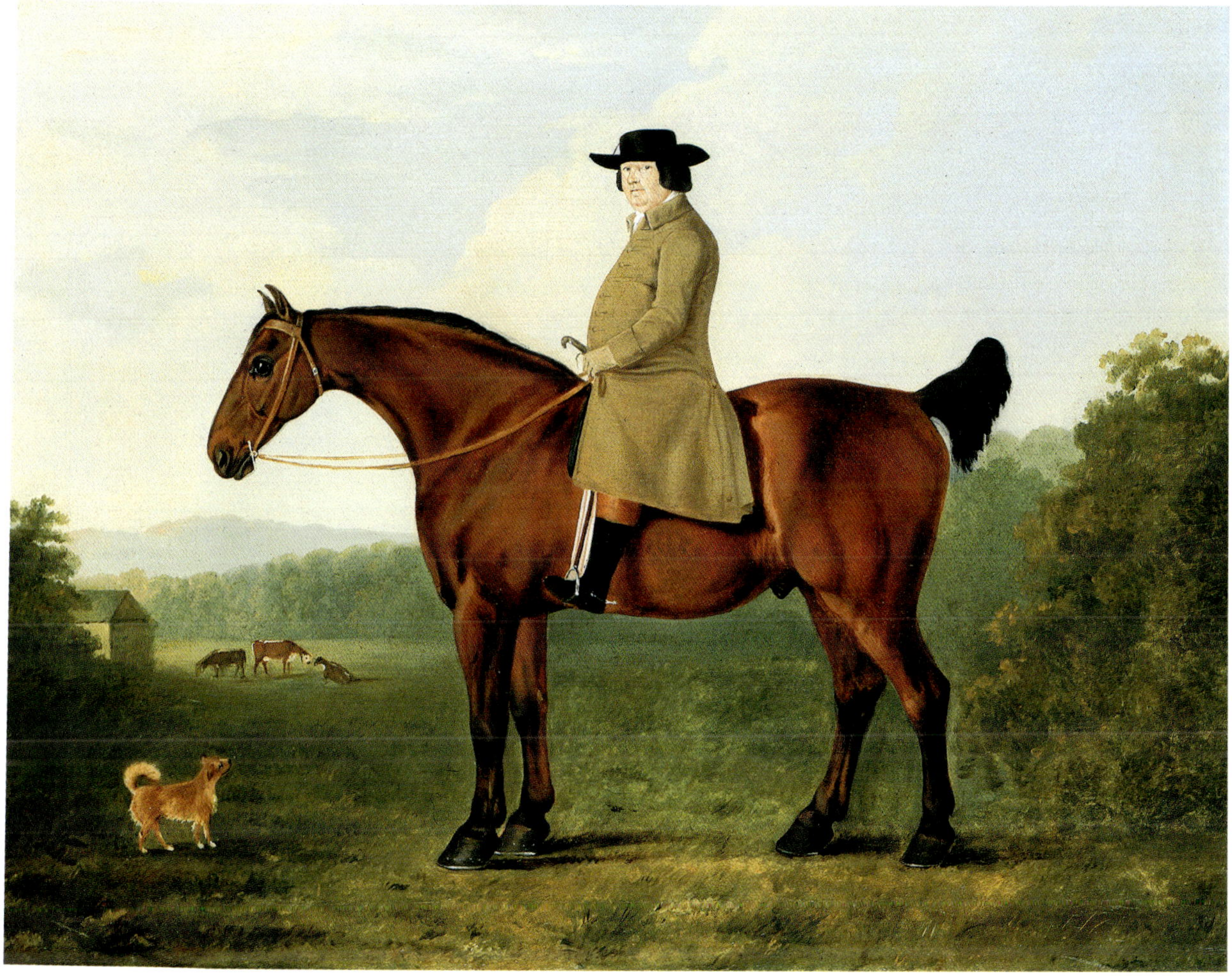

WILLIAM HENRY BROOKE, 1834

Robert Owen

(1771-1858)

Oil on canvas, 273 × 216 mm (10¾ × 8½ ins)
(NPG 943)

A manufacturer and millowner of decency and great talent, and a social and economic theorist of breathtaking simplicity, Robert Owen was born the son of a saddler in Newtown, Montgomeryshire. As a young man he worked for a time for a business specializing in women's clothing, but his organizing abilities and managerial skills soon set him apart and, graduating through the ranks of apprentice, manager and partner, he finally became co-owner of the New Lanark Mills with which his social experiments are most famously associated.

Owen's great faith lay in the education of children and the shaping influence of environment, and at the New Lanark works he had the opportunity to test his theories. For most of his life he was successful enough as a businessman to underwrite his social experiments, but although his benevolent paternalism earned him a temporary influence in Tory circles, his increasingly radical socialism and anti-religious views gradually marginalized him as a genuine influence or power for practical good.

Owen continued to make important contributions to the nascent Co-operative Movement, but after New Lanark his most important experiment came when he sailed for America in 1824 and bought the village of Harmony to put his communist visions into practice. On this first visit to America he was famous enough to speak before the President in Washington, but although he made several more trips in an attempt to bolster his project, 'New Harmony' was doomed by the impracticality which undermined all his later schemes.

Owen is shown here at the age of sixty-three. With its raised eyebrows and curious asymmetry, Brooke's portrait suggests something of that simple and impractical benevolence that even his most contemptuous critics allowed him.

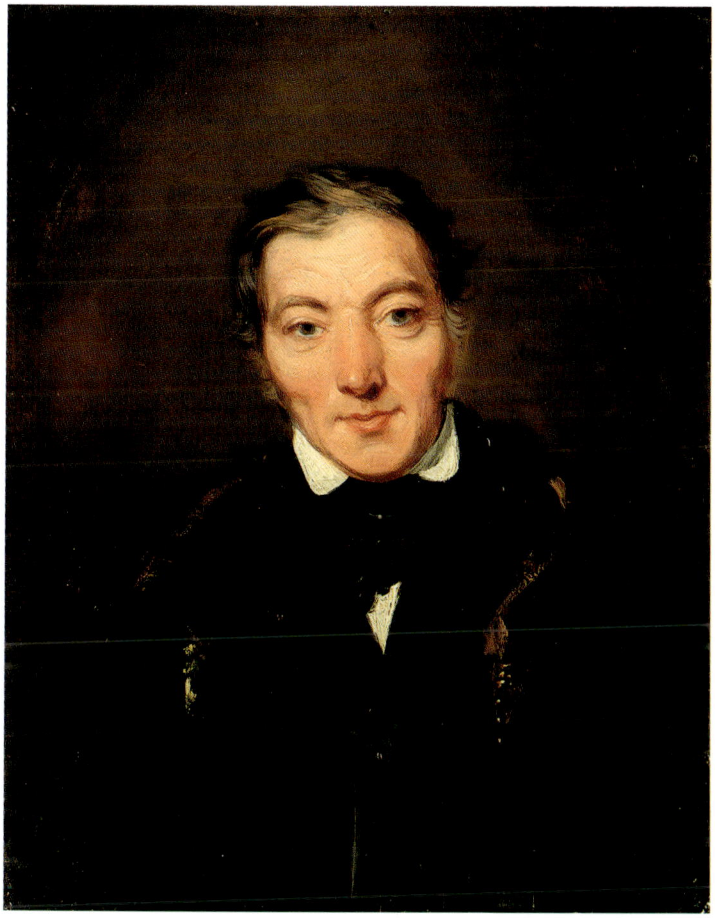

JAMES NORTHCOTE, 1803

Edward Jenner

(1749-1823)

Oil on canvas, 1270 × 1016 mm (50 × 40 ins)
(NPG 62)

The son and the grandson of Gloucestershire vicars, Edward Jenner was born in Berkeley, but went to London as a young man. There he studied under John Hunter and worked preparing specimens brought home from Cook's voyages for Sir Joseph Banks, before he returned to his birthplace to practise medicine and make the discovery of vaccination for which he is most famous.

There was a local belief that dairymaids who had suffered from cowpox did not contract smallpox, and after observation and discussion, in 1796 Jenner tested his growing conviction that this was true by vaccinating a boy first with one disease and then the other. At that time the innoculation of a healthy child with a disease they were almost certain to contract was accepted practice, and when the eight-year-old James Phipps took cowpox but not the subsequent smallpox, Jenner's belief was justified.

There were inevitably setbacks – usually caused by the mistaken use of smallpox pustules – before his discovery was generally accepted, but the recognition was worldwide. Within ten years of his first experiment the use of vaccination was made compulsory in Bavaria, and although Britain did not follow suit until 1853, Oxford University, Royalty and Parliament had all recognized the importance of one of the great medical discoveries of the eighteenth century. 'I never knew a man of simpler mind or warmer heart than Dr Jenner,' Dibdin wrote of him. Careful of his appearance, he used to ride to see his patients dressed in a blue coat and yellow buttons, buckskins and well-polished jockey boots with silver spurs. Northcote's portrait, the background finished after Jenner's death, celebrates his great achievement. 'On a table in the picture', Northcote wrote, 'I have introduced the bones and joints of a Cows hoof and in a glass case the Cows hoof injected, all which is to show which were his peculiar Studies.'

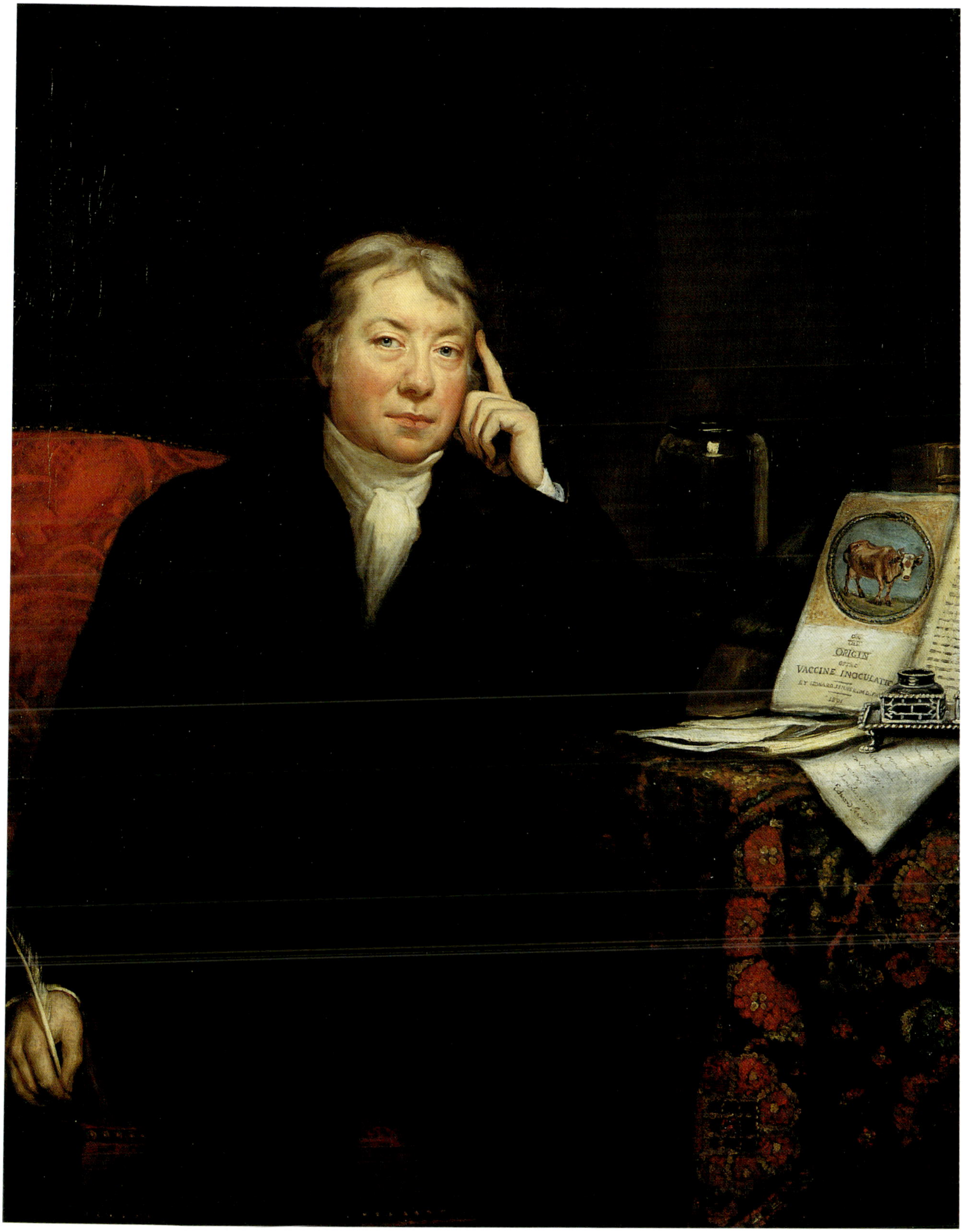

HENRY HOWARD, 1803

Sir Humphry Davy, Bt.

(1778-1829)

Oil on canvas, 1283 × 1029 mm (50½ × 40½ ins)
(NPG 4591)

The relationship between art and science, and the Romantics' simultaneous love and fear of scientific discovery, forms one of the most interesting cultural exchanges of the nineteenth century. As late as the 1840s Byron's talented but wayward daughter Ada was still dreaming of a theory that would yoke the worlds of the imagination and mathematics, and if she had been looking for a source of inspiration – or proof of what was lost when poetry and science parted company – she could have done no better than to turn to Sir Humphry Davy.

The President of the Royal Society, the inventor of the Davy Safety Lamp, and the close friend of Coleridge and Wordsworth, the 'Man of Chemistry', was the greatest British scientist of his day and a poet and writer of genuine talent. An unhappy marriage (the marriage of 'Conceit and Chemistry' as Byron dubbed it) and worsening health darkened his last years, but his pioneering work in electro-chemistry and his apprehension of the physical universe in terms that could excite the poetic imagination make him the quintessential scientist of the Romantic Age.

Honoured in both France and England, knighted in 1812, and created baronet in 1818, Sir Humphry Davy was later painted both by Sir Thomas Lawrence and Thomas Phillips (who showed him seated with his Davy lamp) but, with the exception of a satirical etching by Gillray, Henry Howard's is the earliest portrait of the young scientist. Even in his mid thirties Davy retained 'all the freshness and bloom of five-and-twenty', and Howard's 1803 portrait well captures the strong good looks that made George Ticknor, the American visitor and recorder of London Regency life, call him 'one of the handsomest men I have seen in England.'

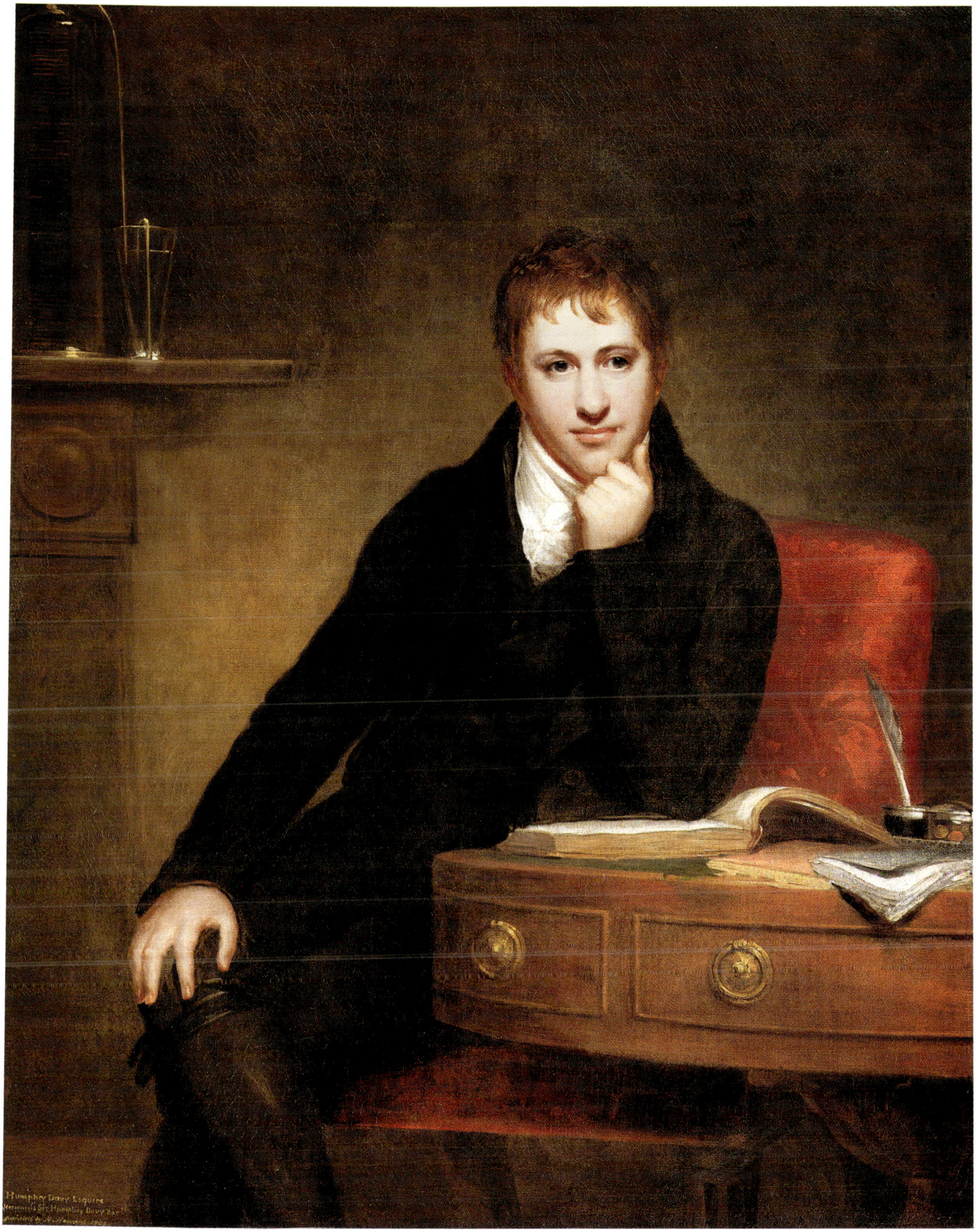
Humphry Davy Esquire

UNKNOWN ARTIST, *c.*1830

John Loudon McAdam

(1756-1836)

Oil on canvas, 895 × 692 mm (35¼ × 27¼ ins)
(NPG 3686)

The name of John Loudon McAdam – 'The Colossus of Roads' – has entered into the language by way of the invention that revolutionized the techniques of road building and, in the age before the railway, made the coaching network possible. The descendant of Scottish Covenanters, McAdam made his fortune during the American War of Independence as an 'agent for the sale of prizes' in New York. Then, on the victory of the Americans, he returned to Britain to immerse himself in the reform of the roads that had fascinated him since childhood.

In an age of growing industrialization, the condition of the country's roads – 'expensive, tedious, and dangerous to travel on, and very costly to repair' – was in urgent need of improvement. Between 1798 and 1814, McAdam travelled over 30,000 miles on the roads of Britain, spent 2,000 days on his tours of inspection and more than £5,000 of his own money as he later told a committee of the House of Commons. In the beginning there was some opposition to his methods and theories, but by 1823 the macadamization of roads had been widely accepted both in the country and in towns. The process involved raising, draining and laying down roads made of successive layers of small, broken stones that would then be compacted naturally by the passage of traffic.

Generous and honourable in public and private life, McAdam could also be a stonily formidable opponent, a quality readily apparent in this anonymous portrait of him painted when he was in his mid seventies. In the distance workmen can be seen laying down one of his roads, and beyond them the city of Bristol where he first put his new construction ideas into extensive practice.

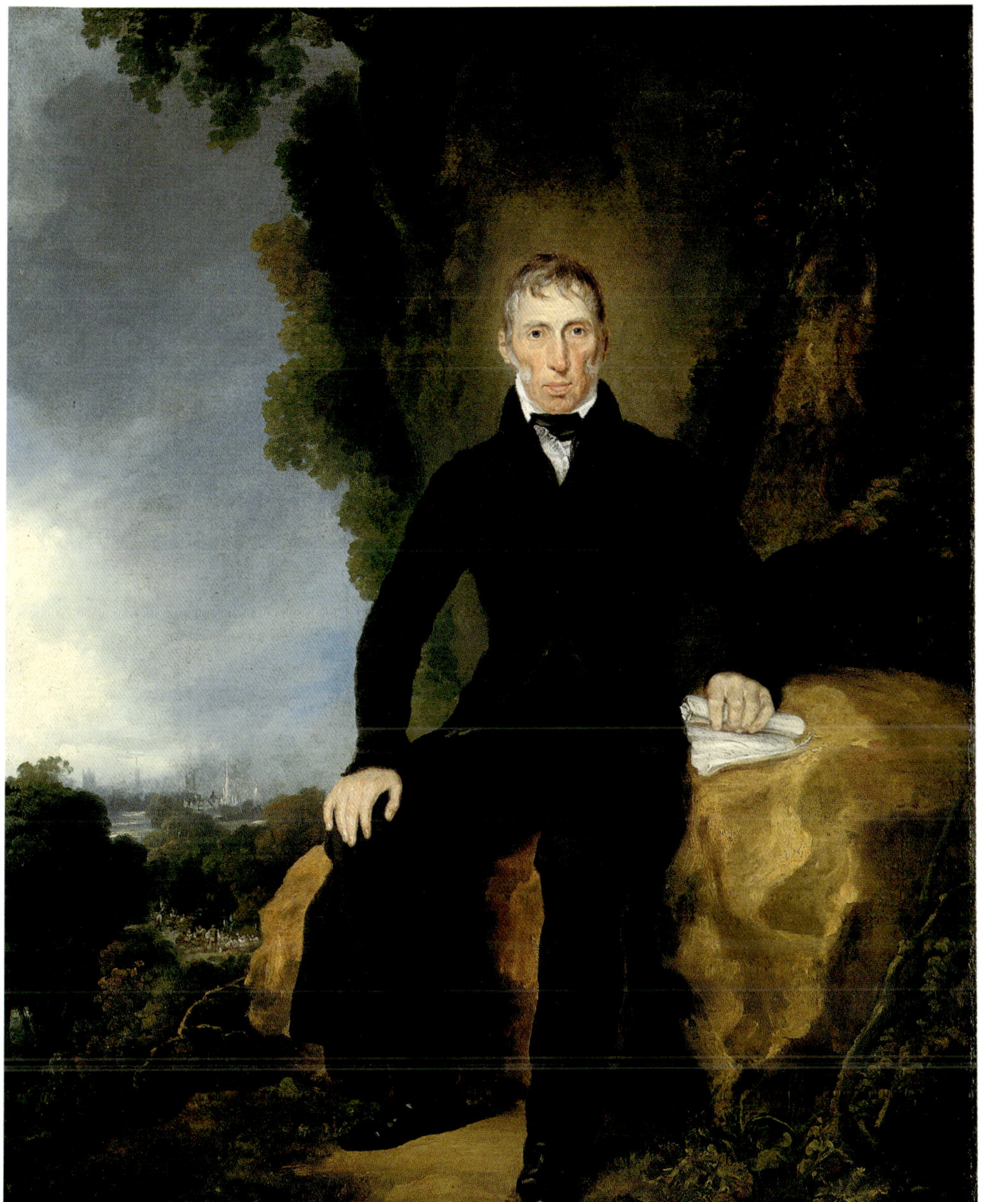

SAMUEL DRUMMOND, *c.*1835

Sir Marc Isambard Brunel

(1769-1849)

Oil on canvas, 1270 × 1016 mm (50 × 40 ins)
(NPG 89)

Eclipsed now by the reputation of his son, Isambard Kingdom (the designer of the Clifton Suspension Bridge, shipbuilder and engineer to the Great Western Railway), Sir Marc Isambard Brunel was himself one of the most distinguished engineers of his day. Born in Normandy and educated for Holy Orders at Gisors and Rouen, Brunel served for six years in the French army before emigrating to America in 1793, where he practised as a civil engineer and architect and planned the defences of New York.

In 1799 Brunel came to England to patent his machinery for making ships' blocks, and over the following years turned his engineering skills to a variety of problems, including experiments in steam navigation and new techniques in sawmills. During the Napoleonic Wars he worked on improving the machinery at the Chatham dockyards and later did the same at Liverpool, but it is for the design of the Thames Tunnel that runs from Rotherhithe to Wapping that he is now best known.

'Below middle stature,' Richard Beamish recorded, ' his head was conspicuously large though without destroying the symmetry of his person; so striking indeed was his forehead that an Irish friend of mine, after his first introduction, was tempted to exclaim, "Why, my dear fellow, that man's face is all head!"'. Brunel's family always preferred the earlier Northcote portrait, but Drummond's painting captures Brunel at the height of his success, exactly midway through the building of his Thames Tunnel and six years before his work was recognized with a knighthood. On the table beside him are manuscripts, plans, a model for a lighthouse, a cotton-winding machine and a safety lamp. On the wall behind him is the painting of the Thames Tunnel done by Thomas Bury.

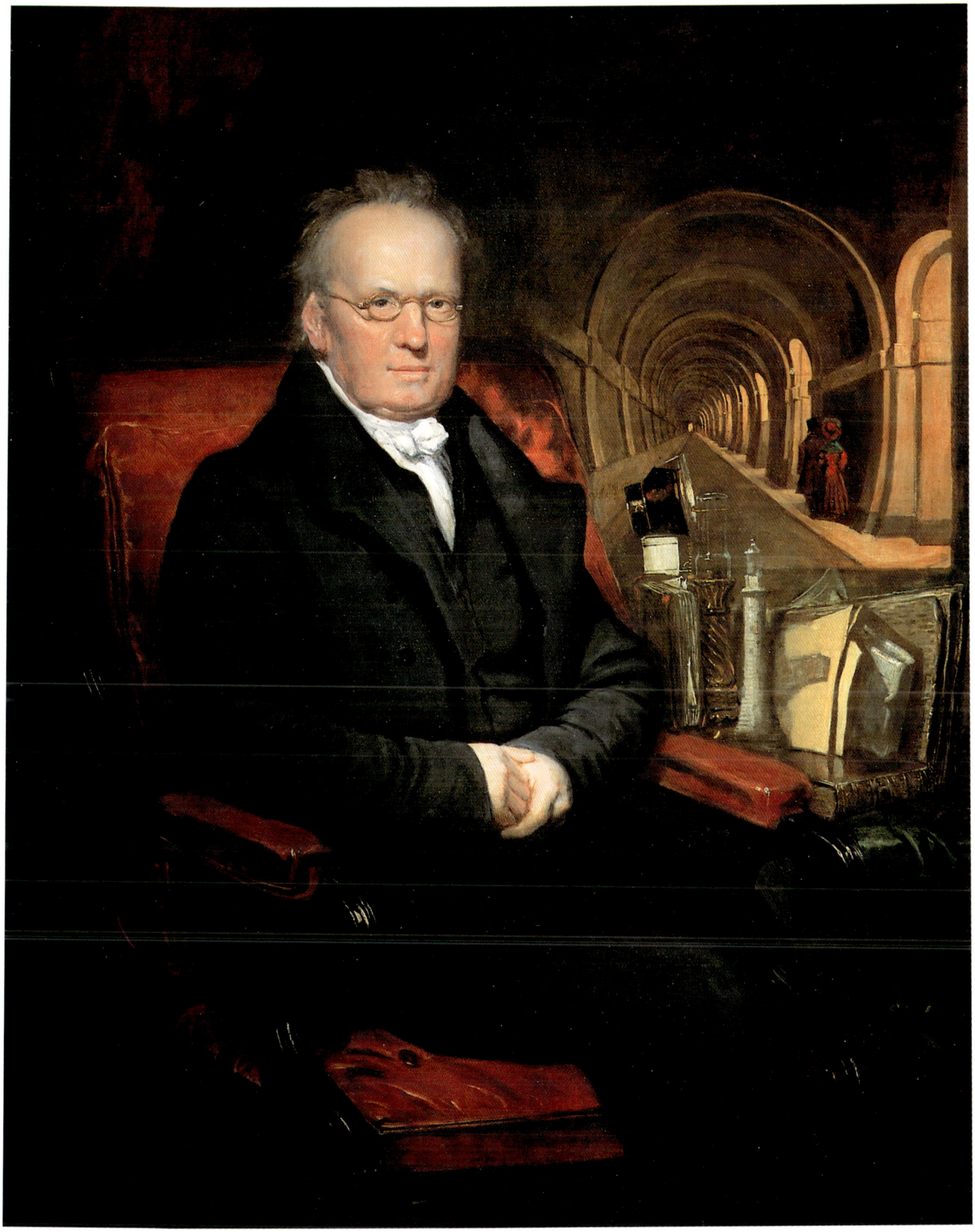

HENRY WILLIAM PICKERSGILL, *c.*1845

George Stephenson

(1781-1821)

Oil on canvas, 1118 × 870 mm (44 × 34¼ ins)
(NPG 410)

The son of a fireman, the inventor, engineer and founder of railways, George Stephenson began his working life in his father's colliery in the north-east of England. An engine-man at twenty-one and an engine-wright five years later, Stephenson successfully tested his first locomotive in 1814 and took out a patent on his engine with steam-blast a year later.

Between 1819 and 1823 a railroad was laid down for Hetton Colliery under Stephenson's direction, but it was his Stockton and Darlington Railway – opened in 1825 – which signalled the future expansion of the railway system that would transform the British countryside and economy. In 1826 he became engineer for the future Manchester and Liverpool Line, and over the next years supervised the spread of railroads that linked Britain's midland and northern cities, increasing the speed of his locomotives in the process to twenty-nine miles per hour and fuelling the manic speculation that Dickens satirized in his novel, *Dombey and Son* (1847-8).

The inventor of the famous 'Rocket', and the first President of the Institution of Mechanical Engineers, Stephenson was one of those practical geniuses who, along with such men as McAdam and the Brunels, did for nineteenth-century Britain what the great agrarian reformers like Bakewell did for the eighteenth-century economy. Honoured abroad for his achievements – he refused domestic decorations – Stephenson is seen here at about the age of sixty-four. The actor and writer Fanny Kemble described him as 'a rather stern-featured man with a dark and deeply marked countenance.' 'His fair, clear countenance was ruddy and seemingly glowed with health', Samuel Smiles wrote of him, 'The mouth was firmly marked and shrewdness and humour lurked there as well as in the keen grey eye.'

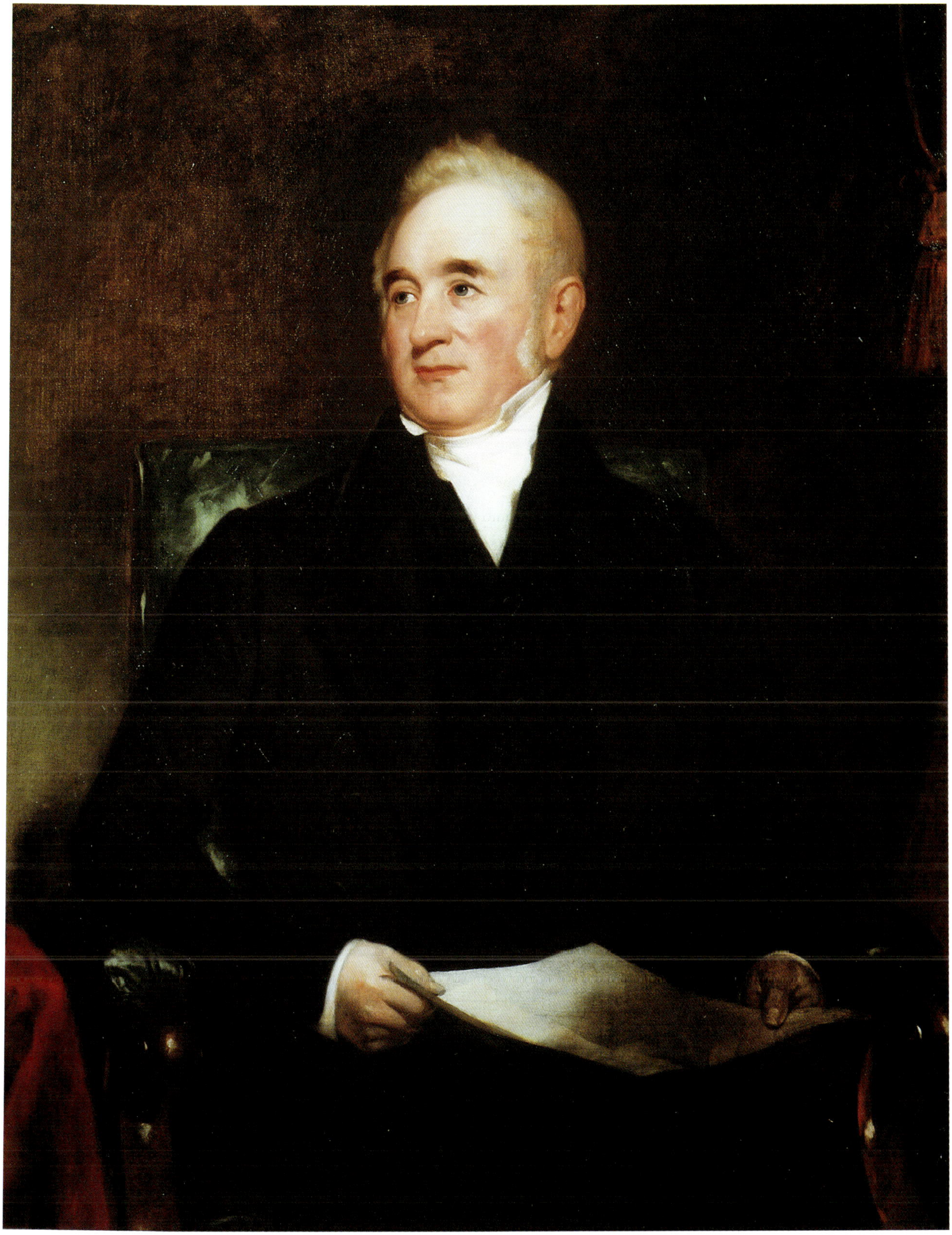

Select Bibliography

Washington Allston, *The Life and Letters of Washington Allston* ed. Janet Flagg (New York, 1893)

Jane Austen, *Emma* (1816)

Thomas Belcher, *The Art of Boxing* (*c*.1820)

T.A.J. Burnett, *The Rise and Fall of a Regency Dandy* (OUP, 1983)

Lord Byron, *Lord Byron's Letters and Journals*, ed. Leslie A. Marchand, 12 vols (London, 1973-82)

William Cobbett, *Rural Rides* (1830)

Hubert Cole, *Beau Brummel* (London, 1977)

Linda Colley, *Britons: Forging the Nation, 1707-1837* (Yale University Press, 1992)

Thomas Creevey, *The Creevey Papers* (London, 1903)

Thomas Dibdin, *Reminiscences of a Literary Life*, 2 vols (London, 1836)

Pierce Egan, *Boxiana* (London, 1812)

Pierce Egan, *Life in London*, illustrated by George Cruikshank (London, 1821)

Joseph Farington, *The Farington Diary*, ed. J. Greig, 8 vols (London. 1922-8)

Benjamin Robert Haydon, *Autobiography and Journals, 1786-1846* (London, 1853)

William Hazlitt, *Conversations of James Northcote* (London, 1827)

William Hazlitt, *The Spirit of the Age* (London, 1825)

William Hazlitt, *Essays on the Fine Arts* (London, 1873)

Christopher Hibbert, *George IV, Regent and King* (London, 1973)

Richard Holmes, *The Romantic Poets and Their Circle* (National Portrait Gallery, London, 1997)

Washington Irving, *The Sketch Book of Geoffrey Crayon, Gent.*, 2 vols (London, 1822)

Edward Bulwer Lytton, *England and the English* (London, 1833)

Venetia Murray, *High Society in the Regency Period, 1788-1830*, (Penguin Books, London, 1999)

James Northcote, *Conversations of James Northcote, Esq.*, R.A. (London, 1827)

John Opie, *Lectures on Painting, (with a Memoir by Amelia Opie)* (London, 1809)

Richard Ormond, *Early Victorian Portraits*, 2 vols (National Portrait Gallery, London, 1987)

Thomas Love Peacock, *Nightmare Abbey* (London, 1818)

David Piper, *The English Face* (London 1957)

Henry Crabb Robinson, *Diary, Reminiscences and Correspondence*, ed. Edith Morley, 3 vols (London, 1938)

Mary Shelley, *Frankenstein, or The Modern Prometheus* (London, 1818)

Percy Bysshe Shelley, *Poetical Works*, ed. Mary Shelley (London, 1839)

Robert Southey, Life *of Nelson*, 2 vols (London, 1813)

William Makepeace Thackeray, *Vanity Fair* (London, 1847)

George Ticknor, *Life, Letters and Journals of George Ticknor*, 2 vols (London, 1876)

Richard Walker, *Regency Portraits*, 2 vols. (London, 1985)

Harriette Wilson, *The Memoirs of Harriette Wilson, Written by Herself*(London, 1825)

Robert Woof and Stephen Hebron, *Romantic Icons* (The Wordsworth Trust, 1999)

Index

Exhibition portraits are shown in **bold** type.